Defenders or Intruders?

About the Book and Author

Following Dr. Nelson's *A History of U.S. Military Forces in Germany,* this book examines contemporary socioeconomic problems created by the stationing of U.S. troops in West Germany (FRG). The issues are magnified by the FRG's strategic importance to the United States, the large number of U.S. troops stationed in the FRG, and the length of time they have remained there. Dr. Nelson assesses the strategic relationship of the two countries against the backdrop of the FRG's security dependency, which adds a unique psychological dimension to the relationship and has created severe strains in the alliance.

Dr. Nelson analyzes the sociological dynamics of the military relationship, clarifying their effect on the political and diplomatic relationship between the two nations. His focal point is the morale of U.S. troops stationed in West Germany, which he studies in relation to military readiness and the acceptability of U.S. forces in German society. The study of morale leads, in turn, to an investigation of some fundamental aspects of the all-volunteer force, which since 1973 has supplied the majority of U.S. military personnel. The book concludes by offering policy recommendations for maintaining West Germany's acceptance of U.S. forces and, thus, preserving the integrity of the military alliance between the United States and the FRG.

Daniel J. Nelson is professor of political science at Auburn University. He is the author of *A History of U.S. Military Forces in Germany* (Westview, 1987) and *Wartime Origins of the Berlin Dilemma* (1978) as well as many articles in scholarly journals.

Defenders or Intruders?

The Dilemmas of U.S. Forces in Germany

Daniel J. Nelson

Westview Press • Boulder & London

Copyright © 1987 by Westview Press, Inc.

Published in 1987 in the United States of America by Westview Press, Inc.; Frederick A. Praeger, Publisher; 5500 Central Avenue, Boulder, Colorado 80301

Library of Congress Cataloging-in-Publication Data
Nelson, Daniel J.
  Defenders or intruders.
  Includes index.
  1. United States—Armed Forces—Germany (West)
2. United States—Military relations—Germany (West)
3. Germany (West)—Military relations—United States.
I. Title.
UA26.G3N43 1987   355′.032′43   86-34024
ISBN 0-8133-0501-2

Printed and bound in the United States of America

 The paper used in this publication meets the requirements of the American National Standard for Permanence of Paper for Printed Library Materials Z39.48-1984.

10   9   8   7   6   5   4   3   2   1

To Helmut and Herta Schuler,
Germany's finest citizens

Contents

Figures and Tables

Preface

Research projects have a way of outgrowing their original boundaries. The idea for this book emerged during the author's period of service in West Germany from 1978 to 1980 as Visiting Professor of International Relations in the Boston University Overseas Graduate Program. The students in the Boston program were primarily U.S. military personnel, both noncommissioned officers (E5 to E8) and commissioned officers (second lieutenant to lieutenant colonel). As the relationships between students and professor lengthened and matured, I became utterly fascinated with the types of relationships that existed between U.S. military personnel and the West German civilian population. The higher up the military rank ladder, the better things seemed to be. Officers at the higher ranks often had extensive contacts in the West German community. They were well acquainted with national and local political figures, possessed considerable knowledge of German history, culture, and traditions, and had many close friendships with Germans. The junior officers, and some of the noncommissioned officers, also tended to socialize frequently with Germans, though their range of contacts was more restricted. The enlisted personnel, by and large, had fewer contacts in German communities and seemed to view military service in the Federal Republic much less sanguinely. At the bottom of the rank ladder were the young recruits having their first experience in a foreign country. Most of them seemed to know only a few Germans, if any at all, and many seemed lonely, confused, and isolated. Among these recruits were the "barracks rats," who remained totally isolated in military ghettos and expressed open hostility toward any and all Germans.

My original intention was to do some research on the sociology of relationships between West Germans and U.S. military personnel to assess the social acceptability of U.S. forces in contemporary West Germany. Sociology and politics, however, maintain a union that any political scientist finds intriguing. As the project matured, it developed into a more general evaluation of the problems and prospects of the U.S. military presence in the Federal Republic in the context of the overall political and diplomatic relationship between the two nations.

Any research project is based upon multiple sources of information. Four sources, however, proved to be especially valuable for this study. The files of West German newspaper clippings at the Federal Press and Information Office in Bonn were a rich source of editorial opinion and general commentary on U.S. forces, especially for the period from the late 1960s to the present time. Data on public opinion were gathered from several excellent public opinion research institutes and archives. Interviews with West German citizens, ranging from government officials to homemakers and students, also constituted a valuable source of opinions and views. Finally, various offices of the U.S. Department of Defense were helpful in providing a rich field of data for analytical purposes.

Two items require specific mention. All translations from German sources into English, including translations of government documents and articles in the press, are my own. I accept full responsibility for the accuracy of the translation as well as the sense or contextual meaning of the original source. Endnotes that cite articles from the West German press give the name of the newspaper and the date of publication, but not the page of the material quoted. This is because the filing system for newspaper clippings at the Federal Press and Information Office in Bonn is organized topically according to date and name of newspaper, but without exact page numbers.

It is impossible to accord proper recognition to all the people whose assistance proved so valuable in the research and writing of this book. Mention of any of them risks the omission of others whose help may have been equally indispensable. The record would not be complete, however, without acknowledgment of the individuals and institutions whose support made possible the completion of this manuscript.

First and foremost, I am indebted to the Hoover Institution on War, Revolution and Peace, Stanford University, which supported the project with funding for a full year of unencumbered research and writing. It was during the period of my appointment as Edward Teller National Fellow at the Hoover Institution that much of the manuscript was written. The excellent facilities and genial ambience provided an atmosphere most conducive to the scholar's craft. I extend many thanks to my colleagues and Senior Fellows at Hoover—Lewis Gann, Peter Duignan, Dennis Bark, and Seymour Martin Lipset—for advice, aid, and encouragement during many months of labor. I am indebted also to Auburn University, which provided a faculty research grant-in-aid for several months of field research in West Germany in 1982. Several offices and individuals at the Department of Defense in Washington assisted the project by generating extensive datasets according to difficult specifications. Special thanks go to Stuart Rakoff, director of Manpower Planning and Analysis, Military Personnel and Force Management, Office of the Assistant Secretary of Defense for Manpower, Reserve Affairs and Logistics, and to Alex Sinaiko at the Defense Manpower Data Center for data on the demographic characteristics of U.S. forces in West Germany; to Msgt. Wiley Myrick, Jr., chief of Management Analyst AMJAMS, Office of the Judge Advocate General, USAF, for data on military justice in the U.S. Air Force; to Col. Thomas A. MacDonnell, chief, Office of Army Law Enforcement, Office of the Deputy Chief of Staff for Personnel, for data on military justice in the U.S. Army; and to Helen Gouin, director of the Drug Abuse Program and Technical Activity, U.S. Army, for data on enrollments in the army's drug and alcohol abuse programs. My two talented research assistants at Stanford University provided indispensable help. Manuel Ebner processed hundreds of tables for the database on public opinion in Chapter 3. David Hyde constructed the demographic tables in Chapter 2 and did much useful bibliographic work. My three research assistants at Auburn University also helped to advance the project with incredible skill and talent. Jason Williams accomplished much useful bibliographic work. Pamela Vines constructed tables and processed material on morale factors in Chapters 5 through 8. Michael Rasmussen assembled the bibliography in final form, rebuilt hundreds of tables, and did much useful editorial work. William C. Flick, computer systems support specialist at Auburn University, contributed his special genius to the management and use of complex data sets on a mainframe computer.

Several people at Headquarters, United States Army, Europe, in Heidelberg, provided wise counsel and useful data. Dr. Robert C. Larson, the U.S. forces liaison officer for Baden-Wuerttemberg, provided useful insights, in lengthy conversations, on many aspects of U.S.–West German relations and helped me thread my way through the military bureaucracy by arranging access to important military leaders. Benton G. Moeller, William Gerling, and Arthur Booth, three very able political affairs analysts in the Bureau of Governmental Affairs, Division of Wartime Host Nation Support, all contributed much to my knowledge of U.S.–West German military relationships by challenging my thinking on any number of issues. LTC Michael Farmer and LTC Ronald M. Joe, chiefs (at different periods) of research and evaluation in the Office of the Deputy Chief of Staff for Personnel, with the able assistance of Cpt. Loggie, generated several vital datasets on the demography of U.S. forces in West Germany. Robert Shackelton, U.S. forces liaison officer for Hesse and Rhineland-Palatinate, provided useful information on several aspects of U.S.–West German relations. Truman R. Strobridge, command historian at Headquarters, United States European Command in Stuttgart, provided much useful historical and statistical material. Col. Mack J. Gibson, military attaché at the U.S. embassy in Bonn, helped to arrange access to military leaders and contributed informed perspectives on several important issues.

Conducting research in the Federal Republic of Germany is always a joyful experience because there are so many able German scholars who willingly give of their time and expertise to facilitate research by U.S. scholars. The excellent research institutions in the FRG are also unfailingly cooperative and helpful. I am deeply indebted to Herr Günter Wickert and the Wickert Institute in Tübingen for conducting a study of German public opinion exclusively for this study. All of the tables for Chapter 12, as well as Table 3.56, were constructed from data generated in the Wickert Institute study of April 1983. The Institut für Demoskopie, Allensbach, graciously allowed me to use all of their studies on West German public opinion in reference to the U.S. military presence. Many of the tables in Chapter 3 were taken from the Allensbach files. I wish to express my profound thanks to Professor Elisabeth Noelle-Neumann and her colleague, Herr Rüdiger Schulz, and others at the Allensbach Institute who facilitated my research in such a charitable manner. I extend special thanks also to *Der Speigel* magazine institutionally and to its editor, Herr Werner Harenberg, personally for granting permission to use all five volumes of the public opinion study entitled "Aufrüstung und Pazifismus." Though the data were generated by the EMNID Institute in October 1981, *Der Speigel* contracted the study and owns the exclusive rights to its use. Other data produced by the EMNID Institute in Bielefeld and now in the public domain also proved highly useful. Many thanks are due to the Zentralarchiv für Empirische Sozialforschung (ZA) in Cologne for extensive use of their public opinion files. The director of ZA, Herr Ekkehard Mochmann, and his colleague, Herr Horst Weinen, facilitated the use of the files with formidable expertise. Frau Klimmer at the Federal Press and Information Office in Bonn provided abundant help with the newspaper clippings files of the West German federal government. Frau Ilsemarie Querner, senior librarian, provided extensive help with the use of materials at the library of the Bundestag in Bonn. My special thanks are accorded to these talented and gracious ladies. Finally, this study could not have been undertaken without the assistance of my friend and colleague Herr Klaus Schuler, senior analyst, Legislative Reference Service, the Bundestag, Bonn. Herr Schuler rendered indispensable help by arranging interviews with government officials and members of the Bundestag. In addition, with his abundant expertise in West German politics and diplomacy, he was a constant source of valuable information. Herr Helmut Schuler and Frau Herta Schuler have provided a wonderful second home for me in Germany since my student days at the University of Bonn.

Despite help from these and many others, I assume full responsibility for the accuracy of the data and for any errors of fact or judgment. The views expressed in this book do not represent the views of the Hoover Institution or any other research institution that rendered assistance.

Daniel J. Nelson

Acronyms

AAFCE	Allied Air Forces, Central Europe
AFCENT	Allied Forces, Central Europe
AFNORTH	Allied Forces, Northern Europe
AFSOUTH	Allied Forces, Southern Europe
AFQT	Armed Forces Qualification Test
AVF	All-volunteer force
CDU	Christian Democratic Union
CENTAG	Central Army Group
CSU	Christian Social Union
DCINCEUR	Deputy Commander in Chief, Europe
FDP	Free Democratic Party
FRG	Federal Republic of Germany
NATO	North Atlantic Treaty Organization
NORTHAG	Northern Army Group
SACEUR	Supreme Allied Commander, Europe
SHAPE	Supreme Headquarters, Allied Powers, Europe
SPD	Social Democratic Party
USAFE	U.S. Air Force, Europe
USAREUR	U.S. Army, Europe
USCINCEUR	U.S. Commander in Chief, Europe
USEUCOM	U.S. European Command
USNAVEUR	U.S. Naval Forces, Europe

Introduction:
The FRG-U.S.
Security Relationship

This book is a case study of the sociopolitical problems associated with the stationing of U.S. military forces abroad. The country in focus is the Federal Republic of Germany (FRG). West Germany represents, perhaps, the most important case study for three reasons: the length of time U.S. forces have remained, the size of the forces, and the importance of the country to U.S. strategic interests. Because a vast literature exists on U.S.-West German nuclear issues, the discussion in this book concerns only U.S. conventional forces.

U.S. forces swarmed over Germany in 1945 as a conquering force. They remained as an army of military occupation for four years. Even after the political and economic reconstruction of West Germany was completed, however, they did not return home. Occupation became defense; the builddown of the late 1940s became the buildup of the early 1950s. The U.S. forces have now been there for forty years. Until some settlement of major East-West issues is achieved, U.S. forces will continue to be stationed in West Germany for the indefinite future. In a sense, things have never been completely normal there since the end of the war. The people are physically and politically separated from their compatriots living on the other side of the border in a separate state. Both German states are hosts to enormous foreign military forces. The world's two largest alliance systems face each other head to head at the dividing line of East and West that runs through the center of Germany. Outside the Soviet bloc no other country in the world has served as host to such a large foreign military presence for such a protracted period of time.

The FRG is also the European anchor point of the Atlantic Alliance. The country possesses the largest and strongest economy in Western Europe; it is politically one of the most stable regimes in Europe; it has Europe's largest and best-trained armed forces; and it sits astride the primary East-West dividing line. In addition, its people have a strong psychological attachment to the United States. If there is one country that must remain in a strong alliance with the United States in the interest of European security, it is this one. Its detachment from the North Atlantic Treaty Organization (NATO) would be a catastrophic blow to the integrity of the alliance and would place in jeopardy the security of all other Western European nations. No other country occupies such a strategic position within the alliance.

In this study there are two normative assumptions that clarify the research focus and influence the interpretation of the data. Because the assumptions flow from value judgments rather than empirical observations, they are neither true nor false on their merits, merely more or less defensible philosophically. The author's major obligation, at any rate, is to articulate them. One assumption is that the FRG and the United States need each other in a vital way, as their relationship is the very touchstone of NATO. West Germany cannot do without the security guarantee of the United States any more than the United States can do without the loyalty of the West German government and people. In terms of policy this means that both governments must be peculiarly sensitive to the maintenance of cordial political and diplomatic relations and must do whatever is necessary to keep the relationship in good working order. Flowing from this assumption is another, equally important—that the NATO alliance has served its purpose well in the past and can continue to do so in the future. The Soviet Union has not attempted any military aggression against Western Europe since the founding of NATO, and it is unlikely to contemplate any military adventures in Western Europe as long as the deterrent value of NATO remains intact. This means that the maintenance of a large contingent of U.S. forces in West Germany since World War II has been essential to U.S. security and will continue indefinitely to be so. As long as no general settlement can be reached on the fundamental issues dividing East and West, there is simply no choice.

The strategic relationship of West Germany to the United States has an interesting and peculiar psychological dimension, which is crucial to the sociopolitical analysis presented here. In this study it is referred to as security dependency. What is implied is that the Germans have no way to guarantee or safeguard their country's security from external threat without a firm military relationship with the United States. True, the West Germans have the largest armed forces in Europe. Combined with those of other West European states, the military power available is a formidable aggregation. On the other side of the internal border, however, are nineteen Soviet divisions, with many more in neighboring states and the western portions of the Soviet Union. West Germany's military power has no credibility as a deterrent to the Soviet Union unless it is backed by a U.S. guarantee based on conventional and nuclear weapons. First and foremost, West Germany's security depends upon the stationing of a large number of U.S. troops on German soil. This is supplemented and cemented by the nuclear guarantee in case conventional forces should prove insufficient for the country's defense against Soviet aggression. The conventional guarantee is the subject of our analysis. Questions relating to nuclear weapons are treated only insofar as they relate to conventional forces.

There are, of course, other states that also rely upon a U.S. guarantee, such as Japan, South Korea, and some states in Europe. West Germany is, however, a special case, owing to the division of the country and the presence of large foreign military forces in both Germanies. If a conventional attack were to occur in Western Europe, it would most likely occur through the accessible land corridors in West Germany—the Hof Corridor, the Fulda Gap, or the North German Plain. Hence the Soviet military threat possesses an immediacy in West Germany much greater than in any other country. In addition, West Germany has a special and peculiar psychological relationship with the United States that stems from the period of the military occupation. The mantle of military protection placed by the United States around West Germany in the early years after World War II remained in place during the period of economic and political reconstruction. The West German economy was rebuilt with the massive Marshall Plan aid extended by the United States. The FRG recovered its sovereignty and acquired its authority under the tutelage of the United States. The West German armed forces were eventually rebuilt with the blessing of the allied powers under the watchful eye of the United States. For at least the first twenty-five years of its existence the Federal Republic existed in a kind of younger brother relationship with a stronger sibling. When the country finally emerged as a major world power in the 1970s, it assumed responsibility for its own welfare with the exception of its security, which still remained heavily dependent upon the presence of U.S. forces. The circumstance of security dependency had a permanency that no wishful thinking could alter.

Security dependency has an unpleasant psychological dimension that can manifest itself in malevolent ways. No person individually or no people collectively enjoys being dependent upon someone else for protection or security. Dependency means not being fully in control of one's fate, an inability to be wholly self-sufficient. It leads sometimes to outbursts born of frustration. For reasons not well understood by psychologists, a dependent who may have been extremely well cared for by a benefactor over a long period of time may suddenly and without provocation turn against the benefactor. Relationships of dependency are difficult to manage in any case, and those involving a security factor are probably even more difficult than others. Inevitably, West German security dependency upon the United States was bound to lead to stresses and strains. Such stresses became noticeable in the 1970s, and they have become stronger in the 1980s. The German-American political relationship has become much more difficult to manage than it was a generation ago.

In this book I analyze the sociological dynamics of the military relationship between West Germany and the United States in an attempt to understand how these dynamics affect the political and diplomatic relationship between the two countries. The study of social interaction between U.S. troops and the West German population leads us, most fundamentally, to inquire into the morale of U.S. troops stationed in the FRG. Several aspects of morale illlustrate the crucial link between the psychosociological condition of U.S. forces and the perceptual images Germans form of the U.S. military presence. The investigation of morale leads, in turn, to a study of the all-volunteer force (AVF) that, since 1973, has been the basic U.S. military personnel structure. The essential question that arises in the latter portions of the study is how the AVF structure affects the morale of U.S. forces stationed abroad and, as a consequence, how the AVF affects the long-term viability of the U.S. military presence in West Germany.

The book aims to present a general "report card" on the status of the U.S. military presence in Germany in sociopolitical terms. Major changes are occurring on the German political scene as well as in the United States. The stresses and strains in the NATO alliance call into question the feasibility of maintaining large U.S. forces in Germany over the long term. Hence, a general assessment of the political problems and prospects associated with the maintenance of the American presence in Germany is necessary.

The viability of the U.S. presence is the central focus of the analysis. Has the viability been eroding in recent years? Is erosion occurring today? What can be done to prevent such erosion in the future? Most essentially, the viability of the U.S. presence depends upon its popular acceptance and approval by the West German population. The master variable is, of course, politics. The political process in Germany and the United States will decide the future of the U.S. presence in Germany. This means that the West German people must be convinced of the reality of the Soviet threat and must understand clearly the role of U.S. forces in German defense. On the U.S. side it means that the people and the Congress must be willing to make a commitment that is viewed as absolutely reliable by the West Germans and must be willing to back up that commitment with the necessary personnel, funds, and facilities.

1

The Structure of NATO and
U.S. Forces in Europe

Though the United States has military forces stationed throughout the world, the majority are in or near Europe. Table 1.1 gives the figures for U.S. forces stationed in foreign countries, particularly Western and Southern Europe. By translating the numbers to percentages, we can see that in the case of army ground forces, 85% of all army forces stationed outside the United States are in Western and Southern Europe and 82% of all foreign-based army forces are in the Federal Republic of Germany and West Berlin. Of the army ground forces stationed in Western and Southern Europe, 96% are located in West Germany. In the case of the air force, 69% of all personnel located outside the United States are stationed in Western and Southern Europe, but only 32% of air force units outside the United States are in West Germany. Of the air force personnel stationed in Western and Southern Europe, 47% are located in West Germany.

The extent to which West Germany accounts for the great bulk of U.S. forces stationed in Europe is shown in Table 1.1. The army and the air force account for 87% of U.S. forces in Europe, whereas the navy and the marines account for 13%. Approximately 68% of naval personnel are afloat as part of the Sixth Fleet in the Mediterranean; the largest land-based naval contingents are located at bases in Italy, Spain, and the United Kingdom. Hence, most army forces and about half the air forces in Europe are stationed in West Germany, while most of the navy and marine forces are stationed elsewhere, though the latter two constitute only a small percentage of the total U.S. forces committed to Europe. West Germany, then, is clearly the central focus of the U.S. military presence in Western Europe. As only 288 naval personnel and 90 marines are stationed in the FRG, the U.S. military presence in Germany means, in effect, the U.S. Army and the U.S. Air Force.

The Structure of NATO

A brief discussion of the European structure of NATO is necessary in order to understand how U.S. forces in West Germany relate broadly to the NATO alliance. The apex of European NATO is the Supreme Allied Commander, Europe (SACEUR), by custom always a four-star U.S. general. In peacetime the forces of the six nations stationed on German soil remain under national command, even though the commands themselves constitute part of the integrated NATO command structure. In wartime or other emergency, as well as during joint NATO maneuvers, these forces come directly under the jurisdiction of the integrated NATO command structure. The sole exception is France, whose forces since 1965 have remained exclusively under national command, though French troops have taken part in joint NATO maneuvers in recent years. The headquarters of SACEUR are known as Supreme Headquarters, Allied Powers, Europe (SHAPE), located near Casteau, Belgium. SHAPE and its commander SACEUR are responsible for three military regions in wartime: AFNORTH (Allied Forces, Northern Europe), which includes Norway, Denmark, and Schleswig-Holstein (the northernmost state of the FRG), with headquarters at Kolsas, Norway; AFCENT (Allied Forces Central Europe), which includes the Netherlands, Belgium, Luxembourg, and the FRG (excluding the northernmost state), with headquarters at Brunssum, the Netherlands; and AFSOUTH (Allied Forces, Southern Europe), which inlcudes Italy, Greece, Turkey, and the Mediterranean, with headquarters at Naples, Italy. U.S. forces in West Germany are assigned to AFCENT, to which Canada and the United Kingdom also contribute forces as noncontinental members. All of the integrated NATO commands are combined commands, including army, navy, and air force units.

The ground forces of AFCENT are organized into two groups: NORTHAG, the Northern Army Group, and CENTAG, the Central Army Group (see Figure 1.1). NORTHAG is divided into four corps, which are responsible for the defense of northern Germany (excluding Schleswig-Holstein, which belongs to AFNORTH) from the northern coastal area and the Elbe River in the north to a line running from Aachen to Göttingen in the south. These four corps are Dutch, West German, British, and Belgian, arranged along the border with East Germany in that order, north to south. Measured at the border, the NORTHAG front extends about 400 kilometers (250 miles) from Lübeck to Göttingen. CENTAG likewise is divided into four corps, which are responsible for the defense of West Germany from the NORTHAG line in the north to the Austrian and Swiss borders in the south. Two of these corps are West German and the other two belong to the United States (the Fifth and Seventh Corps). The U.S. corps are located more or less in the center of the CENTAG area, which covers most of the southern half of the Federal Republic; the West German corps are on the flanks, one contiguous to the Belgians in the north and the other located along the southern border with Austria. A small Canadian contingent and a larger French contingent are located in the southwestern corner of West Germany. U.S. forces occupy the most important forward positions in the CENTAG area, whose front, measured at the borders with East Germany and Czechoslovakia, extends for about 600 kilometers (375 miles). The terrain and demography of NATO center were aptly described by Richard Lawrence and Jeffrey Record:

From the Elbe River in the north to the Harz Mountains near the NORTHAG-CENTAG boundary, the land is generally flat or gently rolling and is crisscrossed by numerous small water obstacles. The north-south road network in this area is excellent, although from east to west it is less extensive. About sixty miles west of the border, the land is very flat and low, with many canals and rivers. As one approaches the Rhine River, small communities and farmlands give way to large cities and major industrial concentrations in the Ruhr River basin and along the North Sea coast. This northern portion of the Central Region is known as the North German Plain and is considered the most favorable route for a Warsaw Pact attack, because of its flat and open terrain, excellent network of roads, and proximity to the coast and to major communications centers along the Rhine. From the Harz Mountains southward (the CENTAG area), the initial line of contact would be along a mountainous and wooded border with only two narrow potential corridors of invasion: the Fulda Gap, aimed at the Frankfurt area, and the broader, more open approach from the Thuringer mountain–Hof area to Würzburg and Nuremberg. Along the border areas in this region, the terrain is rough, heavily wooded, and crisscrossed by streams and small rivers. The east-west road network is generally good, but distances to the Rhine from this sector are considerably greater than from the sector to the north. Most roads are sandwiched in between the surrounding hills and mountains. The CENTAG area is therefore more favorable to the defense than NORTHAG.[1]

The military forces of six non-German nations are stationed on West German soil (Table 1.2). In 1982, foreign military personnel numbered approximately 391,400, to which must be added 325,000 military dependents and 31,130 civilian employees of the six countries. Gathered into one place, the 748,030 foreign military-related persons would constitute West Germany's fourth largest city (after Hamburg, Munich, and Cologne), larger than Frankfurt, Duesseldorf, or Stuttgart. In modern history, no other country in the world has been subject to such a prodigious foreign military presence over such a protracted period of time.

U.S. Forces in Europe

The extent of the U.S. presence is impressive. Americans constitute more than half of the total foreign military presence, and U.S. soldiers and air force personnel represent approximately 60% of the foreign military personnel. The Americans are not, however, spread throughout West Germany. Their presence in the northern half of the country is minimal compared to that in the southern half. The largest installation in the north is the brigade stationed at Garlstedt, near Bremen, in new facilities constructed in 1978. Located at Bremerhaven are major supply and communcations facilities; smaller communications and intelligence gathering facilities are located at Kalkar, Hessisch-Oldendorf near Hameln, Noervenich near Cologne, and Jever near Wilhelmshaven. The lion's share of the U.S. facilities, however, is south of a line stretching from Trier in the west to Fulda near the East German border. Even in this portion of the country, there are very few U.S. bases in the extreme south, where units of the West German army are based, or in the southwestern corner of the country, where the French and Canadian forces are stationed (see Figure 1.2). West Berlin constitutes a special case. Forces of the three major western allies—the United States, United Kingdom, and France— are stationed there in substantial numbers, though there are no West German forces, owing to the city's peculiar political status. In West Germany proper, U.S. forces are not generally concentrated in the larger cities, with certain exceptions. It is true that a few cities, such as Frankfurt, Wiesbaden, Nuremberg, and Stuttgart, have a large U.S. military presence, but the biggest concentrations are in smaller towns with interesting, even exotic, names such as Grafenwöhr, Ansbach, Schwäbisch-Gmünd, or Bad Kreuznach.

Heidelberg conjures up romantic images in the minds of millions of Americans. A picturesque, medieval city on the banks of the Neckar River, it is an ancient citadel of learning. Its famous university was immortalized in Sigmund Romberg's "Student Prince," and the city, with its famous castle and charming, narrow streets, is a mecca for tourists. But Heidelberg is also the headquarters of the U.S. Army, Europe (USAR-EUR) and hence home to thousands of U.S. military personnel. Even the casual tourist, driving in and around the city, is struck by the fact that every third automobile or so carries the familiar green plates of U.S. forces and that parts of the city in and around the base areas are not at all unlike sections of Los Angeles or Des Moines. Frankfurt, home of Fifth Corps headquarters, has a distinctly Americanized flavor. Signs in English direct American guests to important military installations, and most Germans are able to understand at least some English, which is not so in other parts of West Germany. The sprawling Rhine-Main Air

Base is nearly as large as Frankfurt International Airport, Western Europe's busiest air terminal. In certain of the smaller towns where U.S. forces are based—such as Grafenwöhr, Hohenfels, or Vilseck—Americans may constitute as much as 30 to 50% of the population.

In terms of the command structure of U.S. forces in West Germany, the highest command is the United States European Command (USEUCOM) located at Patch Barracks in Stuttgart, the erstwhile home of Hitler's Panzer Regiment 7.[2] USEUCOM's area of responsibility extends from Britain through Western Europe to the Mediterranean and the Persian Gulf, though its primary focus remains Western Europe. The same U.S. general who serves as SACEUR for the NATO alliance also serves as the commander of USEUCOM, with the official title of United States Commander in Chief, Europe (USCINCEUR). Because of the magnitude of this dual assignment, which remains controversial in high military circles, USCINCEUR usually delegates broad authority for the direction and control of the USEUCOM staff to the Deputy Commander in Chief, Europe (DCINCEUR). Or, to use the military vernacular, USCINCEUR has to function most of the time as SACEUR at SHAPE headquarters in Belgium, leaving the bulk of day-to-day USEUCOM responsibility to DCINCEUR in Stuttgart.[3] USEUCOM is distinctive as one of the few unified commands composed of senior commanders of all four military services. Generally the post of USCINCEUR-SACEUR is held by a four-star army general, whereas DCINCEUR is most often a four-star air force general. Approximately 450 military personnel are assigned to USEUCOM: 170 army, 80 navy, 185 air force, and 20 marines. In addition, about 125 civilians of the Department of Defense are on the staff. Daily coordination between USEUCOM and SHAPE assures that, in the event of war, the transfer of U.S. forces to the integrated SHAPE commands of NATO would occur smoothly.[4]

Because USEUCOM is the highest U.S. military command in Europe, the three individual senior service commands for Europe are directly subordinate to it: USNAVEUR (United States Naval Forces, Europe), headquartered at London; USAFE (United States Air Forces, Europe), headquartered at Ramstein, West Germany; and USAREUR, headquartered at Heidelberg. The most vital component of USNAVEUR is the Sixth Fleet, which controls the U.S. ships, personnel, and aircraft that patrol the Mediterranean. Only about 288 naval personnel are assigned to duty in West Germany, plus about 90 marines. Most of these are assigned to USEUCOM, to a small naval detachment at Bremerhaven, or serve as liaison officers to various other army and air force commands. As naval and marine personnel constitute less than two-tenths of 1% of U.S. military personnel stationed in Germany, they are excluded from this study. For all intents and purposes the U.S. presence in Germany means the army (USAREUR) and the air force (USAFE).

Of the approximately 309,000 army and air force troops stationed in European NATO countries, approximatley 83%—or 256,000—are located in the Federal Republic of Germany. Of the approximately 256,000 military personnel in Germany, over 85%—or 218,000—are army troops under the command of USAREUR. The principal USAREUR and USAFE commands are given in Tables 1.3 and 1.4. Because of the number and variety of army units and facilities, Table 1.3 lists only the major commands. Commands dealing principally with nuclear weapons remain classified information, for obvious reasons. Table 1.4 does not list the air force communications and support facilities or other units handling highly classified work. Nevertheless, the tables give an accurate picture of the most important U.S. military commands in West Germany.

In the event of war or a crisis involving NATO, most elements of USAREUR would come under the command of the Central Army Group (CENTAG), which in turn is a NATO subordinate command of AFCENT. As in the case of the highest command level, SACEUR-USCINCEUR, double hats are also worn at subordinate commands. The commander in chief of CENTAG is the U.S. commander in chief of USAREUR. Army air defense units in Germany in war or emergency would be directed by the commander, 4th Allied Tactical Air Force, a NATO subordinate command of Allied Air Forces, Central Europe (AAFCE), whose supreme commander is also the supreme commander of USAFE. The army armored brigade at Garlstedt, near Bremerhaven, however, would come under the command of NORTHAG. The commander in chief of NORTHAG is also the commander in chief of British forces in Germany (the British Army of the Rhine). In peacetime, most U.S. Air Force units in West Germany are under the command of the 17th Air Force, a subordinate command of USAFE, with headquarters at Sembach Air Base. In case of war most elements of the 17th Air Force would come under the direction of AAFCE.[5]

Notes

1. Richard D. Lawrence and Jeffrey Record, *U.S. Force Structure in NATO: An Alternative* (Washington, D.C.: The Brookings Institution, 1974), pp. 28–29.

2. According to a popular rumor, Patch Barracks was Field Marshal Erwin Rommel's headquarters during World War II and the officers' club was his living quarters. In actual fact, however, Rommel had no connection with Kurmärker Kaserne, as the installation was known during the war, and there is nothing to indicate that he even visited it. The rumor may have arisen from the fact that Rommel was once commanding general of the 7th Panzer Division, of which the 7th Panzer Regiment was never a part. See Truman Strobridge, *History of Patch Barracks* (Stuttgart: USEUCOM, 1982), p. 24.

3. In early 1983, General Bernard W. Rogers held the dual post of SACEUR and USCINCEUR, having succeeded General Alexander Haig in 1980. An illustrious series of U.S. generals have held the post through the years, beginning with General Dwight Eisenhower, and including Generals Matthew Ridgway, Alfred Gruenther, Lauris Norstad, Lyman Lemnitzer, and Andrew Goodpaster. The post of DCINCEUR in 1983 was occupied by General William Y. Smith.

4. Truman Strobridge, "USEUCOM," *Armed Forces*, April 1982, p. 107.

5. U.S., Congress, Senate, Committee on Foreign Relations, *United States Foreign Policy Objectives and Overseas Military Installations*, 96th Cong., 1st sess., April 1979 (Washington, D.C.: Government Printing Office, 1979), pp. 35–37. A report prepared by the Foreign Affairs and National Defense Division, Congressional Research Service, Library of Congress.

Figure 1.1.
NATO FORCE SECTORS

SCHLESWIGHOLSTEIN
(AFNORTH)

Bremerhaven

NORTH GERMAN PLAIN

Major U.S. Line
of Communication

NETHERLANDS

GERMAN
DEMOCRATIC REPUBLIC

Ruhr

Harz Mountains

Göttingen

Cologne NORTHAG

CENTAG

Elbe

FULDA GAP

BELGIUM

Thuringian
Forest

Rhine

HOF CORRIDOR

Frankfurt

LUXEMBOURG

CZECHOSLOVAKIA

Darmstadt

Würzburg

Heidelberg

Nuremberg

Stuttgart

FRANCE

FEDERAL REPUBLIC
OF GERMANY

Munich

SWITZERLAND

AUSTRIA

Source: Adapted from Richard D. Lawrence and Jeffrey Record. U.S. Force Structure in NATO: An Alternative. (Washington: The Brookings Institution, 1974), p. 30.

Figure 1.2.
MAJOR U.S. MILITARY INSTALLATIONS IN WEST GERMANY

Source: Adapted from United States Foreign Policy Objectives and Overseas Military Installations, Committee on Foreign Relations, U.S. Senate, by the Foreign Affairs and National Defense Division, Congressional Research Service, Library of Congress, April, 1979, p. 36.

Table 1.1. Department of Defense Active Duty Military Personnel Strengths by Regional Area and by Country (September 30, 1982)

A. Army
B. Air Force
C. Navy
D. Marine Corps

Regional area/country	Total	A	B	C	D
Total Worldwide	2,108,612	780,391	582,845	552,996	192,380
Ashore	1,879,729	780,391	582,845	333,801	182,692
Afloat	228,883	–	–	219,195	9,688
Total Foreign Countries	528,484	267,138	118,166	104,506	38,674
Ashore	448,094	267,138	118,166	33,804	28,986
Afloat	80,390	80,390	–	–	9,688
(1) Western &					
Southern Europe	355,633	227,270	81,575	39,564	7,224
Austria	33	6	2	–	25
Belgium*	2,261	1,469	645	115	32
Cyprus	14	2	2	–	10
Denmark*	131	5	19	18	89
Finland	19	5	2	2	10
France*	95	42	12	9	32
Germany (Fed. Republic					
& West Berlin)*	256,391	218,215	37,798	288	90
Gibraltar	1	–	–	1	–
Greece*	3,540	663	2,472	390	15
Greenland*	325	–	325	–	–
Iceland*	2,871	2	1,052	1,708	109
Ireland	8	2	–	–	6
Italy*	13,055	4,538	4,257	3,999	261
Luxembourg*	6	–	–	–	6
Malta	2	2	–	–	–
Netherlands*	2,578	779	1,775	15	9
Norway*	194	35	115	31	13
Portugal*	1,505	62	1,083	347	13
Spain*	8,950	22	5,084	3,650	194
Sweden	18	1	8	2	7
Switzerland	28	7	3	–	18
Turkey*	5,162	1,229	3,837	77	19
United Kingdom*	25,893	184	23,084	2,291	334
Afloat	32,553	–	–	26,621	5,932
*European NATO A/					

A/ Includes data for the first time on Spain, which became a member of NATO on May 30, 1982.

Source: "U.S. Military Strengths - Worldwide - as of September 30, 1982," Department of Defense, Fact Sheet, No. 518-82, December 1, 1982.

Table 1.2. Foreign Military Forces Stationed in the Federal
Republic of Germany

	Military Personnel	Dependents	Civilian Employees
U.S.A.			
1. U.S. Army Europe (USAREUR)			
HQ: Heidelberg	200,000	113,000	14,500
2. U.S. Air Force Europe (USAFE)			
HQ: Ramstein	33,000	48,000	2,300
Total	233,000	161,000	16,800
United Kingdom			
1. British Army of the Rhine (BAOR) (Including Berlin Brigade)			
HQ: Mönchengladbach	56,000	76,000	2,300
2. Royal Air Force (RAF)			
HQ: Mönchengladbach	9,000	14,900	100
Total	65,000	90,900	2,400
France			
French Forces in Germany (Forces Françaises en Allemagne)			
HQ: Baden-Baden	50,000	32,000	9,000
Belgium			
Belgian Corps			
HQ: Cologne-Junkersdorf	32,000	28,000	1,600
The Netherlands			
1. 41st Tank Brigade			
HQ: Seedorf	5,000	2,500	50
2. 12th Artillery Group			
HQ: Bramsche	1,700	3,500	80
Total	6,700	6,000	130
Canada			
Canadian Forces Europe			
HQ: Lahr	5,400	7,600	1,200
Grand Total	391,400	325,500	31,130

Note: Figures are approximate and rounded off.

Source: German Federal Press and Information Office, "Die
Aliierten Streitkräfte in der Bundesrepublik Deutschland,"
Aktuelles Basismaterial Chroniken, Nos. 5/82,
17 February, 1982.

Table 1.3. Principal USAREUR Commands in West Germany

Type of unit	Unit	Location
1. Headquarters (approx. 650 personnel each)	HQ, USAREUR	Heidelberg
	HQ, V Corps	Frankfurt
	HQ, VII Corps	Moehringen
	7th Army Training Command	Grafenwoehr
2. Armored Division (approx. 16,000 personnel each)	1st Armored Division	Ansbach
	3rd Armored Division	Frankfurt
3. Infantry Division (approx. 15,000 personnel each)	3rd Infantry Division	Wuerzburg
	8th Infantry Division	Bad Kreuznach
4. Armored Cavalry Regiment (approx. 3600 personnel each)	2d Armored Cavalry Regiment	Nuernberg
	11th Armored Cavalry Regiment	Fulda
5. Artillery (approx. 5000 each)	V Corps Artillery	Frankfurt
	VII Corps Artillery	Moehringen
	56th Artillery Brigade	Schwaebisch-Gmuend
6. Commands (approx. 5000 personnel each)	2nd Support Command	Nellingen
	3rd Support Command	Frankfurt
	21st Support Command	Kaiserslautern
	Medical Command Europe	Heidelberg
	U.S. Command Berlin (includes Berlin Brigade)	Berlin
7. Brigades (approx. 4000 personnel each)	3rd Brigade, 2nd Armored Division	Garlstedt*
	4th Brigade, 4th Infantry Division	Wiesbaden
	3rd Brigade, 1st Infantry Division	Goeppingen
8. Air Defense (approx. 12,000 personnel)	32nd Air Defense Command	Darmstadt

*Relocated from Grafenwoehr

Source: Committee on Foreign Relations, United States Senate,
96th Congress, 1st Session, United States Foreign Policy
Objectives and Overseas Military Installations, Prepared
by the Foreign Affairs and National Defense Division,
Congressional Research Service, Library of Congress,
April 1979, p. 37.

Table 1.4. Principal USAFE Commands in West Germany

Unit	Base	Aircraft type	Mission
26th TRW	Zweibruecken	RF-4C	Tactical Reconnaissance
36th TFW	Bitburg	F-15	Air superiority
50th TFW	Hahn	F-4E	Close air support/intercept
52nd TFW	Spangdahlem	F-4C/F-4D	Do
86th TFW	Ramstein	F-4E	Do
435th TAW	Rhein-Main	C-130/C-9	Tactical airlift
601st TCW	Sembach	OV-10/CH-53	Command, control and communications
	Lindsey AS	None	Do
	Hessischoldendorf AS	None	Do
350th ABG	Tempelhof	None	Support
606th TCS	Bremerhaven	None	Tactical air control

Source: Committee on Foreign Relations, United States Senate,
96th Congress, 1st Session, United States Foreign Policy
Objectives and Overseas Military Installations, Prepared
by the Foreign Affairs and National Defense Division,
Congressional Research Service, Library of Congress,
April 1979, p. 37.

2

The Demographic Composition
of U.S. Forces in West Germany

The U.S. military population in West Germany is a highly peculiar population simply by virtue of the fact that it constitutes a military presence of a foreign state. We can surmise a great deal about the character and quality of this population by studying its demographic characteristics. Tables 2.1 to 2.12 display this demography for enlisted personnel (E1–E9), and Tables 2.13 to 2.23 do the same for officers (W1–W4 and O1–10). Each table for enlisted personnel has a corresponding table for officers for the same demographic characteristic. The only exception to this scheme is that Table 2.8, showing Armed Forces Qualification Test (AFQT) scores for enlisted personnel, is not replicated for officers, as officers are not subjected to these tests.

The data in these tables, generated by the Defense Manpower Data Center, reflect the structure of the forces as of the spring of 1983. They include all U.S. military personnel in army and air force units stationed in the Federal Republic of Germany. Data for naval personnel were not generated, as fewer than 400 naval personnel are stationed there. For purposes of this study, we will focus on those data that seem important to an analysis of the character and quality of the U.S. military presence in the FRG and to the long-term viability of that presence as it is affected by social relationships between the Germans and U.S. military personnel.

Armed Service

A total of 251,161 U.S. Army and U.S. Air Force personnel were stationed in West Germany as of the spring of 1983 (combined totals from Tables 2.1 and 2.13). Together with spouses and dependents, the military community comprised nearly a half million people, a formidable military presence indeed in a small, densely populated country of 61.5 million inhabitants. Table 2.1 shows that nearly 86% of enlisted personnel were in the army, with the remaining 14% in the air force. Of the officers serving in West Germany, 79% were army officers and 21% were air force officers (Table 2.13). Thus, although the great bulk of the U.S. military presence in Germany was accounted for by the army, the air force had a higher ratio of officers to enlisted personnel. We may assume that the image most West Germans have of the U.S. military presence is formed more by perceptions of the army than of the air force.

Grade

Tables 2.2 and 2.14 show the distribution of enlisted personnel and officers by grade. The lowest four grades (E1–E4) are commonly referred to as the enlisted troops; grades E5–E9 are usually referred to as the noncommissioned officers or the career force. The data in Table 2.2 show that the army had a higher proportion of personnel at the lowest grades (E1–E2) than did the air force—9% as opposed to 5.3%. Thus, a slightly higher proportion of army personnel than air force personnel possessed a minimum level of experience and were perhaps somewhat less prepared for the vagaries of living and working in a foreign country. Looking at enlisted troops as a whole, we find also that the army had a slightly higher proportion of these grades than the air force—approximately 61% as opposed to 55%—but the air force had a higher proportion of noncommissioned officers. Insofar as these data relate to experience, maturity, and preparation for a foreign experience, similar conclusions emerge from an overview of the data on years of service displayed in Tables 2.6 and 2.18.

If we look at the distribution of officers by grade or rank (Table 2.14), we find that the army had a significantly higher proportion of lower-ranking officers (second and first lieutenants), while the air force had a higher proportion of higher-ranking officers (captains, majors, lieutenant colonels). Hence, the officer corps of the air force in West Germany was somewhat older and more experienced than the officer corps of the army. At the highest ranks, the army had forty-one generals stationed in the FRG, and the air force had thirteen.

Marital Status

The data for marital status, as shown in Tables 2.3 and 2.15, confirm one feature of U.S. force structure well understood by military analysts and often commented upon in the West German press. As compared to the conscription forces prior to 1973, the all-volunteer-force structure had a much higher percentage of married personnel, even in the lower enlisted ranks.

In 1983, army enlisted personnel were approximately evenly divided between being married and single. Among air force enlisted personnel, a slightly higher proportion were married—55% as opposed to 45% single. As might be expected, much higher percentages of the officers were married: 80% of air force officers and 73% of army officers. A much higher percentage of officers had dependents than did enlisted personnel (Tables 2.4 and 2.16). A higher percentage of army officers than air force officers had no dependents—32% as opposed to 25%. Among officers 30.5% had no dependents, compared to 51.3% of enlisted personnel. But if we consider that only 25.5% of officers were single, whereas 49.6% of enlisted men were single, we see that a slightly higher proportion of married officers postponed having children than did married enlisted personnel. Although the data do not indicate what proportion of these dependents are present in Germany, other evidence confirms that the vast majority of them have in fact been living with their military sponsors at or near military bases there. For U.S. forces in Germany, this means a substantially greater burden of providing for dependents abroad than was the case before 1973.

Privileges are authorized according to rank. In the case of the army, there is no authorization for government-subsidized housing until the rank of E5, the lowest rank of the noncommissioned officer corps. If a lower-ranking soldier brings a spouse and/or children to Germany, the family will have to find non-government-subsidized housing on the Germany economy. Given the chronic shortage of housing in the Federal Republic in areas close to military bases and the extremely high rental prices of suitable apartments, soldiers below E5 rank are discouraged by their commanders from bringing families with them. They are not prohibited from doing so, however, and a very large proportion of the lower-ranking soldiers do bring their families. This situation has created a nightmare for military authorities, especially during periods when the U.S. dollar was weak in its exchange rate with German marks.

Thus, living quarters, educational facilities, PX and commissary facilities, recreational programs, and the like have to be found or created for spouses and children who accompany their sponsors. For enlisted personnel at rank E5 or above, round-trip transportation for family members is provided between the United States and Germany. The logistical and support requirements for all of these functions constitute an enormous burden for the Department of Defense.

Gender

Although U.S. forces in Germany are overwhelmingly male, the percentage of female personnel is by no means insignificant, a fact that the Germans find at once puzzling and intriguing. Table 2.5 shows that in 1983, 10.3% of the enlisted personnel were female and 89.7% were male. Sex distribution differed for the army and the air force: 13.6% of enlisted air force personnel, but only 9.8% of enlisted army personnel, were female. These figures are similar to figures for U.S. armed forces as a whole, indicating that under the regime of the AVF, the air force has recruited more female personnel than has the army.

When we look at the sex distribution for officers (Table 2.17), we find that the total percentage of female officers, 9.5%, is not far below the total percentage of enlisted female personnel. Again, however, there is a striking difference between the air force and the army: Whereas 12.6% of air force officers were female, only 8.7% of army officers were female. Not only has the air force been able to enlist more females than has the army, it has also been able to attract more females into the officer corps. Whether the data merely confirm the popular image or whether the image is in fact strengthened by knowledge of the data is a question we cannot answer here. It remains, however, a bit of popular military folklore that the air force is a better place for women than the army, both in terms of life style and promotion possibilities.

The Germans are highly cognizant of female personnel in the U.S. armed forces, especially as the West German army, by contrast, has only a few thousand female volunteers, many of whom hold part-time positions. West German public opinion appears to be divided as to the wisdom or efficacy of females in military service. Liberals and progressives tend to view female participation in the military as a women's rights issue and favor such participation out of a concern for human rights, equal opportunity, and, more specifically, women's status in society. Conservative opinion, more concerned with security than opportunity, takes a dim view of women in military service. One critical strain of opinion that emerges clearly in the German press from time to time sees the inclusion of women in the military forces as a distinctly weak link in the U.S. conventional guarantee of West German security. Also, the fact that over 10% of U.S. military females in the Federal Republic are pregnant at any one time has been widely noted in the West German press and has no doubt increased the level of doubt about the propriety and credibility of U.S. forces stationed in Germany. U.S. commanders may claim, of course, that the incidence of pregnancy within their forces is none of the Germans' business. But as long as U.S. forces are housed on German real estate and constitute an integral part of the tapestry of U.S.-West German relations, then social relations within the U.S. forces are legitimately a German concern. Social relationships and force credibility are issues that cannot be divided into separate compartments.

Years of Service

The data shown in Tables 2.6 and 2.18 give us a rough idea of the level and/or depth of experience of U.S. forces stationed in the FRG. The great bulk of enlisted troops in Germany are relatively inexperienced, which is not unexpected, and holds true in greater or lesser degree for the armed forces of any country stationed anywhere. Armies are, by their nature, composed largely of young people serving for relatively short periods of time. It is also not surprising that the army troops are, in general, less experienced than the air force units; however, the difference in level of experience is rather major. As the data in Table 2.6 indicate, 46.6% of army enlisted personnel had less than one to three years of military service, but the corresponding figure for the air force is much lower—35.2%. This same 11-point spread is seen in the category for nine to twenty years off service. Whereas 30.2% of air force enlisted personnel possessed this higher level of experience, only 19.2% of army enlisted personnel were so experienced.

Similarly, among army officers, 38.8% had from less than a year to five years of experience, but only 23.6% of air force officers were at this less-experienced level. Conversely, higher percentages of air force officers had from six to ten years of experience (24.5%) or eleven to twenty years of experience (41.8%) than their counterparts in the army, whose percentages for these categories were 21.9% and 34.3%, respectively. Hence, the experience levels of air force personnel, both officers and enlisted, were higher than those of army personnel. This may be a factor that has some bearing upon the army's greater problems with crime, indiscipline, and social relations with West Germans.

Level of Education

The level of education among enlisted personnel is always a highly sensitive subject for Pentagon leaders, especially since the advent of the all-volunteer force in the early 1970s. The Department of Defense expends a considerable amount of time and effort attempting to demonstrate that educational levels of various ranks and age groups of military personnel compare favorably with those in civilian life. Nevertheless, the data in Table 2.7 leave no room for comfort, at least in reference to U.S. forces stationed in West Germany. We may begin by noting that among enlisted personnel in the army, less than 10% possessed any education beyond high school; 76.3% possessed a high school diploma; and 13.8% had not finished high school. Although no one would argue that all recruits into the armed forces need to possess a high school diploma, it is nevertheless obvious that the forces' problems with illiteracy and minimum knowledge are compounded by larger numbers of recruits without a high school education. That 13.8% of army enlisted personnel were without a high school diploma, though short of a disastrous situation, leaves little room for enthusiasm. Armed forces are, after all *armed* and need many kinds of expertise in order to defend territory or prosecute a war successfully.

The 76.3% of army enlisted personnel with only a high school diploma is the subject of lively debate. This may be interpreted, on the one hand, as a great success story, because within the civilian labor force as a whole, 23% are non-high-school graduates and 41% possess only a high school diploma.[1] On the other hand, it may be argued plausibly that, given the technological sophistication of armed forces in today's world, the 13.8% of enlisted personnel without a high school diploma represents an uncomfortably high proportion of troops with very little education. The real value of a high school diploma as preparation for military service is also subject to wide disparities of interpretation. Critics of the present quality of U.S. forces point to the worthlessness of the diploma as preparation for anything but minimal tasks. Many high school graduates are barely able to read at the eighth-grade level. Optimists, on the other hand, stress the fact that the considerably higher proportion of military recruits possessing a high school diploma, as compared to the civilian labor force as a whole, attests well to the general quality of U.S. forces. Air force enlisted personnel are somewhat better educated than their army counterparts (Table 2.7). Whereas only 1.6% did not possess a high school diploma, 19.1% had some education beyond high school (as compared to 9.9% for the army). Clearly, the air force, in terms of the educational background of enlisted personnel, is in a somewhat better position to accomplish its military mission in West Germany.

The educational level of the officer corps (Table 2.19) presents a rather impressive picture. Only 3.7% possessed only a high school diploma; 8.1% had some college training; an additional 58.6% were college graduates; and 29.9% possessed advanced degrees beyond the undergraduate degree. Again, air force officers as a group displayed somewhat higher levels of education than did army officers. Whereas 4.7% of the army officers possessed only a high school diploma, only 0.1% of the air force officers remained at this educational level. A slightly higher percentage of air force officers were college graduates (60% as compared to 58.2% of army officers), and a significantly higher percentage of air force officers possessed advanced degrees (38.7% as compared to 26.7% of army officers). A higher percentage of air force officers than might be expected even held doctoral degrees—1%; the corresponding figure for army officers is 0.5%. Hence, the educational background of U.S. officers serving in West Germany is a matter about which Pentagon leaders are justifiably proud. Educational level is, no doubt, a major factor that explains the ease with which U.S.

officers interact with the West German population while a large portion of the enlisted personnel remain completely isolated.

Armed Forces Qualification Test

Armed Forces Qualification Test (AFQT) scores are used in conjunction with educational, medical, and moral standards to determine eligibility to enlist in military service and assignment to occupation. Although the test is a kind of general intelligence and general aptitude test combined, the services use AFQT scores as a primary measure of trainability. Enlisted personnel with higher test scores tend to be assigned to more complex jobs. The test scores are grouped into five broad categories. An AFQT percentile score of 50 is average for the population, that is, for new recruits being tested for general intelligence and suitability for military service. Recruits with scores of 50 and above—Categories I, II, and IIIA—are considered above average; scores in Categories IIIB, IV, and V are below average. Persons who score in Category V—the first through the ninth percentiles—are not eligible for military service; also excluded are persons who score in Category IV but who are non-high-school graduates as well as Category IV high school graduates who score in the tenth to fourteenth percentile range. These excluded groups represent approximately 21.5% of the youth population tested. Congress has established ceilings on the percentage of Category IV's that may be enlisted: 25% for each service in fiscal year 1982 and 20% starting with fiscal year 1983.[2]

Table 2.8 shows the distribution of AFQT test scores by category for enlisted personnel in West Germany. What stands out immediately is the wide disparity in test scores between army and air force enlisted personnel. The scores for army enlisted personnel tend to confirm the worst suspicions regarding the mental abilities of a large portion of army enlisted personnel in the FRG. Over a third, 34.2%, were in the lowest category eligible for military service, Category IV (with scores from 15 to 30); another 26.7% were in Category IIIB (31 to 49). Thus, 60.9% of the enlisted army personnel in West Germany were below average in general mental ability, whereas 39% were above average. Only 20.1% scored in Category II (65 to 92), and a very small group, 2.5%, scored in the highest category (93 to 99).

The figures in the column for air force enlisted personnel present a much brighter picture. Whereas 31.9% scored below average in general mental ability (Categories IV and IIIB), 68% scored above average. The air force had a somewhat higher percentage of enlisted personnel in Category I than did the army (5.1% vs. 2.5%) and a much higher percentage in Category II (38.9% vs. 20.1%). The air force also had lower percentages in the below-average categories; most striking is the much lower percentage of air force personnel in Category IV as compared to the army (7.9% vs. 34.2%).

The portrait of U.S. enlisted personnel in the Federal Republic derived from an analysis of AFQT scores yields significant insight into the various problems of the army and air force in the realm of German perceptions and German-American social relations. The opinion of West German newspaper commentators that much of the U.S. army in the FRG is drawn from a kind of American underclass is given some credence by AFQT scores. Both U.S. military leaders and the West German population have posed two kinds of questions: one concerns the adaptability of army enlisted personnel to living and working in a cultural environment vastly different from that of their homeland and the other concerns the trainability—and hence the military readiness—of U.S. ground forces in Germany.

Insofar as the image of U.S. forces has become more negative during the period of the AVF over the last twelve years, this negative image derives from the army much more than from the air force. A review of AFQT scores explains some of the reasons why the army's image problems are so much more pronounced. The army has to cope with considerably higher levels of substance abuse and indiscipline than does the air force, and this compounds its problems of maintaining cordial relations with the German population near U.S. bases. The army is a larger catch-all force and has greater difficulty meeting its recruitment quotas than either the air force or the navy; it is consequently less able to select out the brightest and most able recruits. And in Germany, the army's problem of coordinating an enormous organization of 214,000 people is obviously a more complicated task than that of the air force, which must organize a mere 37,000 older and more experienced personnel.

Age

Data for the age distribution of enlisted personnel, as shown in Table 2.9, appear to confirm the popular image of the U.S. military as a force of very young people. In 1983, in the army, 42.8% of the enlisted personnel were twenty-two years of age or younger; in the air force the corresponding figure was 37.1%. However, the force of army enlisted personnel in West Germany is not quite as young as we might guess at first glance. The second largest age cohort—with 39.9%—was of personnel twenty-three to thirty years of age in the army. The same was true for the air force, where the twenty-three to thirty age cohort comprised 35.9% of the force.

If we compare the age distribution of army and air force enlisted personnel, we see that the air force was in general a somewhat older force. The air force had 26.6% of its enlisted personnel in the older age categories (thirty-one to forty-eight years of age); the army had only 16.9% of its enlisted personnel in these categories. To the extent that age indicates level of maturity and/or experience, we can say that the air force had a significantly higher percentage of more mature people in the enlisted ranks. Conversely, the army had a higher percentage of less mature personnel in the enlisted ranks than did the air force. These statistics tend to reinforce the conclusions we reached based on AFQT scores. The higher proportion of younger, less mature people is surely a factor that makes for greater drug abuse and indiscipline problems in the army.

Table 2.18 gives the age distribution of the officer corps. The air force had a somewhat older, more mature group of officers in West Germany than did the army. The army had a substantially higher percentage of officers in the youngest age group (48.4%) than did the air force (34.3%), and the air force had higher percentages of officers in the age categories above thirty. Hence, both enlisted personnel and officers in the air force in the Federal Republic are somewhat older, and presumably more mature and experienced, than their counterparts in the army.

Home of Record by State

Table 2.10 gives the distribution of enlisted personnel in West Germany by home of record—the fifty states, the District of Columbia, and five U.S. territories. The corresponding distribution of officers is shown in Table 2.21. In both tables the population of each state or territory is given as well as the area's percentage of total U.S. population, so that the reader may see whether enlisted personnel or officers from any given state or territory are overrepresented or underrepresented among the forces serving in the FRG.

Region

Of greater interest for purposes of our analysis is the distribution of forces in West Germany by region of the United States, as shown for 1983 in Tables 2.11 and 2.22. Eight regions are specified, with a ninth region comprising the five U.S. territories or possessions (Virgin Islands, Guam, Puerto Rico, American Samoa, and the Canal Zone). Table 2.11 displays the regional distribution of enlisted personnel. Somewhat underrepresented were New England, the mid-Atlantic states, and the Midwest; significantly underrepresented were the Pacific states, which contained

14.2% of the U.S. population but provided only 11.5% of enlisted personnel in Germany. The regions that had approximately equal percentages of U.S. population and enlisted troops in Germany were the north-mid-central states, the south central states, and the Mountain states. The two regions that were overrepresented were the U.S. possessions and the South, which was significantly overrepresented, with 15.3% of total U.S. population but 22.8% of enlisted troops in Germany.

The U.S. regional distribution of the officer corps in West Germany is shown in Table 2.22. Two regions were significantly underrepresented: the Midwest, with 19.7% of U.S. population but only 15.1% of officers; and the Pacific region, with 14.2% of U.S. population but only 10.9% of officers. Four regions provided officers in West Germany in approximate proportion to their populations: the New England states, the mid-Atlantic states, the north-mid-central states, and the U.S. possessions. Three regions were overrepresented: the South, the south central states, and the Mountain states.

Both tables show two regions as significantly underrepresented: the midwestern states and the Pacific states. Four regions were represented in approximately the same proportion as their share of U.S. population in respect to both enlisted personnel and officers: the New England states, the mid-Atlantic states, the north-mid-central states, and the U.S. possessions. Most significantly, only one region of the United States appears in both tables as overrepresented: the South. The South, in fact, provided a larger percentage of enlisted personnel in West Germany than did any other region of the United States, as well as the second largest component of officers, the largest coming from the mid-Atlantic states. But a much smaller percentage of the nation's population lives in the South (15.3%) than in the mid-Atlantic states (21.5%), so that the South was significantly overrepresented among the officers, whereas the mid-Atlantic region was not. These data for U.S. forces in the Federal Republic provide some confirmation to the popular impression concerning U.S. forces in general, namely, that southerners are the largest regional group among the enlisted ranks and that they also constitute the backbone of the U.S. officer corps.

Ethnic and Racial Origin

The racial/ethnic composition of the U.S. military has become a highly quarrelsome issue since the advent of the AVF in 1973. As the portion of U.S. forces coming from minority groups rose substantially from 1973 to the early 1980s, criticism of the increasingly unrepresentative character of the U.S. military became more strident. Whether the forces need to be or ought to be racially representative of U.S. society as a whole is a question that will be raised in Chapters 7 and 12. A major item of concern in this study, however, is the effects of a racially unbalanced force structure on U.S.–West German relations and, hence, on the long-term viability of the U.S. presence in the Federal Republic.

Tables 2.12 and 2.23 display the racial and ethnic composition of U.S. forces stationed in the FRG. Table 2.12 indicates that in 1983 61% of enlisted personnel were white, 31.4% were black, 4.2% were of hispanic origin, and 3.4% were of other ethnic groups or of unknown racial/ethnic origin. Important to note, however, is the enormous difference in racial composition of the army and the air force. Whereas blacks comprised 34% of enlisted personnel in the army, they represented only 15.5% of air force enlisted personnel. The army also had a slightly higher percentage of Hispanics (4.3%) than did the air force (3.6%); the air force had a slightly higher percentage of Native Americans, Alaskan natives, and Asian/Pacific islanders (2.5%) than did the army (1.3%). The major difference, then, between the racial/ethnic structures of the army and the air force in the enlisted ranks in Germany is the substantially larger proportion of blacks in the army.

The racial/ethnic composition of the officer corps is shown in Table 2.23. Immediately evident is the underrepresentation of minority groups among the officers, who were 87.7% white in the army and 92.2% white in the air force. The army appears to be further advanced than the air force in the process of racially integrating the officer corps: Whereas 8.8% of army officers were black, still a very low proportion, only 4.5% of the air force officers were black. The air force had slightly higher proportions of other ethnic groups in the officer ranks than did the army, though these percentages for both services were miniscule.

An analysis of these tables yields some strong clues as to the origin of some of the racial strife in the forces in Germany in recent years. The large component of black enlisted troops in the army was commanded by an officer corps that was only 8.8% black. The smaller black enlisted component in the air force was also commanded by an officer corps that included few blacks—4.5%. The increasing proportion of minorities among U.S. forces stationed in Germany caught the attention of the West German press and public after the mid-1970s. As we shall see in Chapter 8, German discrimination against U.S. service personnel has become an increasingly thorny problem. Also, the tendency for West German political leaders and press commentators to question the wisdom of U.S. military personnel policy and, indeed, the quality of AVF forces stationed in the FRG has increased the level of tension in the political relationship between the two countries.

Summary of Force Demography

The tables we have examined give data for the demographic structure of U.S. forces stationed in Germany in 1983. These data do not indicate whether or how the demography of the forces in Germany differs from that of U.S. forces as a whole, though other demographic tables[3] reveal that U.S. forces in Germany are substantially similar to all U.S. forces for most characteristics. In the Federal Republic, the great bulk of the U.S. military presence—over 80%—is accounted for by the army, so that German perceptions of the character and quality of the U.S. military derive more profoundly from impressions of army personnel than air force personnel. In 1983, a very high percentage of service members were young and inexperienced, and about half of them were married, a fact that has often been noted in the West German press. The forces were overwhelmingly male, though female personnel constituted approximately 10% of the force structure, another characteristic widely debated in the West German press. In terms of education and intelligence test category (AFQT), the enlisted personnel tended to be neither highly educated nor of above average intelligence, though these characteristics are not unexpected for a large military establishment; the significance of this is a subject of intense debate among military analysts. The officer corps, on the other hand, displayed an impressive level of educational achievement. The racial/ethnic structure of the forces was skewed by the presence of a high percentage of minority groups, particularly among enlisted personnel. As for regional distribution, the midwestern states and the Pacific states were underrepresented among both enlisted personnel and officers, whereas the southern states were overrepresented.

Notes

1. U.S. Department of Defense, Military Manpower Task Force, *A Report to the President on the Status and Prospects of the All-Volunteer Force* (Washington, D.C.: Government Printing Office, October 1982) p. II-2.

2. *Military Manpower Task Force*, p. II-7.

3. See the demographic tables in Gary R. Nelson, "The Supply and Quality of First-Term Enlistees Under the All-Volunteer Force," in William Bowman, Roger Little, and G. Thomas Sicilia, eds., *The All-Volunteer Force After a Decade: Retrospect and Prospect* (Elmsford, N.Y.: Pergamon–Brassey's International Defense Publishers, 1986), pp. 23–81.

Table 2.1. Enlisted Personnel by Service

	Army	Air Force	Total
N	195,813	32,125	227,938
%	85.9	14.1	100

Source: Derived from 1983 data provided by Defense
Manpower Data Center.

Table 2.2. Enlisted Personnel by Grade

Grade	Army		Air Force		Total %
	Number	%	Number	%	
E1	6,356	3.2	244	0.8	2.9
E2	10,254	5.2	1,441	4.5	5.1
E3	41,587	21.2	8,661	27.0	22.0
E4	61,311	31.3	7,382	23.0	30.1
E5	37,019	18.9	7,162	22.3	19.4
E6	23,082	11.8	3,708	11.5	11.7
E7	11,912	6.1	2,479	7.7	6.3
E8	3,599	1.8	724	2.3	1.9
E9	693	0.3	324	1.0	0.4
Total	195,813	100.0	32,125	100.0	100.0
E1-4	119,508	60.9	17,728	55.3	60.1
E5-9	76,305	38.9	14,397	44.8	39.7

Adjusted Number = 227,938
Mean   = 4.3065
Standard Deviation = 1.4965

Explanation of Grades:
E1-Private
E2-Private
E3-Private First Class
E4-Specialist 4
E5-Sergeant
E6-Staff Sergeant
E7-Sergeant First Class
E8-Master Sergeant
E9-Sergeant Major

Source: Derived from data provided by Defense Manpower Data
Center.

Table 2.3. Enlisted Personnel by Marital Status

Marital Status	Army %	Air Force %	Total %
Single	50.4	44.8	49.6
Married	49.6	55.2	50.4

Adjusted N = 227,892

Source: Derived from data provided by Defense Manpower Data
Center.

Table 2.4. Enlisted Personnel by Number of Dependents

Number of Dependents	Army %	Air Force %	Total %
None	51.6	49.6	51.3
One to Three	41.1	41.8	41.2
Four to Fifteen	7.2	8.7	7.5

Mean   = 2.1356
Standard Deviation = 1.4350
Adjusted N   = 227,714

Source: Derived from data provided by Defense Manpower Data
Center.

Table 2.5. Enlisted Personnel by Sex

Sex	Army %	Air Force %	Total %
Male	90.2	86.4	89.7
Female	9.8	13.6	10.3

Adjusted N = 227,938

Source: Derived from data provided by Defense Manpower Data
Center.

Table 2.6. Enlisted Personnel by Years of Service

Years of Service	Army %	Air Force %	Total %
Less than One to Three	46.6	35.2	45.1
Four to Eight	32.1	28.1	31.6
Nine to Twenty	19.2	30.9	20.8
Twenty to Twenty-Eight	2.0	5.5	2.5
*			

Mean   = 6.1516
Standard Deviation = 5.2419
Adjusted N   = 227,930

*An additional category could be included for 29-35
years of service. Approximately 167 enlisted personnel fall
into this category. However, since they constitute
less than 0.1% they have not been included in these figures.

Source: Derived from data provided by Defense Manpower Data
        Center.

Table 2.7. Enlisted Personnel by Highest Year of Education

Highest Education Completed	Army %	Air Force %	Total %
Did Not Finish High School	13.8	1.6	12.0
High School Graduate	76.3	79.3	76.7
Completed Some College	8.4	16.9	9.6
Undergraduate Degree	1.4	1.9	1.5
Advanced Degree	0.1	0.3	0.1

Adjusted N = 227,606

Source: Derived from data provided by Defense Manpower Data
        Center.

Table 2.8. Enlisted Personnel by Armed Forces Qualification
            Test Category

Category *	Army %	Air Force %	Total %
I	2.5	5.1	2.9
II	20.1	38.9	22.6
IIIA	16.4	24.0	17.4
IIIB	26.7	24.0	26.3
IV	34.2	7.9	30.7

                Mean   = 5.2168
                Standard Deviation = 1.5001
                Adjusted N   = 213,724

*Categories are defined by percentile rankings achieved
on the AFQT Test:

Cat. I   = 93-99 percentile
Cat. II   = 65-92 percentile
Cat. IIIA = 50-64 percentile
Cat. IIIB = 31-49 percentile
Cat. IV   = 10-30 percentile
Cat. V   = 1-9 percentile (Not eligible for military service;
                              hence not included in Table 2.8.)

Source: Derived from data provided by Defense Manpower Data
        Center.

Table 2.9. Enlisted Personnel by Age

Age	Army %	Air Force %	Total %
17-19	9.6	7.7	10.2
20-22	33.2	29.4	32.8
23-30	39.9	35.9	39.4
31-40	14.9	23.0	16.1
41-48	2.0	3.6	2.3
*			

                Mean   = 25.3536
                Standard Deviation = 5.9587
                Adjusted N   = 227,914

*Ages range up to 65 years. However, there is less
than 0.1% of the total enlisted force above the age of
48. The actual number of enlisted personnel above age
48 is 310, with only 12 of these over the age of 55.

Source: Derived from data provided by Defense Manpower Data
        Center

Table 2.10. Enlisted Personnel by Home of Record (State)

State or U.S. Possession	Pop. of State	% of U.S. Pop.	Army %	Air Force %	Total %
Alabama	3,890,061	1.7	3.1	2.0	2.9
Alaska	400,481	0.2	0.1	0.1	0.1
American Samoa	32,297	0.01	0.1	0.0	0.0
Arizona	2,717,866	1.2	1.2	1.4	1.2
Arkansas	2,285,513	1.0	1.3	1.2	1.3
California	23,668,562	10.3	7.6	9.0	7.8
Canal Zone*	*	*	0.0	0.0	0.0
Colorado	2,888,834	1.3	1.3	1.4	1.3
Connecticut	3,107,576	1.4	0.8	1.2	0.9
Delaware	595,225	0.3	0.3	0.3	0.3
District of Columbia	637,651	0.3	0.4	0.2	0.4
Florida	9,739,992	4.2	5.6	6.0	5.7
Georgia	5,464,265	2.4	4.1	2.5	3.9
Guam	105,979	0.05	0.3	0.1	0.3
Hawaii	965,000	0.4	0.6	0.5	0.6
Idaho	943,935	0.4	0.4	0.5	0.4
Illinois	11,418,461	5.0	3.8	3.5	3.8
Indiana	5,490,179	2.4	2.5	2.3	2.4
Iowa	2,913,387	1.3	1.0	1.3	1.1
Kansas	2,363,208	1.0	0.7	1.0	0.7
Kentucky	3,661,433	1.6	1.8	1.4	1.7
Louisiana	4,203,972	1.8	1.8	1.6	1.7
Maine	1,124,660	0.5	0.6	0.8	0.7
Maryland	4,216,446	1.8	2.3	1.6	2.2
Massachusetts	5,737,037	2.5	1.6	2.5	1.7
Michigan	9,258,344	4.0	3.8	3.9	3.8
Minnesota	4,077,148	1.8	1.4	1.8	1.5
Mississippi	2,520,638	1.1	1.7	1.1	1.6
Missouri	4,917,444	2.1	2.4	2.4	2.4
Montana	786,690	0.3	0.3	0.4	0.3
Nebraska	1,570,006	0.7	0.6	0.6	0.6
Nevada	799,184	0.3	0.2	0.4	0.3
New Hampshire	920,610	0.4	0.5	0.6	0.5
New Jersey	7,364,158	3.2	2.2	2.4	2.2
New Mexico	1,299,968	0.6	0.6	0.7	0.7
New York	17,557,288	7.6	6.3	7.0	6.4
North Carolina	5,874,429	2.6	4.1	2.8	3.9
North Dakota	652,695	0.3	0.2	0.2	0.2
Ohio	10,797,419	4.7	4.7	5.1	4.8
Oklahoma	3,025,266	1.3	1.1	1.1	1.1
Oregon	2,632,663	1.1	1.0	1.3	1.1
Pennsylvania	11,866,728	5.2	4.3	6.0	4.5
Puerto Rico*	*3,196,520	*1.4	2.0	0.2	1.8
Rhode Island	947,154	0.4	0.3	0.5	0.3
South Carolina	3,119,208	1.4	2.6	1.6	2.5
South Dakota	690,178	0.3	0.3	0.4	0.3
Tennessee	4,590,750	2.0	2.3	2.0	2.3
Texas	14,228,383	6.2	5.7	6.9	5.8
Utah	1,461,037	0.6	0.4	0.4	0.4
Vermont	511,456	0.2	0.2	0.3	0.2
Virginia	5,346,279	2.3	3.3	2.1	3.1
Virgin Islands	96,569	0.04	0.1	0.0	0.1
Washington	4,130,163	1.8	1.6	2.1	1.6
West Virginia	1,949,644	0.8	0.9	0.9	0.9
Wisconsin	4,705,335	2.0	1.5	2.1	1.6
Wyoming	470,816	0.2	0.1	0.1	0.1

*Population figures for Canal Zone and Puerto Rico are combined.
Data for populations of states and territories are from U.S. Department
of Commerce, Bureau of the Census, Statistical Abstract of the United
States, National Data Book and Guide to Sources, 103rd edition,
1982-1983.

Source: Derived from data provided by Defense Manpower Data Center.

Table 2.11. Enlisted Personnel by Region of United States

Region of U.S.	Pop. of Region	% of U.S. Pop.	Army %	Air Force %	Total %
New England States	12,348,493	5.4	4.0	5.9	4.3
Mid-Atlantic States	49,533,419	21.5	20.0	20.5	20.0
Southern States	35,199,343	15.3	23.5	18.0	22.8
Mid-Western States	45,331,191	19.7	18.1	18.3	18.1
North-Mid-Central States	17,184,066	7.5	6.6	7.7	6.8
South Central States	23,743,134	10.3	9.9	10.8	9.9
Mountain States	10,569,146	4.6	4.3	4.9	4.4
Pacific States	32,596,053	14.2	11.1	13.4	11.5
U.S. Possessions	3,431,365	1.5	2.5	0.3	2.2

Adjusted N = 221,354

Regions are defined as follows:

New England States
Maine
New Hampshire
Vermont
Massachusetts
Rhode Island
Connecticut

Mid-Atlantic States
New York
Pennsylvania
New Jersey
Delaware
District of Columbia
Maryland
Virginia
West Virginia

Southern States
North Carolina
Alabama
South Carolina
Florida
Tennessee
Mississippi
Georgia

Mountain States
New Mexico
Arizona
Colorado
Utah
Wyoming
Idaho
Montana

North Mid-Central States
Kansas
Missouri
Nebraska
Iowa
South Dakota
North Dakota
Minnesota

Mid-Western States
Wisconsin
Illinois
Michigan
Indiana
Ohio
Kentucky

South Central States
Louisiana
Texas
Arkansas
Oklahoma

Pacific States
Washington
Oregon
California
Nevada
Alaska
Hawaii

U.S. Possessions
Virgin Islands
Guam
Puerto Rico
American Samoa
Canal Zone

Data for populations of regions derived from U.S Department of Commerce, Bureau of the Census, Statistical Abstract of the United States, National Data Book and Guide to Sources, 103rd edition, 1982-1983.

Source: Derived from data provided by Defense Manpower Data Center.

Table 2.12. Enlisted Personnel by Ethnic and Racial Origin

Ethnic Origin	Army %	Air Force %	Total %
White	58.3	77.9	61.0
Black	34.0	15.5	31.4
Hispanic	4.3	3.6	4.2
Am. Ind./			
Alaskan Nat.	0.3	1.2	0.5
Asian/			
Pacific Island	1.0	1.3	1.0
Other/Unknown	2.1	0.5	1.9

Adjusted N = 227,938

Source: Derived from data provided by Defense Manpower Data
Center.

Table 2.13. Officers by Service

	Army	Air Force	Total
N	18,335	4,888	23,223
%	78.9	21.0	100

Adjusted N = 23,223

Source: Derived from data provided by Defense Manpower
Data Center.

Table 2.14. Officers by Grade

Rank	Army		Air Force		Total	
	N	%	N	%	N	%
Warrant I	660	3.6	--	--	660	2.8
Warrant II	1564	8.5	--	--	1564	6.7
Warrant III	1031	5.6	--	--	1031	4.4
Warrant IV	240	1.3	--	--	240	1.0
2nd Lieutenant (01)	1474	8.0	221	4.5	1695	7.3
1st Lieutenant (02)	3612	19.7	818	16.7	4430	19.1
Captain (03)	5741	31.3	2113	43.2	7854	33.8
Major (04)	2284	12.5	964	19.7	3248	14.0
Lieutenant Colonel (05)	1279	7.0	542	11.1	1821	7.8
Colonel (06)	399	2.2	217	4.4	616	2.6
Brigadier General (07)	32	0.2	10	0.2	42	0.2
Major General (08)	13	0.1	1	0.0	14	0.1
Lieutenant General (09)	5	0.0	1	0.0	6	0.0
General (4 Star) (10)	1	0.0	1	0.0	2	0.0

Adjusted Number = 23,223

Source: Derived from data provided by Defense Manpower
Data Center.

Table 2.15. Officers by Marital Status

Marital Status	Army %	Air Force %	Total %
Single	26.9	20.5	25.5
Married	73.1	79.5	74.5

Adjusted N = 22,082

Source: Derived from data provided by Defense Manpower
Data Center.

Table 2.16. Officers by Number of Dependents

Number of Dependents	Army %	Air Force %	Total %
None	32.0	24.7	30.5
One to Three	54.8	60.1	55.9
Four to Fifteen	13.2	15.2	13.5

Mean   = 2.7740
Standard Deviation = 1.5716
Adjusted N   = 23,219

Source: Derived from data provided by Defense Manpower
Data Center.

Table 2.17. Officers by Sex

Sex	Army %	Air Force %	Total %
Male	91.3	87.4	90.5
Female	8.7	12.6	9.5

Adjusted N = 23,223

Source: Derived from data provided by Defense Manpower
Data Center.

Table 2.18. Officers by Years of Service

Years of Service	Army %	Air Force %	Total %
Less than One to Five	38.3	23.6	35.2
Six to Ten	21.1	24.5	21.8
Eleven to Twenty	34.3	41.8	36.1
Twenty-one to Thirty-two	5.9	9.9	7.0
*			

```
Mean                 = 9.9219
Standard Deviation = 6.6402
Adjusted N           = 23,217
```

*This table ends at 32 years of service. Some 24 officers
have 33-36 years of service.

Source: Derived from data provided by Defense Manpower
        Data Center.

Table 2.19. Officers by Highest Year of Education

Highest Level of Education Completed	Army %	Air Force %	Total %
High School Graduate	4.7	0.1	3.7
One to Four Years College	9.9	1.3	8.1
College Graduate	58.2	60.0	58.6
Masters or other Professional Degree	26.2	37.7	29.0
Doctorate	0.5	1.0	0.6

Adjusted N = 21,930

Source: Derived from data provided by Defense Manpower
        Data Center.

Table 2.20. Officers by Age

Age	Army %	Air Force %	Total %
21-30	48.4	34.3	45.4
31-40	41.2	49.9	43.1
41-50	9.4	14.2	10.4
51-56	0.8	1.0	0.9
*			

```
Mean                 = 32.1994
Standard Deviation = 6.6255
Adjusted N           = 23,158
```

*One officer is 19 years of age and five are 20 years of
age. A total of twenty-eight officers fall in the category
of 57-63 years of age. However, given the total number,
all of these comprise less than 0.1%.

Source: Derived from data provided by Defense Manpower
        Data Center.

Table 2.21. Officers by Home of Record (State)

State or U.S. Possession	Pop. of State	% of U.S. Pop. %	Army %	Air Force %	Total %
Alabama	3,890,061	1.7	2.6	2.0	2.5
Alaska	400,481	0.2	0.2	0.0	0.2
American Samoa	32,297	0.01	0.0	0.0	0.0
Arizona	2,717,866	1.2	1.4	1.4	1.4
Arkansas	2,285,513	1.0	1.7	1.0	1.5
California	23,668,562	10.3	6.2	7.8	6.5
Canal Zone*	*	*	0.0	0.0	0.0
Colorado	2,888,834	1.3	1.3	1.9	1.4
Connecticut	3,107,576	1.4	1.4	1.4	1.4
Delaware	595,225	0.3	0.4	0.2	0.3
District of Columbia	637,651	0.3	0.3	0.2	0.3
Florida	9,739,992	4.2	5.7	5.2	5.6
Georgia	5,464,265	2.4	2.9	2.1	2.7
Guam	105,979	0.05	0.1	0.0	0.1
Hawaii	965,000	0.4	0.6	0.4	0.5
Idaho	943,935	0.4	0.6	0.6	0.6
Illinois	11,418,461	5.0	3.4	4.2	3.6
Indiana	5,499,179	2.4	1.6	2.4	1.7
Iowa	2,913,387	1.3	1.3	1.7	1.4
Kansas	2,363,208	1.0	1.3	1.6	1.4
Kentucky	3,661,433	1.6	1.5	1.2	1.4
Louisiana	4,203,972	1.8	1.4	1.9	1.5
Maine	1,124,660	0.5	0.8	0.4	0.7
Maryland	4,216,446	1.8	2.0	1.9	2.0
Massachusetts	5,737,037	2.5	2.2	2.7	2.3
Michigan	9,258,344	4.0	2.3	2.5	2.4
Minnesota	4,077,148	1.8	1.2	1.9	1.3
Mississippi	2,520,638	1.1	1.3	0.9	1.2
Missouri	4,917,444	2.1	2.4	2.0	2.3
Montana	786,690	0.3	0.6	0.7	0.6
Nebraska	1,570,006	0.7	0.8	1.2	0.9
Nevada	799,184	0.3	0.4	0.2	0.3
New Hampshire	920,610	0.4	0.6	0.9	0.7
New Jersey	7,364,158	3.2	2.8	3.4	2.9
New Mexico	1,299,968	0.6	0.7	0.9	0.7
New York	17,557,288	7.6	5.9	5.5	5.8
North Carolina	5,874,429	2.6	2.5	2.1	2.4
North Dakota	652,695	0.3	0.4	0.5	0.4
Ohio	10,797,419	4.7	4.0	5.0	4.2
Oklahoma	3,025,266	1.3	1.8	1.5	1.7
Oregon	2,632,663	1.1	1.0	1.8	1.2
Pennsylvania	11,866,728	5.2	5.9	4.8	5.7
Puerto Rico*	*3,196,520	*1.4	0.8	0.2	0.7
Rhode Island	947,154	0.4	0.4	0.1	0.4
South Carolina	3,119,208	1.4	1.9	2.0	1.9
South Dakota	690,178	0.3	0.7	0.5	0.7
Tennessee	4,590,750	2.0	2.6	2.1	2.5
Texas	14,228,383	6.2	7.7	8.3	7.8
Utah	1,461,037	0.6	0.7	0.7	0.7
Vermont	511,456	0.2	0.4	0.2	0.4
Virginia	5,346,279	2.3	4.3	2.5	3.9
Virgin Islands	96,569	0.04	0.0	0.0	0.0
Washington	4,130,163	1.8	2.2	2.3	2.2
West Virginia	1,949,644	0.8	0.9	0.6	0.8
Wisconsin	4,705,335	2.0	1.9	1.6	1.8
Wyoming	470,816	0.2	0.3	0.4	0.3

Adjusted N = 21,589

*Population figures for Canal Zone and Puerto Rico are combined. Data for populations of states and territories are from U.S. Department of Commerce, Bureau of the Census, Statistical Abstract of the United States, National Data Book and Guide to Sources, 103rd edition, 1982-1983.

Source: Derived from data provided by Defense Manpower Data Center.

Table 2.22.   Officers by Region of United States

Region of U.S.	Pop. of Region	% of U.S. Pop.	Army %	Air Force %	Total %
New England States	12,348,493	5.4	5.8	5.7	5.9
Mid-Atlantic States	49,533,419	21.5	22.5	19.1	21.7
Southern States	35,199,343	15.3	19.5	16.4	18.8
Mid-Western States	45,331,191	19.7	14.7	16.9	15.1
North-Mid-Central States	17,184,066	7.5	8.1	9.4	8.4
South Central States	23,743,134	10.3	12.6	12.7	12.5
Mountain States	10,569,146	4.6	5.6	6.6	5.7
Pacific States	32,596,053	14.2	10.6	12.5	10.9
U.S. Possessions	3,431,365	1.5	0.9	0.2	0.8

Adjusted N = 21,589

Regions are defined as follows:

New England States
Maine
New Hampshire
Vermont
Massachusetts
Rhode Island
Connecticut

Mid-Atlantic States
New York
Pennsylvania
New Jersey
Delaware
District of Columbia
Maryland
Virginia
West Virginia

Southern States
North Carolina
Alabama
South Carolina
Florida
Tennessee
Mississippi
Georgia

Mountain States
New Mexico
Arizona
Colorado
Utah
Wyoming
Idaho
Montana

North Mid-Central States
Kansas
Missouri
Nebraska
Iowa
South Dakota
North Dakota
Minnesota

Mid-Western States
Wisconsin
Illinois
Michigan
Indiana
Ohio
Kentucky

South Central States
Louisiana
Texas
Arkansas
Oklahoma

Pacific States
Washington
Oregon
California
Nevada
Alaska
Hawaii

U.S. Possessions
Virgin Islands
Guam
Puerto Rico
American Samoa
Canal Zone

Data for populations of regions derived from U.S Department of Commerce, Bureau of the Census, Statistical Abstract of the United States, National Data Book and Guide to Sources, 103rd edition, 1982-1983.

Source: Derived from data provided by Defense Manpower Data Center.

Table 2.23. Officers by Ethnic and Racial Origin

Ethnic Origin	Army		Air Force		Total	
	N	%	N	%	N	%
White	16,075	87.7	4,506	92.2	20,581	88.6
Black	1,612	8.8	219	4.5	1,831	7.9
Hispanic	227	1.2	72	1.5	299	1.3
Am. Indian/ Alaskan Native	23	0.1	23	0.5	46	0.2
Asian/Pacific Islands	138	0.8	49	1.0	187	0.8
Other/Unknown	260	1.4	19	0.4	279	1.2

Adjusted N = 23,223

Source: Derived from data provided by Defense Manpower Data Center.

3

U.S. Forces and
West German Public Opinion

In a democratic state, public opinion is one of the principal variables that affect the formulation and implementation of public policy. If a government is responsive to the values of the citizenry that sustains it, it must, at some point, respond to the wishes or demands of the citizens, whether wise or unwise, whether expressed or inchoate. Wise governments are well aware of this, with the result that many of them in Western Europe and elsewhere spend enormous amounts of time and money attempting to ascertain what the structure of public opinion is on important public policy issues. Governments do not, of course, really ever know objectively what public opinion actually is on any issue, for the simple reason that public opinion is rarely a monolith. On most issues it is a vast array of views, reactions, opinions, and feelings, based on a multitude of perceptions that may or may not relate to objective facts. But if democratic governments wish to remain in office, they are obliged to pay homage to it in some fashion or another. Public opinion not only sets the outside parameters for the decisions governmental leaders make; it also represents a kind of retaining wall leaders may not breach if they wish to avoid a flash flood of public condemnation.

An analysis of West German public opinion in reference to the major national security issues raised by U.S. forces on German soil is essential to an understanding of the complex political relationship between the United States and the Federal Republic. If the presence of U.S. forces is to remain viable over the long term, then it must be sanctioned by the general approval of the West German people. If it should happen that public opinion was sharply divided on the issue for a protracted period of time or if it became evident that public opinion had decisively shifted against the continued stationing of U.S. forces, then the government of the FRG would sooner or later be obliged to liquidate the U.S. presence.

General Impressions
of the United States and the Soviet Union

Tables 3.1 to 3.15 record impressions about the United States and the Soviet Union held by West Germans. German fondness for Americans increased substantially after the mid-1950s and, with the end of occupation and complete recovery of political sovereignty in 1955, continued to increase consistently until the mid-1960s, reaching a high point of 58% in 1966. During the late 1960s and most of the decade of the 1970s, U.S.-West German relations were strained—by the Vietnam War, Watergate, stresses within the NATO alliance, offset payments crises, etc. By the late 1970s, however, several of the worst sources of stress had been removed, and German fondness for Americans tended to increase again, reaching another high point of 56% in the fall of 1981. We may also note (Table 3.1) that there has never been a large segment of West Germans who said that they did not like Americans; the proportion was highest in the late 1960s and early 1970s (24%), but declined to 18% by 1981.

Comparative data from several European countries may be found in Tables 3.2, 3.3, and 3.4. These data are particularly interesting, and perhaps particularly credible, because they emanate from three different polling organizations. Asked who were the most likeable people (Table 3.2), 38% of German respondents rated the Swiss as their favorite friends, though the Americans and the French tied for second place with 20% each; no other nationality gained particular favor at all. Only 1% of the Germans said that they found the Russians the most likeable. When the question was asked in terms of countries rather than peoples, the results were surprisingly different (Table 3.3). In response to which country they considered the Federal Republic's best friend, Germans chose the United States ahead of any other country, with France a distant second. However, the percentage favoring the United States declined by a few points from 1980 (53%) to late 1982 (48%), reflecting, no doubt, increased political tension induced by arguments over the stationing of a new generation of U.S. missiles on German soil. The Gallup International Poll reproduced in Table 3.4 shows that among five major Western European countries, the West Germans overwhelmingly displayed the most favorable attitude toward the United States; 73% expressed a favorable opinion, and only 24% had an unfavorable opinion. When asked their overall opinion of the Soviet Union, a slighly higher percentage of Germans expressed a favorable opinion than did other nationalities, but perhaps more significantly, a higher percentage of West Germans than any other nationality registered an unfavorable opinion. The positive attitudes expressed in these data toward the United States by West Germans are essential to the trust and confidence needed to create a solid security community.

Germans were asked questions that elicited a choice between the United States and the Soviet Union. In deciding between two possibilities for the future (Table 3.5), a majority of Germans, in 1981, opted for a good relationship with the United States, while only a small percentage opted for a good relationship with the Soviet Union; less than a third remain undecided. When asked whether the Federal Republic should work more closely with the United States or the Soviet Union (Table 3.6), only 1 or 2% chose the Soviet Union in most polls; a majority thought the FRG should work more closely with the United States. However, around 40% opted for working closely with both superpowers, refusing to make a clear choice. We might also note that President Reagan's visit to West Germany in June 1982 had the effect of increasing the majority in favor of working more closely with the United States by 3 percentage points.

Two different polling organizations asked West Germans to choose between accepting Soviet domination or fighting a war (Tables 3.7 and 3.8). We can see immediately that the phrasing of the question and the words used had a decisive impact on the results. When the West Germans were asked to make a choice between defending "democratic freedom, even if it leads to nuclear war," or avoiding "war above all, even though it means having to live under a communist government," 48% chose, in May 1981, to avoid war, while 27% chose to defend democracy, and 25% found it impossible to make such a choice. The terminology used by the Allensbach Institute, in which ideologies are the alternatives, undoubtedly skewed the results in this case. In the Gallup International Poll of February 1982, the choice was between fighting "in defense of your country" (compared to defending "democratic freedom") or accepting "Russian domination" (compared to living "under a communist government"). Far higher percentages of West Germans and British opted to fight than did the French and Italians, though the West Germans showed a slightly higher percentage in favor of accepting Soviet domination; far fewer West Germans were undecided than any other nationality. That 74% of the Germans would choose to fight to defend their country while only 19% would allow Soviet domination shows strong evidence of a value system supporting the FRG's membership in the Atlantic Alliance. As might be expected, the United States had the highest percentage opting to fight and the lowest percentage opting to accept Soviet domination. In every case, except Italy, a majority opted to fight. In the straightforward wording of the question in Table 3.8 German sentiment is clear in regard to the avoidance of Soviet domination.

Tables 3.9 and 3.11 present data from the Allensbach Institute on the level of West German confidence in the United States as a world leader;

Tables 3.10 and 3.12 present comparative data from several West European countries on similar questions. Between 1979 and 1981 confidence among West Germans in the world leadership role of the United States increased by several percentage points. In May of 1981, 42% of West Germans were either very confident or fairly confident that the United States was capable of taking a wise leadership role in world problems, while 47% were either not so confident or not at all confident, and 11% remained undecided. Data from answers to a similar question asked in February 1982 in five West European countries show that West Germans displayed a higher level of confidence than did the citizens of the other European countries in the United States' ability to deal wisely with world problems. A majority of 57% had either a great deal or a fair amount of confidence in U.S. leadership, whereas 40% had very little or no confidence at all. By comparing the West German data to data for the other four countries, we see that the Germans had the clearest vision of the necessity or advantages of U.S. leadership in the realm of European security; the British and the French had a much weaker attachment to U.S. leadership. Here is confirmation of the wisdom of U.S. policy in placing the FRG at the forefront of the U.S.-European alliance relationship. The Germans evidently feel confident that their own government's policy of generally deferring to U.S. policy in security affairs is right and proper.

Tables 3.11 and 3.12 also treat the question of confidence in U.S. leadership, though the specific questions here concern the U.S. security guarantee of Western Europe. The data in Table 3.11 indicate that as of August 1981 half of the West German population agreed that the United States had again become a reliable leader for the Western world (after a perceived period of decline during the Carter presidency) and was tending to West German security vis-à-vis the East from a position of strength; 29% did not agree with such a statement, and 21% were undecided. Opinions tended to differ dramatically among adherents of the four political parties: the Christian Democratic Union (CDU), the Christian Social Union (CSU), the Social Democratic party (SPD), and the Free Democratic party (FDP). Although a substantial majority of CDU-CSU adherents agreed that the United States was seeing to West German security from a position of strength, less than a majority of SPD and FDP adherents and only a small percentage of the Greens agreed with the statement. Hence, the credibility of the U.S. security guarantee or perhaps acceptance of the U.S. leadership role was less than convincing to about half the West German population, a conclusion that might modify somewhat the optimistic conclusions derived from the preceding tables.

The question in Table 3.12 attempted to measure the level of confidence within five European countries that the United States would do whatever is necessary to defend them, *even if this risked a direct attack against the United States itself*. Predictably, the level of confidence was highest in West Germany. Great Britain showed the second highest level of confidence, followed by Denmark and Belgium. In West Germany, 62% expressed either a great deal or a fair amount of confidence that the United States would do whatever is necessary to defend their country, which is to say that they accepted the reliability of the U.S. security guarantee without question. The data for Switzerland reveal a set of security orientations wholly different from that of the four other European countries. The historic attachment of the Swiss to a position of neutrality and their tendency to rely only on themselves in security matters were clearly registered.

Few West Germans have any illusions about the fact that they have for years existed in the shadow of the United States when it comes to East-West security issues. A basic question for any West German government is the extent to which the Germans must provide unwavering support for U.S. policies or initiatives outside the security issue area. This is, in a sense, the dilemma faced by any smaller country that has a relationship of security dependency with a larger power. The polls reflected in Tables 3.13 through 3.15 presented respondents with several alternatives, here arranged in an ascending order of specificity. Respondents were asked whether the Federal Republic should always back the Americans in matters of foreign policy, without specifying what foreign policy issues might be involved (Table 3.13). The phrase "in the present situation" refers to anything the respondent might have had in mind, whether the general situation of security dependency upon the United States, the advent of the Reagan administration, the rise of insurgent movements in Central America, or anything else. In May 1981, 28% of the respondents would have opted always to back the Americans, whereas 65% would have chosen to decide from case to case; only 7% remained undecided. The wording of the question—*always* backing the Americans vs. merely deciding *from case to case*—makes the second alternative sound eminently reasonable without any hint of anti-Americanism or disloyalty to the U.S. cause; hence the substantial majority who opted for this alternative.

In another poll, two rather long sentences were given as alternative opinions on the stand the Federal Republic should take in regards to U.S. foreign policy (Table 3.14). These were presented to the respondents on flash cards, following a brief explanation by the interviewer. In May 1981, 20% of the respondents decided that "if we demand that the U.S. stand by us in Europe, then we have to show by our actions that we support their policy in other parts of the world, even if we don't always agree with it and must make some sacrifices." This low figure in agreement may be accounted for by the qualifiers that make this alternative appear unattractive to many people. First, "in other parts of the world" means outside of Europe. Many West Germans undoubtedly failed to see any logical or necessary connection between support for U.S. policy in Europe and support for U.S. policies elsewhere, especially when "we don't always agree." Second, the idea that we "must make some sacrifices" undoubtedly made the alternative seem illogical or foolish to many respondents.

A majority, 68%, chose the second, quite different alternative—"we should naturally show solidarity with the Americans as far as possible, but when they adopt an unreasonable policy, they can't expect of us that we follow with measures that harm our own interests." In this statement the qualifiers would seem to draw the respondent to an eminently reasonable conclusion. This alternative includes the idea of naturally showing "solidarity with the Americans as far as possible"; that is, no offense is meant to the U.S. protector in any case. If, however, the Americans were to adopt a policy that is defined to the respondent as "unreasonable," then it follows that the West Germans ought to have no obligation to give it automatic support, most especially, and here is the decisive element, when the measures *would be harmful to German interests.* Such a statement is difficult to argue with. What is surprising is that 20% of the respondents chose the first alternative and 12% remained undecided.

In Table 3.15 we see results much more favorable to U.S. policymakers. In this case, however, the policy issue area is precisely defined as policy in reference to the Soviet Union. The question concerns what action the West German government should take in case of disagreement with the United States on situations involving the Soviet Union. The question even specifies that "disagreement persists after talks." In October 1981, 51% of the respondents said they would accept U.S. policy, whereas 45% said they would take some distance from U.S. policy; 4% remained undecided. There are several good reasons why a majority chose to defer to the United States in the area of relations with the Soviet Union. U.S.-Soviet relations are a case of one superpower confronting the other, rather than a small country attempting to react to Soviet initiatives. Over one-third of Germany is governed by a regime directly answerable to the Soviet Union and occupied by Soviet troops. The other portion of Germany is protected from possible Soviet expansionist designs by the presence of U.S. troops, coupled with the nuclear umbrella. The viability of West Berlin is assured only by virtue of the U.S. guarantee and the presence of U.S. troops. Without U.S. backing, West German admonitions or threats to the Soviet Union would have no credibility at all. West German policies sharply divergent from those of the United States would surely play into Soviet hands by dividing the Atlantic Alliance and might even threaten the U.S. security guarantee. Given this matrix of factors, it is not surprising that a majority of West Germans opted to accept U.S. policy in situations involving the Soviet Union; the 45% who said they would "take some distance" might be occasion for surprise or dismay.

Threat Perception

Tables 3.16 through 3.25 present data on West German public opinion in reference to various aspects of the Soviet threat. The first two of these survey expectations of another world war. Tables 3.18 to 3.22 probe ideas concerning the threat from the East, the possibility of a Soviet invasion, or the possibility of getting along peacefully with the Soviet Union. The last three tables deal with comparisons of U.S. and Soviet power.

Table 3.16 displays time-series data from the Allensbach Institute beginning in 1961 and ending in 1982. It is interesting to note that West German expectations of a new world war declined consistently from the early 1960s to the mid-1970s. Whereas 46% of the respondents in 1961 thought that "we have to reckon with the prospect of a new world war breaking out again," by 1975 the percentage had declined to 29%. The decline is probably accounted for by factors such as the stabilization of the Berlin situation that occurred in the months following the Berlin Wall crisis in 1961, the beginnings of détente after the Cuban missile crisis of 1962, the end of the Vietnam War in 1973, and the serious pursuit of détente by the Nixon administration in the early 1970s. The expectation of world war began to increase again in the late 1970s, reaching a high point of 46% in July 1981, a few months after President Reagan had taken office, but it declined again to 38% in June 1982. In the 1982 poll, the percentage of respondents not able to decide or offering no concrete response rose to 19%, reflecting the general confusion of the time as a result of acrimonious U.S.-Soviet relations.

The Allensbach data are strikingly similar to data gathered by the EMNID Institute in a 1981 study for *Der Spiegel* magazine (Table 3.17), which attests to the validity of studies produced by these well-respected public opinion organizations. The EMNID data indicate that 52% of the respondents thought that a world war in the next couple of years was either probable or possible, compared with 46% in the July 1981 Allensbach study, in which the range of possible responses was more restricted. In the EMNID study, 47% of the respondents thought that another world war within two years was unlikely, compared with 45% in the Allensbach study who thought no one would risk a world war again. The data in both studies indicate the presence of a strong strain of pessimism in West Germany affecting half the population. Such pessimism may be cause for dismay, but it exists for quite understandable reasons. The entire West German population lives within 150 miles of the dividing line at which a Soviet thrust into Western Europe would be most likely to occur. With nineteen Soviet divisions stationed next door in East Germany, most concerned West German citizens must from time to time worry about the possibility of a world conflagration if Soviet troops were to cross the border or if a nuclear weapon should be fired from West Germany. As a balance to this pessimism, however, we might take some comfort in the fact that 47% in the EMNID study and 45% in the Allensbach study were confident that a world war is extremely unlikely in the near future. Much of this optimism is obviously attributable to the confidence placed in the U.S. security guarantee.

Tables 3.18 and 3.19 also present comparative data from the Allensbach and EMNID institutes, concerning the threat from the East. It should be noted that the terminology in the questions is not at all vague: In the German language the Soviet Union is commonly referred to in the vernacular as simply "the East." Table 3.18 presents time-series data since 1976. The percentage of respondents worried about the threat from the East declined between 1976 and 1979 from 51% to 41% but increased very dramatically, to 65%, in February 1980, probably as a result of fear induced by the Soviet invasion of Afghanistan in December 1979. Thereafter, it declined only modestly to 59% in both 1981 and 1982, a figure strikingly similar to the 55% the EMNID study found were worried about the threat from the East in October 1981. The percentage of respondents who worried about the threat from the East increased with age in both tables, with minor discrepancies in the oldest age categories. Conversely, the percentage of respondents who did not worry decreased with each age category. The age distribution of the responses yields some valuable insight into the political socialization process in West Germany as it relates to memories of the cold war. Older citizens well remember the Soviet coup in Czechoslovakia and the Berlin airlift in 1948, the East German uprising in 1953, the Berlin Wall in 1961, and the Soviet march into Czechoslovakia in 1968, as well as other events of the cold war years. Younger citizens, on the other hand, having come of age during the years of East-West détente and never having witnessed any direct Soviet attempts to threaten or undermine West European governments, are less likely to believe that the Soviet Union represents a direct threat to the country's security. The fact that nearly half of the respondents in their teens or early twenties did not worry about the Soviet threat is unsettling to policymakers on both sides of the Atlantic.

Tables 3.20 and 3.21 deal specifically with the threat of a Soviet attack on Western Europe. Table 3.20 presents data from a study undertaken in the 1960s and now contained in the files of the Central Archive for Empirical Social Research at the University of Cologne. In 1964, 25.5%

of those questioned believed that there was considerable danger of a
Soviet attack occurring within two years; 48.6% thought that the danger
was small or did not exist at all; and 26% were undecided. Though 25.5%
fearing Soviet attack may not seem significant at first glance, it must
be noted that the question specified an attack occurring *within two years*,
a scenario that must have appeared unrealistic to many in the early
beginnings of détente following the Cuban missile crisis. Table 3.21
presents comparative data for 1982 from five West European countries
on a similar question. In this case the time period for a possible Soviet
attack was specified as five years. The results are somewhat puzzling:
West Germans, together with the Danes, showed the lowest percentage
of respondents (15%) believing that a Soviet attack on Western Europe
within the next five years was likely. Conversely, the West Germans also
had by far the highest percentage (81%) believing that a Soviet attack
within five years was unlikely.

Critics might fault the Germans for not being frightened enough of
Soviet intentions, though the figures for the other countries show that
their citizens were frightened by only marginally higher percentages. On
the other hand, the figures might be interpreted as a sign of hard-headed
realism on the part of the Germans. After all, there has not been a
Soviet attack on Western Europe for over forty years, the deterrent value
of the NATO alliance seems fully intact—with a quarter of a million U.S.
military personnel in the Federal Republic—and the Soviets would be
unlikely to undertake any military adventures in Western Europe with
President Reagan in office in the United States. However the figures in
Table 3.21 are interpreted, we must conclude that a substantial majority
of the citizens in all five countries did not, in 1982, fear the likelihood
of a Soviet attack within the next five years. Though the Belgians showed
the lowest percentage of respondents believing a Soviet attack to be
unlikely, the only real difference between them and the West Germans
is that more of the Belgians (24%) were undecided, whereas the West
Germans seemed to have their minds firmly made up on the issue (only
4% undecided). The Germans are, however, much closer to the border
of a possible attack than are the Belgians.

The surveys reflected in Table 3.22 probed one other dimension of
the Soviet threat. Respondents were asked about the possibility of getting
along peacefully with the Soviet Union. It is interesting, if not unexpected,
that the percentage of West Germans who said they believed that the
West could get along peacefully with the Soviet Union *in the long run*
increased slowly after 1956, though a rapid increase did not occur until
the last half of the 1970s, as a result of the optimism bred by détente.
A major setback occurred in the early 1960s, probably as a result of
the frustration and fear engendered by the construction of the Berlin

Wall. By 1979, a majority of 56% of the respondents believed that peaceful relations with the Soviets over the long term were possible, 27% disagreed with that assessment, and 17% remained undecided.

The last three tables of this group present survey data from three different sources on perceived comparisons of Soviet and U.S. power. Data from two surveys from the mid-1960s (Table 3.23) show that approximately 40% of the respondents rated the United States as militarily more powerful than the Soviet Union. Between 10% and 13.8% rated the Soviet Union more powerful; slightly less than a third thought that the superpowers were militarily about equal; and 15% to 17% had no opinion. The important point here is that in the mid-1960s a substantial plurality of West Germans rated the United States as militarily more powerful. The situation appears to have changed dramatically by the mid-1970s, as may be seen in Table 3.24, which presents data beginning in 1976 from the Allensbach Institute. By the mid-1970s, a majority of the respondents rated the East bloc more powerful, whereas a tiny percentage rated the West more powerful. This perception changed by only a few percentage points between 1976 and 1981. The difference in perceptions recorded in Tables 3.23 and 3.24 is, by any standard, rather major. Its importance may, however, be somewhat mitigated by a more precise look at the terms used in the two questionnaires. In the earlier surveys, the respondents were asked to make a direct comparison between the military power of the United States and that of the Soviet Union. In the later polls, by contrast, they were asked to compare blocs. In the European context the terms "East" and "West" refer to the NATO and Warsaw Pact alliances. In the comparison between Soviet and U.S. power, a majority of the respondents believed the United States to be militarily more powerful. In comparing blocs, however, the respondents probably had in mind, among other things, the gross disparity in ground forces in the European theatre, where NATO forces are outnumbered by Warsaw Pact forces approximately three to one. Given the figures on personnel and tanks, widely publicized in the West German press, plus the un-challenged installation in the late 1970s and early 1980s of Soviet SS-20 missiles targeted on Western Europe, it is not surprising that only a small portion of West Germans rated the Western bloc as more powerful. The Allensbach data are corroborated by the data in the EMNID study of October 1981 (Table 3.25). In this survey, 49% of the respondents rated the East as more powerful; 11% rated the West as more powerful; 39% believed that the two sides were equally powerful; and only 1% had no opinion.

The data in tables 3.23–3.25 give evidence of an ominous trend in recent years in West German public perceptions of East-West power relationships. There is little doubt that the Soviet military buildup has altered West German perceptions of the East-West power balance in favor of the Soviet Union. We may also surmise that this perception of Warsaw Pact superiority is a major factor underlying a certain skepticism of the U.S. security guarantee. It also no doubt lends impetus to slowly growing neutralist sentiment in West Germany.

Alliance Relationships

The next group of tables (3.26–3.40) records perceptions of various aspects of West Germany's alliance relationships—NATO and the alliance with the United States—as well as the FRG's capability for self-defense and perceptions of neutralism, pacifism, and anti-Americanism.

The data presented in Table 3.26 show a steadily increasing percentage of West Germans over the years who claim to have some understanding of NATO. Whereas only 56% claimed to know something about NATO in the early period of the mid-1950s, by 1960, 79%, and a decade later in 1971, 85%, believed they understood the meaning of NATO. That figure increased to 93% by 1980. The data do not, of course, give us any idea of the accuracy of these perceptions, but given the FRG's geopolitical situation, we may fairly surmise that West Germans in general are far better informed about NATO than are Americans. More important than the level of accurate information are the impressions West Germans had of the advantages or disadvantages of NATO, recorded in time-series data in Table 3.27. The percentage of West Germans believing that NATO brought more advantages than disadvantages increased substantially in the 1950s, but continued to increase only slowly after that, reaching a high point of 55% in May 1981. The percentage of West Germans believing that NATO brought more disadvantages has shown a wavering pattern between 11% and 14%; however, this group has always been small. Perhaps as significant as this minority is the rather large group of West Germans who have remained undecided on the issue—60% in 1956 declining to 31% in May 1981. In several polls, those who believed in the advantages of NATO were recorded as only a few percentage points more than those who were undecided. Although this might appear to be only lukewarm support of the country's major defense structure, the data given in the next two tables provide a different persective.

In a 1982 Gallup International Poll for *Newsweek* (Table 3.28), 61% of West German respondents expressed either a great deal or a fair amount of confidence in NATO's ability to defend Western Europe against an attack—a higher percentage than that for any of the other four countries polled, though Great Britain, at 56%, ran a close second. The proportion expressing not very much confidence or none at all in NATO's defensive capability was similar in all these countries. Nearly a quarter of the respondents in France, Italy, and Belgium were, unfortunately, unable to answer the question. The French, as expected, were by far the most ambivalent on the issue and expressed the least confidence in NATO. These figures attest to the credibility of West Germany as the most important ally of the United States in the Western alliance.

When confidence in NATO was tested in a different way, by asking whether the Federal Republic should remain a member, the results were stunning, as may be seen in Table 3.29. In all three polls displayed, only a tiny portion of West Germans believed that the country should leave NATO; a majority—78% in 1981—were in favor of remaining a member of the alliance. These results are proof positive, if any is needed, that despite ambivalence about unpleasant choices, the West Germans are solidly convinced of the importance of NATO to their country's security.

The FRG's alliance with the United States is, of course, a more specific aspect of its membership in NATO. The data in Table 3.30 indicate some ambivalence among West Germans on this topic, although the wording of the choices must have influenced the pattern of responses. The first statement was accepted by 47.6% of the respondents, despite its conservative bias (in "thirty years. . . . nothing has changed . . .") and despite its conclusion implying a rather unconditional acceptance of U.S. leadership in all matters related to defense. The second alternative, selected by 35.1% of the respondents, contains some alluring language to the effect that much has changed in thirty years and the Federal Republic has "gained importance in the circle of world powers." Nothing in the statement implies a total rejection of U.S. leadership; it merely says that "it is impossible for us to continue to follow the U.S. as leader all the time." Given the length and complexity of the statements, it is hardly surprising that 17.3% of the respondents were undecided.

Different results appear in Table 3.31; the choices in these polls were between remaining in a strong military alliance with the United States or trying to become completely neutral. In 1981, a majority of 54% opted for a strong military alliance, whereas only 27% opted for neutrality; 19% were undecided. The time-series data also show that the percentage in favor of a strong alliance was somewhat weaker (49%) in 1975, during the heyday of détente. The question shown in Table 3.32 gave respondents a choice between further alternatives—the continuation of a strong alliance with the United States or the formation of a "tight Western European political bloc." Neutrality in Western Europe would be a lonely situation, whereas a Western European political bloc would put the West Germans among friends in an organization presumably opposed to Soviet domination. The political bloc option would seem to be inherently more attractive than isolation, especially if the Europeans could together mount a credible defense posture, which the statement does not assume. The survey results, in any case, did indeed show the option of a Western European bloc to be somewhat more acceptable than neutrality: 31.6% of the respondents chose this alternative; a larger percentage (24.5%) remained undecided on this question as compared to the question in the previous table. Nevertheless, a large plurality of 44.3% elected to maintain the Federal Republic's strong military alliance with the United States; even the attractiveness of an independent European option did not detatch the largest group of West Germans from the security this alliance offers.

Tables 3.33 and 3.34 probe opinions in reference to a closely related question—whether West Germany has the capability to defend itself. In the time-series data in Table 3.33 we see that since 1960 approximately a third of the West Germans believe that they could not defend themselves if the Soviet Union started a war; an increase of 10 percentage points choosing this option was registered between September 1979 and May 1981 (from 31% to 41%). Surprisingly, however, the group of West Germans who agree with this conclusion has never been a majority. Those who believe that "we are well enough armed" to mount a credible self-defense have only once, in January 1980, exceeded 30% of the respondents. More significantly, a large percentage of West Germans, ranging from approximately one-third to just under one-half, have remained undecided or confused on this issue. In any case, the percentage believing that the Federal Republic could not defend itself has always been larger than the percentage believing that the country could mount an adequate self-defense.

The question asked in the survey documented in Table 3.34 was whether Western Europe does enough on behalf of its defense or needs to do more. The question might be interpreted in two ways: as suggesting a European defense effort independent of the United States; or as asking whether the Europeans are making an adequate contribution to the collective efforts of the Atlantic Alliance. The meaning is not clear from the wording, and we cannot presume what meaning may have been conveyed to the respondents from the context of the questionnaire. At any rate, in West Germany the percentage believing that the Europeans were doing enough to defend themselves militarily declined during the decade of the 1970s, from 50% in 1973 to 34% in 1979. Conversely, the percentage believing that the Europeans ought to do more for their defense increased from 26% to 38%. Evidently, the constant Soviet military buildup during that period had a notable impact on West German perceptions in the area of defense efforts. The repeated admonitions from NATO headquarters in Brussels may also have worked to stiffen German resolve. However, the percentage favoring a greater defense effort was, in 1979, and remains, too small to suit planners in the Pentagon and many members of the U.S. Congress. The data should impart a serious message to U.S. policymakers. Unless and until a clear majority of West Germans believe that greater defense efforts are necessary, it will be difficult for any West German government to render a greater contribution. The need is for greater efforts in the areas of public information and education by both the West German and U.S. governments.

The alleged rise of neutralist sentiment in the FRG has occasioned much concern in Washington. Members of Congress, as well as high-ranking members of the administration, have become upset over what they believe is an increasingly unstable situation on the German political scene. Such concern is probably exaggerated, as we may see in the next five tables, which treat a series of questions that we have placed under the rubric of "neutralism-pacifism, anti-Americanism." Neutralist sentiment does exist, and there is some evidence that it has grown moderately in recent years. Before we reach precipitous conclusions, however, a hard look at the data is in order.

Table 3.35 contains the results of a 1982 Allensbach Institute survey that attempted to measure the extent of neutralist sentiment in the Federal Republic. The two statements to which the respondents were asked to react tested the inclination toward neutralist sentiment against the need for the U.S. security guarantee. In June 1982, shortly before President Reagan's visit, 66% of the respondents agreed that "as a neutral state we would be too weak to defend ourselves against an attack." Hence the necessity of maintaining the alliance with the United States. Only 23% felt that "the freedom of the Federal Republic would not be in jeopardy as a neutral state" and that more could be done for peace by remaining outside a major power bloc; 11% were undecided. After President Reagan's visit the group preferring alliance with the United States to neutrality increased by three percentage points, though by December 1982 the percentages returned to about the same level as before the president's visit. The important point is that nearly two-thirds of the respondents clearly opted for maintaining the U.S. alliance over neutrality, whereas just over one-fifth opted for a neutral position in the interests of working toward world peace and understanding.

The Allensbach data are corroborated by the data from the EMNID Institute in the 1981 *Der Spiegel* study, as may be seen in Table 3.36. Though the statements are worded somewhat differently, the choice was essentially similar to that in the Allensbach survey. Just short of a two-thirds majority, 63%, opted for the alliance with the United States, as "a neutral Germany would be isolated and too weak to defend itself from the Soviet pressures." The option of neutrality was selected by 35%; neutrality was in this case presented more positively—as an escape from "the tensions of the superpowers," with the case of Austria cited as an example. Only 2% were undecided. The only differences in the results of the Allensbach and EMNID studies are that a somewhat larger percentage chose the neutral option in the EMNID study than in the Allensbach study—35% vs. 19%—where a larger percentage remain undecided in the Allensbach study (12%) than in the EMNID study (2%). These differences are probably accounted for by the differing contexts in which the questions occurred within the questionnaire and by the fact that the neutral option is presented in a more positive light in the EMNID statement. In both studies a majority of the respondents opted to remain in the alliance with the United States, whereas a minority chose the option of neutralism. Clearly, neutralist sentiment in West Germany did not, in the early 1980s, pose a major threat to the established policy of alliance with the United States.

Neutralism was approached in a very different way in the survey presented in Table 3.37. The respondents were asked to react to the statement "Without the Americans, we would already be lost." The statement does, of course, touch upon the general reputation of the United States as well as the reliability of the U.S. security guarantee. But it also probed neutralist sentiment by eliciting a kind of gut reaction to West Germany's inevitable predicament of living in the shadow of the United States. The responses show an emotional attachment to the United States and, by implication, a disdain for any kind of neutralist stance. A majority—55%—accepted the unqualified statement, and only 26% found the statement false; 18% were indifferent. The results indicate that most West Germans have adjusted to living in the U.S. shadow, and only a quarter of them might wish to change the situation.

Tables 3.38 and 3.39 display various opinions about the peace movement in the Federal Republic. Though the growth of the peace movement after 1979 probably has more to do with feelings about nuclear weapons in West Germany than about the alliance with the United States per se, the movement also connects to the broader perspectives that are the foundation of the neutralist phenomenon. In the 1981 EMNID study, 29% of the respondents did not approve of the peace movement, 61% were indifferent in one way or another, and 9% expressed some degree of active approval. Only 2% said that they already participated in the movement or definitely planned to participate. A similar Allensbach study, in December 1982, found a high percentage of people who expressed outright disapproval of the movement—68%; 29% were more or less indifferent; and 3% said they worked actively with the movement. The range of choice in the EMNID study was much greater, which may account for some of the difference in the results. Nevertheless, the EMNID data indicate more indifference to the movement, whereas the Allensbach study found more disapproval, a difference that is difficult to explain. In both studies only a small portion of respondents admitted to active participation in the peace movement.

As instructive as the comparison of these two tables is the breakdown of opinion by age category, shown in Table 3.39. Age is a very significant factor in opinions about the peace movement. Disapproval of the movement was overwhelming (81%) among people sixty years of age or older, whereas ambivalence toward the movement as well as a higher level of approval (44%) was shown among the youngest group, sixteen to twenty-nine. The percentage of respondents who thought the peace movement was all right decreased, and the percentage who disapproved of the movement increased, with each age category. The percentage of respondents who said they worked actively with the movement was highest among people sixteen to twenty-nine years of age, though even in this group it was very small (6%). These results merely confirm what most observers assume—that the peace movement finds its major support among young people. What this may mean for the future is hazardous to predict. On the one hand, this may portend an emerging groundswell of pacifist-neutralist sentiment in West Germany as the movement catches on as the wave of the future. On the other hand, people change their views as they grow older, sometimes in the direction of moderation or conservatism, and given the present demographic structure of the West German population, aging and with a very low birth rate, there may be scant reason to assume that the peace movement is likely to expand much beyond its present boundaries. In any case, opinions in reference to the peace movement do not tell us very much about the reliability of West Germany as an ally in the NATO alliance. It is quite possible to approve of the peace movement and believe in the necessity of the U.S. security guarantee at the same time. In addition, few people are completely consistent in their political beliefs.

Table 3.40 treats a more specific aspect of neutralism-pacifism, one of primary interest to U.S. policymakers—the phenomenon of anti-Americanism. Much material has appeared in the U.S. press suggesting that a rising tide of anti-U.S. sentiment has been engulfing West Germany in the mid-1980s. Though much of this commentary is exaggerated and simplistic, the data in this table suggest that anti-U.S. sentiment is a factor that cannot be discounted. In October 1981, 21% of the respondents believed that anti-American feelings were forming in the Federal Republic. An additional 53% believed that there was something about the statement that was true. Only 26% believed that the statement was false. Hence, a total of 74%, or nearly three-quarters of the respondents, agreed that anti-U.S. sentiment was an important factor in one way or another, whereas only one-quarter discounted the phenomenon altogether.

Clearly, this is not good news for either policymakers in Washington or U.S. military commanders in the FRG. Nevertheless, the data must be understood in the perspective of the data presented in the other tables. Certain manifestations of anti-Americanism are to be expected as an inevitable psychological result of prolonged security dependency. The good news in West Germany is that, despite manifest strains of anti-Americanism, visible in the Green party and certain sectors of the peace movement, there is no evidence of the kind of vicious and pervasive anti-U.S. sentiment that has taken root in many other countries. The survey results in Table 3.40 display ambivalence: only 21% definitely believed that anti-American feelings are forming. Though it may be true that anti-Americanism is a phenomenon that must be reckoned with, it is also true that the security equation in West Germany as well as the dense network of friendly sociocultural relations established over many years mitigate against the development of strong anti-U.S. sentiment or a mass movement of this persuasion. It is known, for instance, that some of the most radical leaders in the Green party have been sorely disappointed with the public reception of their patently anti-U.S. themes. Hence, the phenomenon of anti-Americanism in West Germany bears watching closely, but there is no reason for exaggerated concern.

U.S. Troops in West Germany

The final group of tables (3.41–3.56) is most closely related to our central topic, the presence of U.S. troops in West Germany. The first eight of these document West German opinion about U.S. troops in 1955. In that year, the Federal Republic had just recovered its full sovereignty from the Allied Powers and the NATO alliance was still in its infancy. Konrad Adenauer was chancellor of the fledgling republic, the West German economy was reaching a takeoff stage, and the cold war was at its height. The tables were found in the files of the Central Archive for Empirical Social Research at the University of Cologne. They provide both an intriguing portrait of West German opinion in the 1950s and a basis for comparison with more recent data.

West Germans in 1955 were still highly ambivalent about the meaning of the U.S. military presence; 34.8% still thought that the U.S. troops were primarily occupation troops, whereas 42.5% believed that the troops were there primarily for protection of their country's security (Table 3.41). The occupation had, of course, ended, but its memory left an indelible imprint on West German minds, and many Germans were not yet convinced that the motives of the Americans were altogether trust-worthy. Nevertheless, a plurality had concluded by this time that the troops were present more for security purposes than for continuation of an occupation regime.

There was also considerable ambivalence about whether the U.S. military presence served to increase or decrease the possibility of war. As shown in Table 3.42, a plurality of 34.6% believed that the U.S. presence decreased the possibility of war, but at the same time a rather large percentage, 23.7%, believed that it increased the possibility of war; 16.4% believed that it had no effect either way, and one-quarter (25.2%) had no opinion at all. These results should not be too surprising in view of the fact that the cataclysm of World War II was then only ten years in the past, and, after the ordeal of military occupation, many West Germans were more concerned about avoiding another war than anything else.

Some comfort may be derived from evidence that, even in this early period, U.S. soldiers enjoyed a relatively respectable reputation. When asked what they thought of the behavior of U.S. soldiers (Table 3.43), a large plurality of West Germans (41.6%) replied that it was good, and another 25.3% said that it was fair, creating a total figure of 67% who were satisfied with the soldiers' behavior. Surprisingly, only about 4% said the soldiers' behavior was bad, though about 30% declined to state an opinion. If we reflect upon the tarnished reputation of U.S. soldiers as expressed in the West German press of the 1970s, the mid-1950s appear to be the good old days.

Social and cultural relations between U.S. troops and the West German population were very good in the mid-1950s, as may be seen in the next two tables. The contacts were, however, not extensive. In a survey of social relations (Table 3.44), 19% of the respondents said that there were no particular social relations, whereas another 54.8% did not know whether social relations existed or not. Similar results are seen in the area of cultural relations (Table 3.45). Among those respondents who believed they knew something about social relations between U.S. soldiers and West Germans, three-quarters said that the relations were either very good or good. Only 3.6% said that social relations were bad or very bad. Even more positive results were recorded for cultural relations—80% described them as good, whereas only 2% described them as bad. In terms of general reputation, and especially in the areas of social and cultural contacts, the mid-1950s were definitely a period of rather good relations between West Germans and U.S. service personnel.

Table 3.46 records impressions of improvement or deterioration in the relations between U.S. soldiers and the West German public between 1953 and 1955. The results are highly favorable. Nearly two-thirds of the respondents (65.5%) believed that relations had improved or remained the same, whereas only 1.7% said that they had deteriorated. Even though nearly a third (32.8%) had no opinion, the general picture in the 1950s was one of steadily improving relations between West Germans and U.S. military personnel.

For those who believe that the Germans' self-image leads them to be a bit standoffish, if not culturally arrogant, some confirmation may be found in Table 3.47, which records responses to a sensitive question about cultural or ethnic intermarriage. What reaction would a West German have if his or her daughter, sister, or other close relative wanted to marry a U.S. soldier? Although 16.6% of the respondents indicated that they would mildly or strongly approve, 40.5% would strongly or mildly disapprove; 34.3% remained indifferent. In interpreting these results a generous measure of empathy is called for. Cultural arrogance, in one form or another, is characteristic of every human society in the world. There are few religions, tribes, nationalities, or cultures whose members overwhelmingly approve of marriage outside the group. The Germans are not an exception here. In addition, the question asks about a relative marrying a U.S. soldier, not a U.S. student, banker, lawyer, or other civilian. Hence, the question probes emotions about military personnel as much as about intercultural marriage. We should also not forget that the data are from a time not far removed from the U.S. occupation, and were likely to have been influenced by various residual emotions concerning the conqueror and the vanquished. With these caveats in mind, the data should hardly occasion surprise. Indeed, they may demonstrate that by the mid-1950s the West Germans' sociocultural attitudes were not much different from those of other Europeans, though only the availability of comparable data from France, Italy, and other countries would permit us to know for sure. At any rate, less than half of the West Germans questioned indicated they would suffer emotional trauma if a close relative married a U.S. soldier, which does not attest terribly negatively to the texture of German-American relations.

The last of the surveys from 1955 (Table 3.48) tested opinion in reference to the overall advantages or disadvantages accruing from the presence of U.S. troops in the Federal Republic. It is interesting to note that even in 1955 a large plurality of West Germans (41.2%) had concluded that the presence of U.S. troops brought more advantages than disadvantages. Only 15.2% believed that the troops brought more disadvantages, 26.6% remained ambivalent, and 17% expressed no opinion. By the mid-1950s the expedience of the U.S. security guarantee through the stationing of a large contingent of U.S. troops on West German soil was becoming clear to a large segment of the West German population.

The general reputation of U.S. troops remained very positive in 1961, according to data in Tables 3.49 and 3.50. When asked whether or not U.S. soldiers behaved well, 82% replied that they did, and only 7% said that they did not. An astounding 92% of respondents said that they had a good impression of U.S. officers, whereas only 3% said that their impression was not good. These results confirm my conclusions in an earlier work that the period from 1955 to 1967 was in many ways the golden period for U.S. troops in Germany, especially in terms of the high regard in which they were held by the mass of the West German population.[1]

The next six tables treat West German public opinion in reference to proposals to withdraw U.S. troops from the Federal Republic. This issue constitutes, in a real sense, the acid test of West German opinion. It may well be that many West Germans regard the presence of U.S. troops as a necessary evil. Even if that were true, the Germans could hardly be blamed for harboring a certain resentment. Does any people want a large contingent of foreign military troops in their midst? The real issue for a democratic state such as the FRG is whether a majority believes that the foreign troops must remain in the interest of the country's security. If a majority does not sanction the foreign presence, then a real question exists as to the legitimacy of the government policies that maintain it. If, however, a majority clearly favors the foreign military presence, the question changes to one of managing the foreign presence intelligently with the least political and cultural interference in the country's social fabric.

We begin this section with a study from 1957. A highly unlikely scenario was presented in which the Soviets would make the following proposal: "Let the U.S. and the British withdraw all troops from the continent and liquidate their military bases, and Russia would withdraw all its troops and armament behind its own borders" (Table 3.51). The interviewer asked the West German respondents whether they would rather have the proposal accepted or denied. The scenario is, of course, altogether attractive. What could be more desirable than the removal of all foreign troops from West German soil while the Soviets at the same time withdrew all their troops and armaments behind their own borders? If the proposal is accepted as representing an effort in good faith, there is hardly any reason to refuse it, and only a minority of West Germans did. Of those questioned, 57.3% opted to accept the proposal, 28.2% refused it, and 14.5% were undecided. If we wish to be critical, we can easily point to the naiveté of the 57.3% who would trust the Soviet Union to withdraw its huge contingent of troops from East Germany. A major uprising against the Ulbricht regime had taken place only four years earlier. On the other hand, it seems reasonable that a majority of Germans would wish to liquidate all foreign military presence from both parts of the country after years of military occupation, political division, and foreign defense presence, if any kind of good-faith initiative can be presumed in the proposal. We must not forget that the survey was made in the first years of the Bonn republic, when democratic political attitudes were in an early stage of maturity and the country was undergoing considerable debate on the outlines of a proper foreign policy. We might take comfort in the fact that, even at this time, 28% found the proposal unacceptable, which demonstrates a rather profound distrust of the Soviet Union.

The data displayed in Table 3.52 date from the early 1970s. The respondents were told to assume that there were no U.S. troops in Germany any more and then asked if they thought the country's military security would still be good enough. In May 1970, half of the respondents thought the country's security would be inadequate without U.S. troops, only 20% thought security would still be good enough, and 30% found it impossible to say. In May 1973, 47% believed that security would be inadequate without U.S. troops and 24% believed it would be good enough. This change is probably accounted for by the expectations generated by East-West détente. The data do show, at any rate, that by the 1970s almost half of the West Germans believed that U.S. troops were absolutely essential to their country's security.

Table 3.53 gives interesting time-series data on a very similar question. The surveys asked for opinions on the withdrawal of U.S. troops from Europe. Most Germans fully realize that most U.S. troops in Europe are, in fact, in West Germany; thus, withdrawal of troops from Europe obviously would mean withdrawal from West Germany also. In the mid-1950s, a majority of West Germans would have approved of a proposal to withdraw all U.S. troops from Europe. The memory of the military occupation was still fresh, and many West Germans were not sufficiently convinced of the seriousness of the Soviet threat. What is important to note, however, is the increase in the percentage of West Germans polled from 1956 to 1965 who would have disapproved of such a withdrawal. By 1965, 59% would have disapproved of U.S. troop withdrawal, while only 12% would have approved. From 1965 to 1973 the percentage of those who would have disapproved went down from 59% to 45%, and the percentage of those who would have approved went up from 12% to 23%. The change is probably accounted for by a period of relatively stable Soviet-U.S. relations and the development of East-West détente after 1969. After 1973, the percentage for those who would have disapproved increased again, reaching a high point of 60% in 1979; the percentage for those who would have approved continued to go down, to a low point of 11% in 1979. It is important to note how small the percentage of West Germans who would approve of U.S. troop withdrawals has been since the 1960s, at most less than one-quarter of the population in 1973 and only a little over one-tenth of the population in 1979. With the passage of time, a majority of West Germans has become convinced of the necessity of maintaining U.S. troops.

In a 1981 study for Der Spiegel (Table 3.54), EMNID found that only 12% of the respondents would have approved of U.S. troop withdrawals from Europe, while 62% would have disapproved; 25% remained indifferent. These data corroborate the Allensbach data found in the previous two tables: Only a small group of West Germans wished to see U.S. troops removed from the country.

Table 3.55 provides comparative data from three European countries and the United States on the issue of troop withdrawals from Europe. In this 1982 poll, a different question was asked—what is the effect of having U.S. troops stationed in Western Europe. The answers indicate that the West Germans viewed the presence of U.S. troops in a much more positive light than did the British or the Danes. Nearly half (48%) of the Germans replied that the presence of U.S. troops provided greater protection, a much higher percentage than in Britain or Denmark. West Germany also had the lowest percentage of respondents (15%) believing that the presence of U.S. troops increased the chances of attack. The Danes were not far behind, with 16%, though the British had 25% in this category. These figures should occasion no surprise. The West Germans have many more U.S. troops in their midst than do any other European people, and they live in the closest proximity to the large concentration of Soviet troops in East Germany. As might be expected, Americans were more convinced than any of the Europeans of the positive effects flowing from the presence of U.S. troops in Europe; 61% believed that the troops provided greater protection, and only 10% believed that the troops increased the chances of attack. Viewed as a group, these last six tables provide confirmation of the premium placed upon the U.S. military presence by the majority of the West German population.

The final question in our study of public opinion approached the issue of U.S. troop withdrawals from an entirely different standpoint. The focus shifts from whether or not the West Germans wish the forces to remain, to whether or not they believe in the reliability of repeated U.S. promises to keep the forces in the Federal Republic. In a survey done specifically for this study by the Wickert Institute in Tübingen, the following question was asked: "Do you believe that the often repeated assurances of the American government, that American troops will remain in Germany as long as the Germans wish them to remain, are absolutely reliable?" The results, displayed in Table 3.56, cannot bring great comfort to U.S. policymakers. Less than a majority, 47%, said they believed that the assurances were either absolutely or fairly reliable; 28% believed that the assurances were either fairly or absolutely unreliable; and another 25% did not know or declined to give an answer. If we add the latter two figures, we see that 53% either distrusted the reliability of U.S. promises or remained unsure.

The breakdown of the data according to various demographic groups provides interesting material for analysis. The most significant demographic characteristics that appeared to account for variation of opinion were sex and region. Males were much more inclined to believe in the reliability of U.S. assurances than were females; 60% of the male respondents found the assurances either absolutely or fairly reliable, as compared to 42% of the females. Confidence in U.S. assurances declined from the south to the north of West Germany. In Bavaria and Baden-Wuerttemberg only 23% of those questioned found the assurances either absolutely or fairly unreliable. In Hesse, Rhineland-Palatinate, and the Saar the percentage increased to 26%. Moving northward to North Rhine Westphalia we find 28% unconvinced of the reliability of the American assurances, while in the northern states of Lower Saxony, Schleswig-Holstein, Bremen, and Hamburg the figure was 38%. This may have something to do with the fact that except for the garrison at Garlstedt near Bremen, the great bulk of U.S. forces are in the southern portion of the Federal Republic. The southern Germans see them and interact with them more frequently, and the Americans constitute an integral part of the normal routine there. If there is any truth to "seeing is believing," it may be that West Germans in the south find it more difficult than those in the north to accept the possibility that the U.S. troops would suddenly be absent from the FRG's economic life or that the FRG would have to tend to its own security without the U.S. forces.

These data indicate, at any rate, that there is at least a mild problem in West Germany with the level of confidence in U.S. assurances. This should come as no surprise. After repeated attempts year after year in the U.S. Congress to withdraw the troops, can anyone wonder that West German confidence in the repeated assurances given by every U.S. president has slowly but surely eroded? Congress may indulge the tendency to threaten or punish the Federal Republic for not always living up to U.S.-defined goals. There is, however, a high price to be paid for this behavior, and Congress ought not be surprised if requital in West Germany comes in the form of reduced confidence in the U.S. conventional guarantee. Reduced confidence, in turn, fuels impulses toward estrangement, neutralism, and detachment from the United States among the Germans and contributes to the erosion of NATO's vitality.

If NATO's credibility is to be preserved, which it must in the interest of the West's security, then it is essential that the alliance between the United States and the Federal Republic be maintained and strengthened. This, in turn, calls for reinforcement, not weakening, of the level of confidence the West Germans have in the U.S. conventional guarantee.

Not only are major efforts by both governments called for, to inform and convince the West Germans of the reliability of U.S. promises, but in word and in deed Congress and the administration must act in concert to demonstrate to the West Germans that Washington will honor its long-standing commitments.

Reflections on West German Public Opinion

The general profile of West German public opinion that emerges from a review of these tables should leave little doubt that the close security relationship between the United States and West Germany is sanctioned by broad public approval. Public opinion in West Germany, as in any democratic state, is hardly monolithic. The West Germans disagree on many important aspects of their political association with the United States. In the area of national security, however, there is broad agreement on the fundamentals of the FRG's association with NATO and its close alliance with the United States.

It should be good news to anyone concerned with U.S. European policy that the Federal Republic provides stable ground for the anchor point of the Western alliance. We have seen from the available data that the West Germans have a basic fondness for Americans that has steadily increased since the end of the occupation regime in the 1950s. Though subject to minor fits and starts, the fondness does not appear to be ephemeral but rather deeply rooted in the German postwar consciousness. In terms of foreign policy and international relations a majority of West Germans believes that the United States is the Federal Republic's best friend. This attitude provides the essential foundation for a viable alliance. The fact that most West Germans would choose to fight to defend their country rather than accept Soviet domination shows dedication to the basic values that support the superstructure of the Western security alliance.

The data show quite clearly that West Germans display, in general, a higher level of confidence in U.S. world leadership than do the citizens of any other European country. In the realm of security policy most West Germans are quite content to defer to U.S. policy in situations that involve the Soviet Union. A higher percentage of West Germans than other Europeans expressed confidence in NATO's ability to defend Western Europe against a possible Soviet attack. This is highly significant in view of the fact that Germans have in their midst the great bulk of U.S. forces stationed in Europe. The Germans see them, know them, and assess them much more closely than do other Europeans.

In regard to NATO and the alliance with the United States, over the years most West Germans have become convinced of the necessity of maintaining U.S. troops in the FRG. Most, by far, favor the Federal

Republic's continued membership in NATO. Despite the growth of neutralist sentiment, with the rise of the Green party, and the divisive debate over stationing a new generation of U.S. missiles on West German soil, a majority of West Germans still choose the alliance with the United States over any kind of neutralism. Perhaps the acid test of West German opinion on security issues comes from questions that survey opinion on the removal of U.S. troops from the FRG. Here we see that a very large proportion of West Germans approves of the continued presence of U.S. troops on West German soil. Only a small percentage would approve of their removal.

The conclusion that emerges from this profile of German public opinion is that the Federal Republic is the European country most ideally suited to play the role it has played for two decades and should continue to play in future years—namely, the bedrock ally of the United States in Europe and the European touchstone of the Atlantic Alliance. What this indicates, in turn, is that policymakers in Washington ought to be highly sensitive to the absolutely strategic nature of U.S.–West German relations for the future health of U.S. security interests in Europe. We cannot afford to alienate the Germans from their attachment to the United States by thoughtless actions that neglect their input in the formulation of Western security policy. We cannot force their adherence to every nuance of U.S. policy by threats, badgering, or diplomatic arm twisting. We must, of course, insist that they continue to render a fair contribution to the burdens of European defense and that they increase their contribution in any way that is politically feasible. Coupled with this insistence, however, must be assurances that the U.S. security guarantee, which has extended to the FRG for over forty years, will not be withdrawn even in times of tension. The solid ground on which the relationship now rests could, even in the face of the FRG's proven reliability, change to shifting sand if the Germans are faced with constant threats by Washington to remove the security guarantee. The better part of wisdom is to manage political relations with West Germany as part of a strategy to maintain that country as the United States' major ally at the very dividing line of East and West.

Notes

1. See Daniel J. Nelson, *A History of U.S. Military Forces in Germany* (Boulder, Colo.: Westview Press, 1987), Chapter 3.

Table 3.1. Fondness for Americans

	Jan 57 %	Apr 61 %	Jul 62 %	May 65 %	Apr 66 %	Jan 67 %	May 73 %	May 75 %	Aug 79 %	Sep 80 %	Sep/ Oct 81 %	Nov/ Dec 82 %
Like Them	37	51	54	58	58	47	48	42	50	51	56	53
Don't Especially Like Them	24	16	18	19	18	24	24	21	23	22	18	22
Undecided	18	17	17	13	15	16	17	21	17	17	17	15
No Opinion	21	16	11	10	9	13	11	16	10	10	9	10

Question: "Do you like Americans or don't you especially like them?"

Source: Archives of the Allensbach Institute, Nos. 1003, 1053,
1067,1070,2002,2014,2023,2095,3012,3072,3084,3098,4000,
4006,4018.

Table 3.2. Most Likeable People

Question: "Which people do you find most likeable?"

Date: October 1981

Swiss	38%
Americans	20%
French	20%
British	12%
Spanish	7%
Polish	5%
Belgians	3%
Russians	1%
No Opinion	4%

Source: EMNID Institute, "Aufrüstung und Pazifismus," Vol. 1,
Table 4, October 1981. Reprinted with permission of
Der Spiegel.

Table 3.3. Federal Republic's Best Friend

Question: "Which country do you consider to be the Federal Republic's best friend?"					
	Sep 77 %	Jan 80 %	Sep 80 %	Aug 81 %	Nov/ Dec 82 %
The U.S.	54	53	51	49	48
France	10	14	17	18	15
Austria	6	5	6	8	6
Switzerland	3	2	2	2	3
England	2	1	2	1	1
Holland	2	1	2	1	1
Belgium	X	X	X	X	X
Italy	1	1	X	X	1
Russia	X	X	X	X	X
Other Countries	5	5	5	6	4
Have No (Best) Friend	9	9	4	9	8
No Response	14	13	14	9	14
	106	104	103	103	101

X=less than 0.5%

Source: Archives of the Allensbach Institute, Nos. 3047, 3077, 3087, 3099.

Table 3.4. Opinion of United States

Question: "What is your overall opinion of the United States?"

Date: February 1982

	Great Britain %	France %	W. Germany %	Italy %	Belgium %
Favorable	46	55	73	63	49
Unfavorable	44	32	24	21	22
Don't Know	10	13	3	16	29

Question: "What is your overall opinion of the Soviet Union?"

	Great Britain %	France %	W. Germany %	Italy %	Belgium %
Favorable	14	13	20	13	11
Unfavorable	74	73	77	68	61
Don't Know	12	14	3	19	28

Source: Gallup International Poll, February 1982; published in Newsweek (Foreign Edition), March 15, 1982.

Table 3.5. Relationship with U.S. or Russia

Question: "If we had to decide between these two possibilities, which is more important for the future of the German people: a good relationship with the U.S. or a good relationship with Russia?"

More important:	May/June 54 %	October 75 %	May 81 %
A good relationship with U.S.	62	52	65
A good relationship with Russia	10	12	6
Undecided	28	36	29

Source: Archives of the Allensbach Institute, No. 4103.

Table 3.6. Foreign Policy Orientation to U.S. or Russia

Question: "A general question concerning foreign policy- Should the Federal Republic work more closely with the U.S. or with the Soviet Union?"

	May 73 %	Oct 77 %	Sep 78 %	Jan 80 %	Jul 81 %	Jan 82 %	Jun* 82 %	Jun** 82 %
More closely with U.S.	36	49	51	49	50	42	51	54
More closely with U.S.S.R.	3	2	1	2	2	2	1	1
Just as closely with both	54	38	36	41	37	44	39	39
Undecided	7	11	12	8	11	12	9	6

*Before Reagan visit
**After Reagan visit

Source: Archives of the Allensbach Institute, Nos. 2131,3049,3060, 3098,3178,4004,4010 before Reagan visit, 4010 after Reagan visit.

Table 3.7. Defense of Freedom vs. Avoidance of War

Question: "No one knows what will happen, but what do you think-if we are confronted with the choice of either letting Europe become Soviet or resisting the move with every means at our disposal, which is more important-to defend democratic freedom, even if it leads to a nuclear war, or to avoid war above all, even though it means having to live under a communist government?"

	May 55 %	Jul 60 %	Mar 76 %	Mar 79 %	May 81 %
Avoid war above all	36	38	52	52	48
Defend Democracy	33	30	28	23	27
Impossible to say	31	32	20	25	25

Source: Archives of the Allensbach Institute, Nos. 4103,3012,3028, 3032,3082.

Table 3.8. Russian Domination vs. Fighting in Defense

Question: "Some people say that war is so horrible that it is better
to accept Russian domination than to risk war. Others say
it would be better to fight in defense of your country than
to accept Russian domination. Which opinion is closer to
your own?"

Date: February 1982

	Great Britain	France	W. Germany	Italy	U.S.
	%	%	%	%	%
Better to accept domination	12	13	19	17	6
Better to fight	75	57	74	48	83
Don't know	13	30	7	35	11

Source: Gallup International Poll, February 1982; published in
Newsweek (Foreign Edition), March 15, 1982.

Table 3.9. Confidence in U.S. Leadership

Question: "How confident are you that the United States is capable
of taking a wise leadership role in world problems today-
very confident, fairly confident, not so confident, or
not at all confident?"

	Aug 79	May 80	May 81
	%	%	%
Very or fairly confident	34	34	42
Not so or not all confident	54	56	47
Undecided	12	10	11

Source: Archives of the Allensbach Institute, Nos. 4103,3072.

Table 3.10. Confidence in U.S. Policy

Question: "In general, how much confidence do you have in the United
States to deal wisely with world problems?"

Date: February 1982

	Great Britain	France	W. Germany	Italy	Belgium
	%	%	%	%	%
A great deal	6	4	6	7	7
A fair amount	29	36	41	36	38
Subtotal	35%	40%	57%	53%	45%
Not very much	39	35	33	18	20
None at all	21	12	7	11	10
Subtotal	60%	47%	40%	29%	30%
Don't know	5	13	3	18	25

Source: Gallup International Poll, February 1982; published in
Newsweek (Foreign Edition), March 15, 1982.

Table 3.11. U.S. as Reliable Western Leader

Question: "If you heard the following: 'The U.S. today has again finally become a reliable leader for the Western world, seeing to our security vis-a-vis the East from its position of strength.'-would you say that's true, or don't you see it that way?"

	May 81 %	Aug 81 %	By party preference CDU/CSU %	SPD %	FDP %	The Greens %
True	47	50	68	42	44	17
Don't see it that way	26	29	15	35	36	75
Undecided	27	21	17	23	20	8

Source: Archives of the Allensbach Institute, Nos. 4103,3099.

Table 3.12. Confidence in U.S. Defense Guarantee (Comparative)

Question: "If your country's security was threatened by a Russian attack, how much confidence do you have in the U.S. to do whatever is necessary to defend your country, even if this risked a direct attack against the U.S. itself?"

Date: February 1982

	Great Britain %	W. Germany %	Belgium %	Denmark %	Switzerland %
A great deal	20	17	12	17	7
A fair amount	36	45	34	32	26
Subtotal	56%	62%	46%	49%	33%
Not very much	28	27	23	25	39
None at all	12	8	10	11	22
Subtotal	40%	35%	33%	36%	61%
Don't know	4	3	21	15	6

Source: Gallup International Poll, February 1982; published in Newsweek (Foreign Edition), March 15, 1982.

Table 3.13. Acceptance of U.S. Leadership Role

Question: "A question about foreign policy: In the present situation, should the Federal Republic always back the Americans in matters of foreign policy, or should it decide from case to case whether it follows the Americans or goes its own way?"

	May 1980	May 1981
Always back the Americans	30%	28%
Decide from case to case	56%	65%
Undecided	14%	7%

Source: Archives of the Allensbach Institute, No. 4103.

Table 3.14. Support for U.S. Policy Initiatives

Question: "One may have various opinions about what stand the Federal Republic should take regarding American policy. Written here are two opinions-which of the two would you tend to agree with?"		
"I think that if we demand that the U.S. stand by us in Europe, then we have to show by our actions that we support their policy in other parts of the world, even if we don't always agree with it and must make some sacrifices."	May 80	May 81
	39%	20%
"We should naturally show solidarity with the Americans as far as possible, but when they adopt an unreasonable policy, they can't expect of us that we follow with measures that harm our own interests."	49%	68%
Undecided	12%	12%

Source: Archives of the Allensbach Institute, No. 4103.

Table 3.15. Acceptance of U.S. Policy on Soviet Union

Question: "Assume that the American and German governments disagree on how to handle a situation concerning the Soviet Union. This disagreement persists after talks. What should the Germans do in such a case?"

	October 1981
Accept the U.S. policy	51%
Take some distance	45%
Undecided	4%

Source: EMNID Institute, "Aufrüstung und Pazifismus," Vol. 3, Table 54, October 1981. Reprinted with permission of Der Spiegel.

Table 3.16. Possibility of World War

Question: "Do you think that we have to reckon with the prospect of a new world war breaking out again, or don't you think anyone will risk a large-scale war again?"									
	Aug 61 %	Jan 63 %	Feb 65 %	Jun 67 %	Dec 75 %	Sep 79 %	May 80 %	Jul 81 %	Jun 82 %
Must reckon with world war	46	42	41	38	29	32	36	46	38
No one will risk it	45	49	48	54	63	59	54	45	43
Other/no concrete response	9	9	11	8	8	9	10	9	19

Source: Archives of the Allensbach Institute, Nos. 1057,1073,1098, 2029,3022,3073,3079,3092,3098.

Table 3.17. Likelihood of World War in Two Years

Question: "Do you believe that there will be another world war within
the next couple years?"

	October 1981
Probably	6%
Possibly	46%
Unlikely	47%
No answer	1%

Source: EMNID Institute, "Aufrüstung und Pazifismus," Vol. 2,
Table 29, October 1981. Reprinted with permission of
Der Spiegel.

Table 3.18. Threat from the East (Allensbach Files)

Question: "Do you worry about our being threatened by the East?"

	Feb 76 %	Jan 78 %	Sep 79 %	Feb 80 %	Jul 81 %	Jan 82 %
Worry	51	44	41	65	59	59
Don't worry	37	43	41	25	24	26
Undecided	23	13	18	10	17	15

By age groups for January 1982:

	Age groups			
	16-29	30-44	45-59	60 and over
Worry	49	59	62	67
Don't worry	34	26	24	20
Undecided	17	15	14	13

Source: Archives of the Allensbach Institute, Nos. 3073,3078,4103,
3098,4003,4004.

Table 3.19. Threat from the East (EMNID Files)

Question: "Do you worry about being threatened by the East?"

	October 1981
Worry	55%
Don't worry	45%
Undecided	1%

Again, by age groups:

	18-21	22-25	26-29	30-39	40-49	50-64	65 +
Worry	45%	48%	48%	57%	60%	53%	59%
Don't worry	55%	51%	52%	42%	38%	47%	41%
Undecided	1%	1%	--	1%	1%	--	--

Source: EMNID Institute, "Aufrüstung und Pazifismus," Vol. 1,
Table 18, October 1981. Reprinted with permission of
Der Spiegel.

Table 3.20. Likelihood of Soviet Attack Within Two Years

Question: "All in all, how great do you think the danger is of a Soviet attack taking place within the next couple of years?"	
Date: February 1964	
Great danger	4.1%
Quite large	21.4%
Subtotal	25.5%
Only small	30.0%
No danger at all	18.6%
Subtotal	48.6%
No opinion/don't know	26.05%

Source: Files of the Central Archive for Empirical Social Research,
University of Cologne, Study 45.

Table 3.21. Likelihood of Soviet Attack Within Five Years

Question: "How likely do you feel it is that the Soviet Union will
attack W. Europe within the next five years?"

Date: February 1982

	Great Britain	W. Germany	Belgium	Denmark	Switzerland
Likely	21%	15%	23%	15%	25%
Not likely	72%	81%	53%	67%	71%
Don't know	7%	4%	24%	18%	4%

Source: Gallup International Poll, February 1982; published in
Newsweek (Foreign Edition), March 15, 1982.

Table 3.22. Possibility of Peace with the USSR

Question: "Do you believe that the West can get along peacefully
with Russia in the long run?"

	Jul 56 %	Apr 59 %	Feb 62 %	Jun 62 %	Jun 76 %	Sep 79 %
Can get along peacefully	46	46	34	36	49	56
Don't believe they can	40	38	46	51	33	27
No opinion	14	16	20	13	18	17

Source: Archives of the Allensbach Institute, Nos. 096,1030,1062,
1066,3030,3073.

Table 3.23. U.S. or Soviet Leadership in Military Power, 1960s

	Feb 64	May 65
Question: "All in all, who do you think leads in terms of total military power, Russia or the U.S.?"		
U.S.A.	41.01%	40.35%
Russia	13.81%	10.21%
Both equal	29.78%	32.46%
No opinion	15.39%	16.99%

Source: Files of the Central Archive for Empirical Social Research, University of Cologne, Studies 428,429.

Table 3.24. U.S. or Soviet Leadership in Military Power, 1970s and 1980s

Question: "A question about armament in the East and West-from all that you've heard, how would you assess the present power relationship? Is the East more powerful, the West more powerful, or are they equally powerful?"

	Feb 76	Oct 77	Sep 79	May 80	May 81	Jul 81
	%	%	%	%	%	%
East bloc more powerful	57	48	48	49	46	52
West more powerful	5	6	5	7	6	6
Equally powerful	24	33	31	27	31	27
Don't know	14	13	16	17	17	15

Source: Archives of the Allensbach Intitute, Nos. 3047,3073,3098,4103.

Table 3.25. Eastern vs. Western Power

Question: "Who is more powerful, the East or the West?"

	October 1981
East is more powerful	49%
West is more powerful	11%
Equally powerful	39%
No opinion	1%

Source: EMNID Institute, "Aufrüstung und Pazifismus," Vol. 2, Table 26, October 1981. Reprinted with permission of Der Spiegel.

Table 3.26. Recognition of NATO

Question: "Do you know what is meant by NATO?"

	Oct 55	Dec 56	Dec 60	Aug 63	Sep 71	Mar 76	Sep 79	Jan 80
Yes	56%	68%	79%	77%	85%	89%	87%	93%
No	44%	32%	21%	23%	15%	11%	13%	7%

Source: Archives of the Allensbach Institute, Nos. 088,1001,1049,1080, 2074,3027,3073,3077.

Table 3.27. Advantages vs. Disadvantages of NATO

Question: "Does NATO bring more advantages or disadvantages to the Federal Republic?"

	Sep 56 %	Aug 59 %	Sep 71 %	Sep 79 %	May 81 %	Dec 81 %
More advantages	29	43	47	48	55	50
More disadvantages	11	6	9	7	14	11
Undecided/ Don't know what NATO is	60	51	44	45	31	39

Source: Archives of the Allensbach Institute, Nos. 099,1029,2074,3073, 4003,4103.

Table 3.28. Confidence in NATO Defense

Question: "How much confidence do you have in NATO's ability to defend Western Europe against an attack?"

Date: February 1982

	Great Britain %	France %	W. Germany %	Italy %	Belgium %
A great deal	12	5	16	16	7
A fair amount	44	34	45	33	36
Subtotal	56%	39%	61%	49%	43%
Not very much	25	29	29	19	24
None at all	10	9	6	9	9
Subtotal	35%	38%	35%	28%	33%
Don't know	9	23	4	23	24

Source: Gallup International Poll, February 1982; published in Newsweek (Foreign Edition), March 15, 1982.

Table 3.29. Maintenance of Membership in NATO

Question: "Should the Federal Republic remain a member of the NATO?"

	Jan 69 %	Sep 71 %	May 81 %
It should remain a member	79	71	78
It should leave the NATO	4	5	6
No opinion/don't know what NATO is	17	24	16

Source: Archives of the Allensbach Institute, Nos. 2048,2074,3073.

Table 3.30. Acceptance of U.S. Leadership

Question: "Of the two following statements, which is closer to your own views?"	
	May 81
"The Federal Republic needs America as security now as much as it did thirty years ago, when the Alliance was founded. Nothing has changed in that respect. Therefore as Germans, we have to continue to stand next to the U.S. and accept them as leaders."	47.6%
"I see it differently. In the last thirty years, many things have changed. The Federal Republic has gained importance in the circle of world powers. With the new German role in world politics, it is impossible for us to continue to follow the U.S. as leader all the time."	35.1%
Undecided	17.3%

Source: Archives of the Allensbach Institute, No. 4103.

Table 3.31. Alliance with U.S. or Neutrality

Question: "What is, in your opinion, the better foreign policy for us: Should we remain in strong military alliance with the U.S. or should we try to be completely neutral?"

	Feb 75 %	Sep 78 %	May 81 %
Military alliance with the U.S.	49	57	54
Try to be neutral	36	27	27
Undecided	15	16	19

Source: Archives of the Allensbach Institute, Nos. 3011,3060,4103.

Table 3.32. Alliance with U.S. vs. Western European Alliance

Question: "Which is the better foreign policy for the Federal Republic: Should we continue a strong military alliance with the U.S. or should we form a tight Western European political bloc?"

Date: May 1981

Military alliance with the U.S.	44.3%
Political block in Europe	31.6%
Undecided	24.5%

Source: Archives of the Allensbach Institute, No. 4103.

Table 3.33. Possibility of Self-Defense

Question: "Assume the Russians would start a war.... Could we defend ourselves?"

	Sep 60 %	Sep 71 %	Mar 76 %	Sep 79 %	Jan 80 %	May 81 %
We could not defend ourselves	37	37	29	31	35	41
We are well enough armed	19	27	26	27	33	25
Undecided/Impossible to say	44	36	45	42	32	34

Source: Archives of the Allensbach Institute, Nos. 2063,3028,3073, 3077,4103.

Table 3.34. Adequacy of Defense Effort in Western Europe

Question: "Does Western Europe do enough at the present time to defend itself militarily, or should it do more?"		
	Mar 73	Sep 79
Does enough	50%	34%
Should do more	26%	38%
Undecided	24%	28%

Source: Archives of the Allensbach Institute, Nos. 2092,3073.

Table 3.35. Alliance with U.S. vs. Neutrality (Allensbach Files)

Question: "With which of the following statements do you tend to agree more?"			
	Jun 82*	Jun 82**	Nov/ Dec 82
"The alliance with the U.S. and other western countries has secured Germany's freedom for the last 30 years. As a neutral state we would be too weak to defend ourselves against an attack."	66%	69%	65%
"The freedom of the Federal Republic would not be in jeopardy as a neutral state. And as a neutral state we could do more for world peace and the understanding between nations than we can when we are allies to a major power-bloc."	23%	19%	22%
Undecided	11%	12%	13%
*Before Reagan's visit **After Reagan's visit			

Source: Archives of the Allensbach Institute, Nos. 4010 (before Reagan's visit), 4010 (after Reagan's visit).

Table 3.36. Alliance with U.S. vs. Neutrality (EMNID Files)

Question: "Which of the following two statements corresponds more more closely with your own views?"	
Date: October 1981	
"For the Federal Republic it would be best if we were a neutral state, then we would not have to suffer as much under the tensions of the superpowers. We see by the example of Austria, that one can get along well with neutrality."	35%
"The Federal Republic needs the political and military alliance with the U.S. and other western countries. A neutral Germany would be isolated and too weak to defend itself from the Soviet pressures."	63%
Undecided	2%

Source: EMNID Institute, "Aufrüstung und Pazifismus," Vol. 1, Table 7, October 1981. Reprinted with permission of Der Spiegel.

Table 3.37. Need for U.S. Security Guarantee

Question: "Do you think the following statement is true or false?" "Without the Americans, we would already be lost." Date: October 1981	
True	55%
False	26%
Indifferent	18%
No response	1%

Source: EMNID Institute, "Aufrüstung und Pazifismus," Vol. 3,
         Table 55, October 1981. Reprinted with permission of
         Der Spiegel.

Table 3.38. Opinions about Peace Movement (EMNID Files)

Question: "Opinions about the Peace movement." Date: October 1981	
Dislike it fundamentally	10%
I have something against it	19%
Subtotal	29%
I am indifferent to it	22%
I think it is O.K. but I would not actively participate	39%
Subtotal	61%
I might participate actively sometime	7%
I will definitely participate eventually	1%
I am already part of the movement	1%
Subtotal	9%
No response	1%

Source: EMNID Institute, "Aufrüstung und Pazifismus," Vol. 3,
         Table 57, October 1981. Reprinted with permission of
         Der Spiegel.

Table 3.39. Opinions about Peace Movement (Allensbach Files)

Question: "Opinions about the Peace movement."

Date: Nov/Dec 1982

	I do not approve of it	I think it's all right	I work actively with it
	68%	29%	3%

	By Age Group			
	16-29	30-44	45-59	60 +
I do not approve of it	50%	70%	77%	81%
I think it's all right	44%	27%	22%	19%
I work actively with it	6%	3%	1%	X

Source: Archives of the Allensbach Institute, No. 4018.

Table 3.40. Extent of Anti-American Feeling

Question: "Often one hears that Anti-American feelings are forming in the Federal Republic. What do you think?"

Date: October 1981

Anti-American feelings are forming	21%
There is something about this statement is true	53%
The statement is wrong	26%
No opinion	1%

Source: EMNID Institute, "Aufrüstung und Pazifismus," Vol. 2, Table 25, October 1981. Reprinted with permission of Der Spiegel.

Table 3.41. Role of U.S. Troops in West Germany

Question: "What is your view of the American soldiers in West Germany? Are they primarily occupation troops or are they here primarily for the protection of the security of West Germany and Europe?"

As occupation troops	34.8%
As protection	42.5%
As both equally	14.1%
No opinion	8.6%

Source: Files of the Central Archive for Empirical Social Research, University of Cologne, Study 432.

Table 3.42. American Presence and Possibility of War

Question: "Do you believe that the American military presence increases or decreases the possibility of war?"

Date: June 1955.

Decreases possibility of war	34.6%
Increases it	23.7%
No effect	16.4%
No opinion	25.2%

Source: Files of the Central Archive for Empirical Social Research, University of Cologne, Study 432.

Table 3.43. Behavior of American Soldiers (1955)

Question: "From all you've seen and heard, what do you generally think of the behavior of American soldiers?"

Date: 1955

It is:

Good	41.6%
Fair	25.3%
Bad	3.9%
No opinion	29.2%

Source: Files of the Central Archive for Empirical Social Research, University of Cologne, Study 457.

Table 3.44. Social Relations between American Soldiers and Germans

Question: "Could you tell me if there are any social relations between American soldiers and the general German public?"	
Date: 1955	
Yes, there are	26.04%
No, there are none	19.10%
No opinion	54.86%

"If you said there are, how would you describe them?"

As being:	
Very good	17.5%
Good	56.5%
Subtotal	74.0%
Mediocre	15.6%
Bad	1.7%
Very bad	1.9%
Subtotal	3.6%
No opinion	6.8%

Source: Files of the Central Archive for Empirical Social Research, University of Cologne, Study 457.

Table 3.45. Cultural Relations between American Soldiers and Germans

Question: "Could you tell me if there are any cultural relations between American soldiers and the general German public?"	
Date: 1955	
Yes, there are	22.15%
No, there are none	20.27%
No opinion	57.58%

"And if you said there are, how would you describe them?"

As being:	
Very good	19.6%
Good	60.4%
Subtotal	80.0%
Mediocre	12.5%
Bad	1.7%
Very bad	0.3%
Subtotal	2.0%
No opinion	5.5%

Source: Files of the Central Archive for Empirical Social Research, University of Cologne, Study 457.

Table 3.46. Development of American Soldier-German
            Civilian Relations

Question: "Do you have the impression that relations between American soldiers and the general public have become better within the last couple years, or have they deteriorated?"
Date: 1955

They have become better	41.8%
They have remained the same	23.8%
They have deteriorated	1.7%
No opinion	32.8%

Source: Files of the Central Archive for Empirical Social Research,
        University of Cologne, Study 457.

Table 3.47. Marriages between American Soldiers and Germans

Question: "Imagine that your daughter, sister or another one of your close relatives wanted to marry an American soldier, would you approve of this?"
Date: 1955

I would very much approve of it	2.8%
I would approve of it	13.8
Subtotal	16.6%
I would not like it too much	26.0%
I would be very opposed to it	14.5%
Subtotal	40.5%
It wouldn't make any difference	34.3%
No opinion	8.6%

Source: Files of the Central Archive for Empirical Social Research,
        University of Cologne, Study 457.

Table 3.48. Approval-Disapproval of American Troop Presence

Question: "All in all, does the presence of American troops have more advantages or disadvantages for us Germans?"
Date: 1955

More advantages	41.2%
More disadvantages	15.2%
Neither/nor	14.4%
Both advantages and disadvantages	12.2%
Subtotal	26.6%
No opinion	17.0%

Source: Files of the Central Archive for Empirical Social Research,
        University of Cologne, Study 457.

Table 3.49. Behavior of American Soldiers (1961)

Question: "Do American soldiers behave very well?"	
Date: 1961	
They behave well	82%
Not so good	7%
Undecided	9%
Other answers	2%

Source: Archives of the Allensbach Institute, No. 1052.

Table 3.50. Impressions of American Officers

Question: "Do you have a good impression of the American officers, or is it not too good?"	
Date: 1961	
Good impression	92%
It is not too good	3%
Undecided	5%

Source: Archives of the Allensbach Institute, No. 1052.

Table 3.51. Reaction to Soviet Neutrality Proposal

Question: "Assume the Russians would make the following proposition: Let the U.S. and the British withdraw all troops from the continent and liquidate their military bases, and Russia would withdraw all its troops and armament behind its own borders. Would you rather have this proposal accepted or denied?"	
Date: May 1957	
Accepted	57.3%
Denied	28.2%
Undecided	14.5%

Source: Files of the Central Archive for Empirical Social Research, University of Cologne, Study 71.

Table 3.52. Link between German Security and American Troops

Question: "Assume there were no American troops in Germany any more, would our military security still be good enough, or would it not be good enough?"		
	May 70	May 73
It would still be good enough	20%	24%
It would not be good enough	50%	47%
Impossible to say	30%	28%
Undecided	--	1%

Source: Archives of the Allensbach Institute, Nos. 2063,2095.

Table 3.53.   Reactions to U.S. Troop Withdrawals
              (Allensbach Files)

Question: "If you read in the newspaper, that the Americans are going
           to withdraw all their troops from Europe, would you approve
           or disapprove of this?"

	Jul 56 %	Dec 57 %	Jun 65 %	Apr 69 %	May 70 %	May 73 %	Jul 76 %	Aug 78 %	Sep 79 %	Sep 81 %
Approve	51	34	12	17	22	23	15	17	11	17
Disapprove	22	34	59	56	51	45	54	57	60	59
Undecided	27	32	29	27	27	32	31	26	29	24

Source: Archives of the Allensbach Institute, Nos. 096,1003,1065,2051,
        2063,2095,3030,3059,3073.

Table 3.54.   Reactions to U.S. Troop Withdrawals (EMNID Files)

Question: "Assume that the U.S. would withdraw its troops from Europe
           for a given reason, would you approve of this or disapprove
           of it?"

Date: October 1981

Approve	12%
Disapprove	62%
Indifferent	25%
No opinion	1%

Source: EMNID Institute, "Aufrüstung und Pazifismus," Vol. 22,
        Table 22, October 1981. Reprinted with permission of
        Der Spiegel.

Table 3.55.   Security Effects of American Troops in Europe

Question: "What is the effect of having American troops stationed
           in Western Europe?"*

Date: February 1982

	Great Britain	W. Germany	Denmark	U.S.
Increases chances of attack	25%	15%	16%	10%
Provides greater protection	24%	48%	33%	61%
No effect	46%	33%	26%	19%
Don't know	5%	4%	25%	10%

*The question was asked only in the countries shown.

Source: Gallup International Poll, February 1982; published in
        Newsweek (Foreign Edition), March 15, 1982.

Table 3.56. Confidence in American Security Guarantee

Question: "Do you believe that the often repeated assurances of the American government, that American troops will remain in Germany as long as the Germans wish them to remain, are absolutely reliable?"
Possible Answers: A. Yes, absolutely reliable   B. Yes, fairly reliable   C. I don't know   D. No, fairly unreliable   E. No, absolutely unreliable   F. No answer

	A %	B %	C %	D %	E %	F %
Total Population	27	20	12	13	15	13
Profession:						
Wage-earners, Salaried						
employees, Civil servants	26	22	13	13	16	10
Self-employed, Retired, Other	31	17	9	12	14	17
Age Groups:						
18-29	27	16	12	14	16	15
30-49	26	27	9	7	19	12
50-69	29	15	15	17	12	12
Education:						
Primary school only	27	21	14	14	16	8
High school, Abitur,						
University degree	28	19	8	11	15	19
Sex:						
Male	42	18	6	15	12	7
Female	21	21	14	12	17	15
Size of Community:						
100,000 inhabitants or less	28	26	13	13	7	13
Over 100,000 inhabitants	23	12	24	11	20	10
Region:						
Schleswig-Holstein, Lower Saxony						
Bremen, Hamburg	37	12	12	21	17	1
North Rhine Westphalia	19	12	16	3	25	25
Hesse, Rhineland-Palatinate, Saar	32	21	5	16	10	16
Bavaria, Baden-Wuerttemberg	26	31	11	14	9	9

Source: Wickert Institute Public Opinion Study, April 1983.

4

The Nexus of Morale Factors

A major purpose of this study is to inquire into the sociological dynamics of the relationship between the West German population and the U.S. military. Whether the United States *ought* to continue to maintain a large-scale military presence in the Federal Republic is a policy question that will be discussed in the final chapter. Whether the U.S. *can* maintain such a presence depends, in turn, upon the quality of the relationship between the West German population and the U.S. military. The long-term viability of the U.S. military presence in the FRG has much to do with the general level of morale of U.S. troops, which influences the tone and texture of the relationship. If U.S. troops are to remain, their presence must be perceived by the Germans as more valuable than the negative effects arising from their incumbency, because no West German government could continue to base the country's security upon a large-scale U.S. military presence if public support for that presence disappeared.

The subject of military morale is inordinately intricate. Morale is, in reality, an entire complex of factors, some objective and others highly subjective. Webster's dictionary defines morale as "the mental and emotional condition (as of enthusiasm, confidence, or loyalty) of an individual or group with regard to the function or tasks at hand" or "the level of individual psychological well-being based on such factors as a sense of purpose and confidence in the future." Morale includes such states of mind or emotions as determination, perseverance, motivation, confidence, resolution, vigor, energy, and devotion to goals. The concept may be applied with validity to either individuals or groups. Given the essential mission of the military—to engage in combat with a hostile enemy—the concept of morale has special importance for military forces. Without a high level of collective morale, they would be unable to sustain combat against a well-prepared or highly motivated enemy. It is as important that morale be sustained at as high a level as possible in peacetime as in time of war, as the essential purpose of peacetime forces is constant preparation for potential or actual combat.

An intense study of morale would draw us into complex sectors of applied psychology, which is not our purpose here. We wish only to understand how certain key factors of morale influence the relationship between West Germans and U.S. military forces. We are interested, first, in what these factors mean in terms of assessing the actual level of morale of U.S. military personnel in West Germany and, second, in West German perceptions of how these factors affect the social and military viability of the U.S. military presence.

The selection of key factors is, at best, somewhat arbitrary. Various analysts, depending upon their interests or research concerns, would be likely to choose very different sets of factors. Even the definition of factors is hazardous, as some factors may be more centrally related to the concept than others. In addition, there is the risk of subsuming some factors as subfactors of others and perhaps excluding other important factors altogether. These methodological caveats, though serious, need not create an insurmountable obstacle for purposes of the inquiry at hand. On the basis of press coverage, interviews, and available sets of data, we can identify six key factors of morale that seem to be particularly important to the U.S. military presence in the FRG: alcohol and drug abuse; crime and indiscipline; race relations within the miliary; the problem of West German discrimination against U.S. military personnel; the problem of terrorism; and the phenomenon of poverty experienced periodically by U.S. forces.

Another methodological problem that need not concern us is the question of whether these factors are in the realm of cause or effect. Whether high levels of drug use, for example, cause a decline in morale or are a manifestation of lower morale is not a highly relevant question for the purposes of our inquiry. Cause and effect are probably closely interwoven. Important is how each of these factors influences the performance of U.S. forces in West Germany, and, even more important, how each influences German perceptions of the effects of the U.S. presence upon German society and upon German-American relations.

Three sources of evidence were of particular importance in analyzing the six factors of morale. First, statistical data provided primarily by the military services (army and air force) were useful in constructing a profile of objective evidence. Second, interviews with West German politicians, military figures, businesspeople, students, and homemakers, as well as with U.S. military personnel, from high-ranking officers to young recruits, were useful in gaining a sense of the gamut of opinion concerning these issues. Finally, West German press coverage was used extensively as a means of observing changes in West German elite opinion over time in reference to each of the morale factors. Each of the following six chapters attempts to construct a general picture of an important facet of the morale of U.S. forces in the FRG from the late 1960s until approximately the mid-1980s. In each case the most important consideration is how the morale factor influenced the tone and texture of German-American relations and, consequently, the long-term viability of the American military presence in the Federal Republic of Germany.

5

Alcohol and Drug Abuse

In the last decade the problem of drug abuse, like other social problems, has tended to wax and wane. There is, however, a singular obstinacy to the problem that has made it impossible for the armed services ever really to come to grips with it, despite herculean efforts. The problem deserves special consideration for two reasons: the effect of drug abuse on the combat capability of the forces and the image the problem creates in the West German mind in reference to the U.S. military presence.

A military organization is different from a civilian organization in that the presence of a drug problem sabotages the purposes and goals of the organization more than is true in other settings. Military forces are, after all, armed forces, possessing all sorts of sophisticated weapons of high explosive power, which must be serviced and maintained as well as used in exercises and war. In many civilian settings, drug use may be tolerated without seriously compromising the work of the organization, especially if the work of the organization does not affect human safety. Salespeople have reported making average or higher sales while using drugs, actors or actresses sometimes turn in exceptional performances while on heavy dosages of drugs; teachers teach, construction workers pour concrete, truck drivers drive, bankers lend money, and business executives close important deals, all while high on drugs. Society worries more about the surgeon who performs delicate operations or the pilot who flies jumbo jets while smoking grass or sniffing cocaine. So much more must society worry about the effects of drug use within the nation's defense establishment. What would happen if the Soviets mounted a full scale invasion of Western Europe, at the same time that a high percentage of U.S. soldiers were strung out on marijuana, coke, or heroin? That is precisely the nightmare of the commanders in Europe. Most military analysts are quite willing to concede that a first-rate military force must be as drug-free as possible if its capability as a fighting force using high-technology weapons is to be taken seriously.

In a democratic society such as the United States it is not realistic, and not healthy, to expect the armed forces to be an island of civilization apart from the society from which they are drawn. Young soldiers are men and women not unlike their counterparts in civilian society. They have hopes and dreams, personal triumphs, and shattered illusions much like other young people. Despite the unrepresentativeness of the military forces under the regime of the AVF, it is still true that the military forces mirror in important ways the larger society. The reason that U.S. military forces have had a serious drug problem since the late 1960s is that U.S. society has had the same serious problem. Indeed, the United States has the most serious drug problem of any advanced, industrialized society in the world. Viewed from this perspective, it should not be surprising that U.S. military forces have a more serious problem with drug abuse than do the forces of any other NATO ally, but it is precisely this circumstance that tarnishes the image of U.S. forces in Europe and heightens the level of suspicion.

Dimensions of the Drug Abuse Problem

Apart from the case of Vietnam, the U.S. military has had more serious drug-abuse problems with the forces stationed in the Federal Republic than anywhere else in the world, including the United States. The reasons for this are complex and not well understood. Part of the explanation rests undoubtedly with the feeling of increasing estrangement that developed between U.S. soldiers and the West German civilian population from the late 1960s onward. Whereas U.S. soldiers felt they understood and were accepted by the West Germans with unabashed affection for the first quarter-century after World War II, the feelings of closeness seemed to dissipate in the decade of the 1970s. Soldiers and air force personnel, feeling isolated and alone, were more prone to find solace and diversion in drugs. The fact that for the last decade or so the Federal Republic has been considered a hardship post by most military personnel sets the stage for problems of drug abuse. The availability of drugs is another important factor. The entire gamut of illegal drugs is available for purchase anywhere in West Germany, though the supply is richer and easier in and around large cities. The Frankfurt central train station, like the Port Authority Bus Terminal in New York, is on any given night beset with legions of drug dealers.

The problem of drug abuse varies inversely with the general level of morale among the troops. During periods of lower morale, problems of drug abuse are more serious and vice versa. Hence, all the factors that contribute to morale—such as perceived opportunity, physical facilities, earning levels, strength of the dollar, and unit cohesion—contribute also to the drug equation. Youth life styles and trends in civilian life affect military life styles as well, though perhaps with a time lag of a few months. Particular drugs may be more popular at one time, whereas others are more in vogue a few years later. Another factor is probably the sheer dimensions of the U.S. presence in Germany. The drug problem is less severe in countries where the U.S. military community represents a tiny minority surrounded by an alien culture, simply by virtue of the fact that the smaller numbers of troops and the alien culture give the local commanders greater possibilities of control. In the Federal Republic, by contrast, the concentration of the U.S. presence, especially in urban areas such as Frankfurt, Stuttgart, Mannheim, and Berlin, creates the illusion of large U.S. ghettos surrounded by the fast-moving life of the cities. This complicates the commanders' problems of control over the troops after duty hours.

Historical Background of Drug Abuse in West Germany

The problem of drug abuse among the troops in Germany ballooned to dimensions that seemed nearly beyond control in the late 1960s and early 1970s.[1] Part of the explanation for this may be found in the "spin-off" syndrome, or the transferrence of problems from Vietnam to the neglected forces in West Germany. Disillusionment with the losing cause in Vietnam and with U.S. foreign policy, coupled with major social change, youth rebellion, civil rights movements, and challenges to authority, produced conditions that were rife for a breakdown of the social order in the military. Drug abuse was simply one manifestation of the prevailing disorder. General Michael Davison, the USAREUR commander in chief in Germany, confirmed that in 1972 and 1973 drug abuse had been "the greatest single threat to the discipline and professionalism" of the army in Europe. An "atmosphere of terror" existed in army barracks because of drugs, and drug-related crimes had increased fourfold in a period of eighteen months.[2]

The contrast between U.S. forces and the forces of other NATO allies in the FRG at that time was particularly poignant. During the same period the British Army of the Rhine reported that it had very little incidence of either drug abuse or alcoholism. A Rhine army spokesman stated that to his knowledge there had been only one hard drug case in the eighteen months preceding the turn of the year 1974. Only sixty-eight British soldiers faced drug charges in 1972, some of whom were acquitted. The rate dropped after that.[3] The West German public at large seemed to be well aware that the military drug problem was primarily American, though during this period drug usage among West German youth was also dramatically on the rise. The West German press, in a report that noted that 4,000 U.S. soldiers had become ill with hepatitis in the year 1973 alone, posited that the drug problems of the Seventh Army had become a serious security risk.[4]

In 1973 the army instituted draconian measures to curb drug abuse among the troops in West Germany. The measures included body searches, unannounced locker inspections and urine tests, and the use of dogs in billets. Commanders were given the authority to force soldiers into rehabilitation programs even on suspicion. The measures had their intended effect, though drug usage probably would have declined to a certain extent anyway because U.S. participation in the Vietnam War ended and drug usage among youth groups in the civilian population also appeared to decline, both in the Federal Republic and the United States. General Davison reported in 1974 that although drug abuse had been detected among 6.27% of all U.S. service personnel in West Germany in the fourth quarter of 1972, the figure declined to only 3.3% in the fourth quarter of 1973.[5]

The army's war on drugs was halted temporarily in early 1974 as a result of a ruling by a federal district court judge in Washington. As a result of a class action suit filed by the American Civil Liberties Union and the Lawyers' Military Defense Committee on behalf of U.S. soldiers stationed in the FRG, the court ruled that almost all of the measures instituted by the army violated constitutional rules, most particularly the rule against unlawful search and seizure without a warrant. The army halted the procedures, but was allowed to resume them seven months later pending a ruling from a higher circuit court of appeals. During the interim when the control measures were suspended, drug use began to escalate dramatically once again. In the appeal to the higher court the army included an emotionally written affidavit from General Davison that pleaded for consideration of the special needs of a military organization. The changes prescribed by the lower court, he argued, would be seen by drug abusers "as almost free rein to continue and to even increase their abuse. . . . While fear of punitive action is not a completely desirable tool, . . . it is sometimes the only effective stimulator for one who is caught up in the insidious clutches of drug addiction."[6]

In September 1975, the circuit court of appeals in Washington reversed the ruling of the lower court. The court ruled that the searches were constitutional in the military context because of the "vital interest of the nation in maintaining the readiness and fitness of its armed forces." Evidence taken in such searches must be considered legally seized and could be used against soldiers in later proceedings. "The soldier cannot reasonably expect the Army barracks to be a sanctuary like his civilian home," the court concluded.[7] Seventh Army headquarters at Heidelberg was naturally relieved by the ruling. Without the power to enforce discipline upon its soldiers, especially in the flourishing drug trade, the generals would have faced a rapid march back into the swamp of the early 1970s, possibly without any exit this time.

The drug trade in West Germany, after a two-year decline, began to bloom again in late 1975, though the situation did not get nearly as out of hand as in the early 1970s. According to the results of a series of random urine tests on personnel twenty-five years of age and younger, released by army headquarters at Heidelberg, a distinct increase in hard drug abuse was noted. Nearly half of the soldiers found to be using drugs had taken methaqualone, a sedative considered dangerous by the military command but sold by prescription in pharmacies in West Germany. The statistics showed that 2.7% of the troops used drugs excessively. The samples confirmed that 1.4% used opiates, barbituates, and amphetamines, and 1.3% used methaqualone. The study also confirmed what most observers expected—that the problem was much worse in the army than in the air force. The figure for hard drug abusers in the air force was found to be 0.1%.[8] Significantly, the army did not release figures relating to either hashish or heroin, a gap that was promptly covered by the results of an independent study conducted by reporters of the newspaper *Stars and Stripes.* They found that 1.7% of U.S. troops were regular users of heroin. Though U.S. authorities in West Germany had confiscated twelve kilograms of heroin during the past year, it was estimated that only 2% of all hard drugs circulating in the military market were confiscated. The newspaper also found a small army of ex-GIs who were living in West Germany illegally and supplying a substantial portion of the heroin to soldiers, largely via the central distribution centers in Amsterdam. A good hit of heroin, usually 1/30th to 1/40th of a gram, cost ten dollars. The investigation also revealed that the army's official urine-testing program was being widely circumvented. It was common practice, according to *Stars and Stripes,* for a heroin addict to purchase on short notice a urine sample from a nonuser or temporarily "clean" buddy at a going price of forty dollars per sample. Conversely, soldiers determined to get out of the service as soon as possible could purchase the sample of a heroin addict for the same price. Not only did the paper find that soldiers in West Germany "make up a significant part of the heroin consumer market in Europe," but "the purchase of heroin is as easy for a knowledgeable user as for a shopper to buy a bag of oranges at the corner fruit stand or a bouquet of roses at the local flower market."[9] When the *Stars and Stripes* story was picked up by the West German press, it was also noted that whereas the number of heroin addicts in the United States was stable or perhaps declining, the number of addicts in the Federal Republic was doubling every year, with a disproportionate amount of addiction occurring among GIs. And, though no evidence was offered to back up the claim, the West German press reported what most Germans suspected to be true, namely, that "most heroin reaches German hands through American drug dealers."[10] The impression, whether true or not, was certainly not calculated to improve the image of the U.S. Army among the West German population.

The problem with drugs seemed to stabilize in the period from 1975 to 1978. Though the problem was never really surmounted or overcome, it was at least kept at manageable levels, and scant attention was paid to it in the West German press. In 1978, however, the problem seemed to get noticeably worse once again. In May, an army general told the House Select Committee on Narcotics Abuse and Control that an army survey showed that 31.2% of enlisted personnel said they used marijuana, and 7.3% admitted using hard drugs such as heroin. In November, a five-member congressional task force visited West Germany to survey the situation. The information collected appeared to be devastating. According to Congressman Glenn English, 20 to 30% of the personnel in some U.S. units in Germany used heroin regularly, and 80 to 90% of the personnel in some units used hashish frequently. "U.S. forces in Europe can perform their mission," Congressman English said, "but there is a drug problem and, unless immediate action is taken, it will be difficult to contain." The task force also discovered that narcotics available to service personnel in West Germany were more potent than those available in the United States. According to Congressman English, the marijuana was "stout stuff" with "10 times the bang that you find from marijuana in the United States." Heroin in the United States was 4 to 5% pure, but "the heroin that is sold to soldiers in Germany is 40 to 50 percent pure."[11]

The difficulty of compiling accurate statistics is well illustrated by the congressional visit. Many observers complain that the military services deliberately underestimate or miscalculate most statistics on drugs, crime, and other matters related to morale. Though such a charge cannot be proven, the Pentagon was patently dismayed by the figures released by the congressional task force. According to a spokesperson for the Pentagon, "We haven't had an opportunity to evaluate Representative English's findings since he returned from Europe. However, current statistics within the Department of Defense indicate a much lower percentage of drug abusers."[12]

Exercising its protective role vis-à-vis U.S. forces, the Federal Republic's defense ministry refused to comment on any of the reports. In mid-December 1978, however, a permanent German-American Working Group on Narcotic Drugs, composed of representatives of the defense ministries of both countries, was established to study the problem intensively and make recommendations to appropriate officials. Throughout 1979 various initiatives were taken to strengthen collaboration between U.S. and West German officials in combating the drug trade, including a series of conferences, increased exchanges of information, and closer collaboration between U.S. military police units and the German police.[13]

In the spring of 1979 the military services began another all-out war against drug abuse, largely as a result of concern expressed by President Jimmy Carter following consultations with Congressmen Lester Wolff and Glenn English. The president let it be known that, in his view, the drug problem in Europe had serious implications for the combat readiness of U.S. troops. He had also apparently received discreet diplomatic warnings from the German government that stronger action should be taken against the drug problem. The army, of course, attempted to play down the problem. A Pentagon spokesperson confirmed that "the army views its drug abuse problem as serious but not of epidemic proportions. The abuse does have some adverse impact on combat readiness, but it is difficult, if not impossible, to establish a definitive causal relationship that can be quantified." The Pentagon's attitude was much too benign, in the view of Wolff and English. In their consultations with the president they warned that the equivalent of perhaps two divisions of U.S. troops in Europe were permanently incapacitated by hard drug addiction.[14]

With prodding from Congress and the White House the military services again gave high priority to the fight against drug abuse among the troops in Europe. Measures for detection of drug abuse were strengthened, and rehabilitation programs for addicts were expanded and revamped. Unannounced urine tests were run frequently, and new units of sniffing dogs were trained to inspect cargo shipments and living facilities. However, the drug problem in the military remains intractable, and there seems to have been very little change in regards to it in Europe. West Germany still ranks number one as the location where the problem is most severe. A congressional report issued in the fall of 1981 again confirmed the existence of the problem in shocking dimensions. According to the report, the use of drugs during duty hours extended to 42.6% of enlisted army personnel in Europe and to 17% of air force personnel. In the barracks at Hanau, Aschaffenburg, Schweinfurt, Bad Kreuznach, and Buedingen, 16% of enlisted personnel smoked marijuana or hashish every single day. Though there was good evidence that heroin usage had declined from 10 to 4% since 1978, usage of all other drugs remained high or had increased.[15]

The East German Drug Connection

Information about the supply of drugs to military personnel in West Germany in recent years reveals a surprising new twist: East Germany has become a major supply route for heroin and other hard drugs coming into West Germany. The focal point of this scenario is West Berlin. As West Berlin's military and political security has come to rest on a sounder basis through the normalization accomplished by the Quadrapartite Treaty of 1971, the East German government's long-term strategy has been to undermine the social stability of West Berlin by permitting a steady stream of Turks and Pakistanis to enter West Berlin via East Berlin. In the past five years the Turkish and Pakistani minority populations in West Berlin have mushroomed, causing serious disruption of the social fabric of the beleaguered city. Every night jumbo jets filled with Turkish and Pakistani passengers land at East Berlin's Schoenefeld Airport on direct flights from Ankara and Karachi on Interflug, East Germany's national airline. They are taken by bus to the border crossing points to West Berlin with instructions on how to find the welfare office. Every morning any tourist or West Berlin resident may witness the long line of new arrivals from Turkey and Pakistan forming at the doors of West Berlin's welfare offices.

Among these people are an unknown number of drug dealers who transport large suitcases of heroin from Schoenefeld Airport to West Berlin. The West Berlin border remains completely unguarded for political reasons, to demonstrate that the Berlin Wall exists to keep East Germans from fleeing to West Berlin, not vice versa, and to maintain the principle of West Berlin as a free and open city. Congressmen Wolff and English estimated, in 1978, that 65% of the heroin used by American GIs in West Germany arrived via East Germany.[16] In late 1978 a congressional delegation met with a group of East German officials and gave them a list of twenty-five suspected drug traffickers who were transporting drugs through East Germany to West Berlin.[17] The East German government refused to take any action, thus implicating itself in the dirty business of the drug trade. West Berlin overflows with drugs as a direct result of this East German policy, and the U.S. forces have a greater problem with the control of drug abuse in Berlin than anywhere else.[18] However, the commanders in West Berlin have done as well as commanders elsewhere in West Germany in keeping some control over the situation.

Statistics generated for this study by the military services present a somewhat different picture of the drug problem from that constructed from press reports. Table 5.1 illustrates the drug problem in terms of rates of punishment for drug offenses for the years 1973–1982. The punishment rate for possession or use of marijuana was higher for the U.S. Army in Europe than for the army as a whole in the years 1974, 1981, and 1982. The rates for USAREUR and the army as a whole were approximately even in 1975 and 1978, and the general army rate was higher than that for USAREUR in 1976, 1977, 1979, and 1980. It must be pointed out, however, that the table shows only the rate of punishments meted out, which may bear little relationship to the incidence of actual usage. Field commanders report that pressure to take action against marijuana may increase or decrease several times in any given year. Some commanders, who take a dim view of drugs in general, may take vigorous action to clean up the company on their own initiative from time to time, whereas others, more concerned with periodic reports on unit readiness, may decide to look the other way at marijuana offenses, so that the reports do not indicate a serious situation. The table also shows an extremely high rate of punishment for marijuana offenses in 1974 (statistics for earlier years are not included), followed by a steadily declining rate from 1975 until 1980. A sharp rise in the punishment rate may be noted in 1981 and 1982, reflecting, perhaps with some time lag, an increase in general drug usage that actually began in 1979, as documented by other types of evidence.

The category of "other drug offenses" reflects the entire panoply of drugs from hashish to heroin, with most of these drugs stronger or more dangerous than marijuana. Throughout the entire period from 1974 through 1982, the rate of punishment for these drug offenses was substantially higher for USAREUR than for the army as a whole, which supports the general thesis that since the early 1970s drug abuse has been a greater problem for the army in West Germany than anywhere else. We may also note, however, that although the punishment rate for this category declined steadily for the army as a whole from 1974 to 1982, it tended to increase and decrease more sporadically for USAREUR from the extremely high rates recorded for the earlier 1970s. And whereas the punishment rate for marijuana increased dramatically in the early 1980s, the rate for other drug offenses tended to decline slightly. Again, however, the punishment rate may or may not be indicative of the actual rates of usage.

Drug Abuse in the 1980s

In the winter of 1982, USAREUR headquarters conducted an opinion survey on major elements affecting morale among both officers and enlisted personnel in USAREUR.[19] Seventy-five questions covered subjects ranging from use of drugs and alcohol to living conditions, unit morale, discriminatory treatment by Germans, use of leisure time, race relations, and other matters. The survey was administered to 5,163 military personnel ranging in rank from private to colonel.[20] There is no way of knowing, of course, how truthfully either officers or troops answered the questions, but the data are the best available, and they allow us to construct a general picture.

The data on drug usage in USAREUR are presented in Tables 5.2 and 5.3. What stands out in the data for officers is the surprisingly high percentage who admitted to using marijuana. Though only 2% or less said they used it frequently (defined as three or more times per week), over 11% admitted to infrequent usage. The table also allows us to see differential rates of usage between blacks and whites (data for other ethnic groups, which constitute a very small percentage of USAREUR personnel—see Tables 2.12 and 2.23—are not included). Among officers, 11.3% of blacks and 13.2% of whites admitted to infrequent usage of marijuana, though we have no way of knowing whether such usage took place mainly while on duty or during off-duty hours. There is vigorous debate within the scientific community about the long-term effects of infrequent marijuana usage. The effects of marijuana usage upon job performance are also not well documented, though it can be fairly assumed that the performance of military officers is not enhanced by smoking dope. In any case, the fact that 11 to 13% of officers reported using marijuana even infrequently is not encouraging news.

Frequent use of the menagerie of other drugs on the list does not appear to be a problem in the officer corps. Black officers recorded slightly higher rates of frequent usage for all of the drugs than did white officers. A more interesting result may be found in the columns for infrequent drug usage. Uppers and cocaine were the most popular drugs used infrequently by black officers, whereas uppers, downers, and LSD were the most popular drugs used infrequently by white officers. However, infrequent use of all of the drugs was substantially higher among white officers than among black officers. For instance, 2% of black officers recorded infrequent usage of uppers, as compared to 5.4% of white officers. Evidently, white officers are more prone to some recreational use of drugs, whereas black officers are slightly more prone to frequent use. Except for marijuana, however, drug use among all officers, black and white, is not a major problem.

Among enlisted personnel, frequent use of drugs, with the exception of marijuana, does not appear to be a problem if the responses of the troops to the questionnaire are to be believed. Less than 2% of the troops used any of the drugs frequently, and the differences in rates of usage between blacks and whites were not substantial. Marijuana was the great exception; 6.1% of black enlisted personnel and 14.5% of white enlisted personnel admitted to frequent use. But if these percentages are added to the percentages for infrequent use, we find that 44.7% of white enlisted personnel and 22.7% of black enlisted personnel smoked marijuana on a recurrent basis. Regardless of how these statistics are interpreted, this means that the army in West Germany, despite progress with control efforts in the early 1980s, still faced a major problem in 1982 with pot smoking among the troops. Critics of marijuana usage in military forces would have no trouble in characterizing the problem as massive.

Many drugs were apparently used by the troops on an infrequent basis, defined as less than three times per week. The most popular drugs used infrequently by whites were uppers, LSD, and cocaine, whereas those most popular among blacks were uppers and cocaine. Most striking, however, is that infrequent usage was much higher among white enlisted personnel than among black enlisted personnel. The reasons for this situation are not readily apparent. It is possible, of course, that black soldiers were less prone to trust the confidentiality of the questionnaire for purely statistical purposes than were white soldiers and were consequently less inclined to admit to drug usage. Other reasons, however, seem more persuasive. It is probably true that a higher percentage of black recruits view military service as an opportunity for mobility, status, or career progress. The competition for jobs in civilian life favors whites, whereas the army represents not only security, but a situation in which young blacks may advance both skills and earning power. The use of drugs would compromise or ruin these possibilities; hence drug use is risky and blacks may be less willing to run the risk than whites. It is also possible that blacks are more fearful of the consequences of getting caught than whites. As the officer corps is heavily white, blacks may believe that they will suffer stiffer penalties than whites if they are caught using drugs. Whatever the reasons may be, the statistics clearly indicate that the use of drugs is more extensive among whites than blacks, both among officers and enlisted personnel. This fact may serve to dispel stereotyped assumptions about the racial basis of disruptive behavior in the army in West Germany.

The Alcohol Problem

That large numbers of soldiers drink large quantities of alcohol is nothing new. The consumption of alcohol always has been and always will be a problem in the military forces of Western countries. The extent to which alcohol consumption represents a serious problem in a military setting is subject to widely divergent interpretations. Most observers would probably agree that alcoholism, as distinct from alcohol consumption, represents a serious problem both at the individual and organizational level. In this sense, a military organization is no different from any other social organization. Given the purpose and mission of military forces, however, alcoholism immediately becomes a serious problem when even a small percentage of officers or troops indulge the consumption of alcohol to excess.

Tables 5.4 and 5.5 present a general picture of alcohol consumption in the U.S. army in West Germany, again based on data from the 1982 USAREUR personnel opinion survey. Table 5.4 shows the frequency of alcohol consumption in 1982 by officers and enlisted personnel. We can see immediately that drinking is a way of life in the army, not unlike U.S. society as a whole. Only small percentages of either officers or troops claimed that they did not drink at all. Substantial percentages of officers admitted to drinking on a frequent basis, defined as three or more days per week. The percentage was higher for white officers (27.9%) than for black officers (20.8%). Nearly two-thirds of the officers said that they drank infrequently, defined as two or fewer days per week.

The picture is more serious for enlisted personnel. Very small percentages claimed not to drink at all—10.7% of blacks and 5.2% of whites. If we look at the data for frequent and infrequent consumption, the contrast between black and white enlisted personnel stands out immediately, similar to the situation with drugs. The percentage of whites who admitted to drinking frequently (40.1%) is nearly double the figure for blacks (21.9%). Conversely, the percentage of whites who said they drank moderately (54.7%) is lower than that for blacks (67.6%). The reasons for these results may be similar to those suggested above in reference to drug abuse. To the extent that excessive drinking entails a perceived risk of descent into alcoholism, the risk is higher for blacks than for whites, as the penalty of expulsion from military service is probably more frightening for blacks than for whites. These statistics may be interpreted in a variety of ways. On the one hand, we might be relieved that the percentages of officers and troops who said they drank infrequently were substantiallay higher than the percentages who drank frequently. On the other hand, we might be dismayed that the percentages of officers and troops who imbibed frequently were depressingly high.

A different picture of alcohol consumption is presented in Table 5.5, which contains data on how much is consumed on days when personnel indulge in drinking. The columns for officers show that 11.4% of white officers and 16.2% of black officers claimed not to drink at all. There is a discrepancy between these data and the data in Table 5.4. Why higher percentages of officers claimed abstinence in the answers documented here cannot easily be explained, as both questions were on the same questionnaire. The results may indicate a lower level of reliability in the data, or they may stem from lack of clarity in the wording of the questions. There is, however, a general consistency in the pattern of answers by blacks and whites. Of the white officers 14.7% admitted to drinking excessively (five or more drinks) on days when they did drink, whereas only 11.5% of the black officers said they drank excessively.

The percentages of officers who claimed to drink moderately are similar— 73.9% for whites and 72.2% for blacks.

A similar inconsistency appears between the two sets of data for abstinence for enlisted personnel. In this case (Table 5.5), 9.6% of enlisted whites, and 16.2% of enlisted blacks claimed not to drink at all. Forty-one percent of whites, compared to only 16.7% of blacks, admitted to drinking excessively on days when alcohol was consumed, a difference of striking proportions. Conversely, a higher percentage of blacks claimed moderation—67.1%, compared to 49.4% for whites.

If we combine the data in Tables 5.5 and 5.4, the picture that emerges is not encouraging. Mainly, it confirms what most observers already know. Officers in West Germany, as elsewhere, consume a generous amount of alcohol, even black officers, the more moderate group. Among enlisted personnel, whites appear to be somewhat awash in a sea of alcohol. No one can prove, of course, that much of this drinking occurs during duty hours, and most observers are willing enough to grant soldiers the pleasure of having a few drinks when not manning tanks or slogging through wet forests. Many would even be so generous as to grant that a good bash now and then is not a bad thing and might even serve to renew the spirits. Nevertheless, it is obvious that alcohol does constitute a problem of some dimensions for the U.S. Army in West Germany. The magnitude or severity of the problem depends upon the values of the observer.

Treatment and Control Efforts

The army's Alcohol and Drug Abuse Control Program is available to any soldier who wishes to enroll. Normally, commanders are content merely to disseminate information about the program to the troops from time to time, leaving it to soldiers themselves to decide whether they need to enroll. At times, however, when senior commanders believe that alcohol abuse is on the increase, active measures are taken to enroll known abusers in the program, and peer pressure is exercised to get officers with an alcohol problem to enroll in the program. The army has an interest, of course, in knowing whether the control programs have any appreciable effect upon alcohol abuse and, hence, troop morale. The USAREUR opinion survey in 1982 included such a question, and the responses are recorded in Table 5.6. The data clearly indicate that the army's efforts in reference to alcohol abuse are given high marks. Nearly three-quarters of the officers agreed that "the Army is concerned with alcohol abuse and is trying to do something about it." Only small percentages of the officers disagreed with the statement—15.7% of white officers and 8.7% of the black officers. Among enlisted personnel, majorities of both racial groups agreed that the army was trying to do something about alcohol abuse; a higher percentage of blacks (67.7%) agreed with the statement than whites (57.4%). Only small percentages disagreed with the statement—15.8% of white enlisted personnel and 10.2% of black enlisted personnel. Clearly, more blacks among both officers and enlisted personnel held the alcohol abuse program in high regard than did whites, though both races believed that the army was doing a good job.

Table 5.7 presents another picture of alcohol and drug problems by indicating the number of clients enrolled in the army's Alcohol and Drug Abuse Control Program from 1978 to 1982. In West Germany the army maintains eighty-four centers for drug and alcohol rehabilitation. The data confirm that drug abuse has not been a major problem in the officer corps, either for USAREUR or the army as a whole, and alcohol has been a troublesome but not overwhelming problem. It is probably true that there is more private drug usage among officers than anyone knows about; nevertheless, extensive interviews with officers at all levels would seem to confirm the general conclusion that a very large percentage of officers, competitive and concerned about their promotions and careers, consider use of drugs altogether counterproductive, unprofessional, or too risky. For enlisted personnel, the table shows that from 1978 through 1980 there were many more soldiers in Europe enrolled in the drug-abuse program than in the rest of the army all over the world, including the United States, though the gap narrowed considerably during that three-year period. In 1981, the enrollment rates for Europe and the rest of the army were approximately equal, and in 1982 the rate armywide was greater than for Europe. The column for the alcohol treatment program shows that the enrollment rate for Europe was smaller than for the rest of the army during the entire period from 1978 to 1982, though the gap between Europe and the rest of the army narrowed from 1978 to 1981. The data are interesting in that they indicate that in the United States and other parts of the world alcohol is the major substance-abuse problem, whereas in Europe drugs represent a much larger part of the army's dilemma. This is not surprising in view of the easier availability of many drugs in Europe at comparatively lower prices.

Data for punishments for alcohol and drug abuse in the air force are presented in Chapter 6 (Tables 6.2 and 6.3). It is difficult to compare the air force data for punishment with the army data for enrollment in treatment programs because the air force data give numbers rather than percentages and do not indicate a comparison between the punishment rate for Europe and the rate for the air force stationed elsewhere. There may also be doubt about the reliability of the data, as, given the total number of air force personnel in West Germany—approximately 37,000— the small numbers translate into miniscule percentages. No explanation can be given for these small numbers, and speculations are hazardous.

It may be, however, that the reports for West Germany are inaccurate or depreciated, that reporting systems for the air force differ materially from those for the army, or that the data do not find their way accurately into the air force's central computers in Washington.

Still, it is clear that the air force's problems with drugs and alcohol are minor compared with those of the army, despite possible problems with the air force data. There are many reasons for this. The army always has been and always will be a much larger, more diverse, catchall service than the air force. The air force, with its spiffy image as a service with high-speed jet aircraft and incredible technological wizardry, has less of a problem recruiting a higher percentage of brighter, more qualified personnel than does the army. The air force also finds it easier to create close unit cohesion within an atmosphere heavy with pride and élan. As a service more conscious of its public image, especially in a foreign setting, there is likely to be more peer pressure in the air force against drug usage as a stain on its professional image.

It is tempting to castigate the army for failing adequately to control its enormous drug problem in West Germany. There is no doubt that the drug problem is a major factor of negative image-building for the army in West German public opinion. But the army has tried, occasionally with the use of stringent measures, to bring the problem under control and remains highly sensitive to the problem's nature and dimensions. Certainly, the army has not been notably less successful in controlling drug abuse than have other large organizations in the United States. Universities, for instance, with rates of drug abuse probably far higher than those of the army, would have little advice to offer the military. Nor, for that matter, would corporations, government bureaucracies, labor unions, or congressional staffs. The problem of drug abuse, in the final analysis, transcends attempts to control it, not because army methods have failed, but because the army reflects the larger problems of American society, of which it is an integral part. As long as drugs are a pervasive, entrenched phenomenon of that society, especially among the youth, we must expect that the army will have to fight a continuing battle against their abuse, sometimes making progress and sometimes losing ground.

In West Germany, the army's problems with drug abuse are augmented by cultural isolation, high availability of drugs, racial discrimination, and feelings of second-class status in a wealthy, sophisticated society. The morale problems caused by decaying, often wretched physical facilities also create a situation rife for drug abuse that can scarcely be overestimated. And, in the opinion of major segments of the West German press as well as many U.S. field commanders, the problems with drug abuse are compounded by the character of the all-volunteer force itself.

Notes

1. See Daniel J. Nelson, *A History of U.S. Military Forces in Germany* (Boulder, Colo.: Westview Press, 1987), Chapter 4.
2. *The Daily Telegraph* (London), February 26, 1974.
3. Ibid.
4. *Frankfurter Allgemeine,* May 31, 1974.
5. *The Christian Science Monitor,* February 20, 1974.
6. Ibid.
7. *International Herald Tribune,* September 5, 1975.
8. Ibid., August 8, 1975.
9. *Die Welt,* September 12, 1975. *International Herald Tribune,* September 5, 1975.
10. *Die Welt,* September 12, 1975.
11. *International Herald Tribune,* December 4, 1978.
12. Ibid.
13. See, for instance, *Allgemeine Zeitung* (Mainz), March 7, 1979.
14. *The Guardian* (Manchester), May 7, 1979.
15. *Frankfurter Rundschau,* September 22, 1981.
16. Ibid., June 3, 1978.
17. *International Herald Tribune,* December 4, 1978.
18. See the statement of Deputy Secretary of Defense Charles Duncan as reproduced in the *International Herald Tribune,* July 28, 1978.
19. The survey was conducted by officers trained in survey research techniques attached to the Research and Evaluation Division of the Office of the Deputy Chief of Staff for Personnel (ODCSPER). I wish to thank LTC Ronald M. Joe for making available the computer printouts from which the tables were constructed.
20. The 5,163 respondents were divided into two major rank groups: 2,742 enlisted personnel at ranks E1–E4 and 2,421 officers at ranks E5–E9, W1–W4, and 01–06. Hence, the "enlisted personnel" referred to in the tables include only the four junior ranks. The "officers" category includes all noncommissioned officers, warrant officers, and commissioned officers through the rank of colonel; general officers were not included in the survey. I do not know the technical details of the selection of the sample population, i.e., stratification of the sample, method of random sampling, etc. The process of survey research in a military environment is constrained by the difficulty of assembling various troop units all in one place at one time. I do know, however, that the opinion survey included units at practically every army base in West Germany. I was assured in conversations with LTC Ronald M. Joe, executive officer of the Research and Evaluation Division of ODCSPER, that all possible precautions were utilized to assure the randomness of the sample, and that, given the constraints of the military environment, an appropriately stratified population sample was achieved in terms of age groups, rank/grade, sex, level of education, race/ethnic group, living unit (on post or off post), length of duty in Europe, and marital status. The first thirteen questions on the questionnaire asked for demographic characteristics. The remaining sixty-

two questions asked for opinion on substantive questions. My conversations with research personnel in the Research and Evaluation Division of ODCSPER also led me to believe that the validity and reliability of their survey research projects would compare favorably with the research efforts of university or research institute teams.

Table 5.1. Punishments for Drug Offenses in US Army Europe
(USAREUR) and Armywide 1973-1982 (Rate per 1,000)

	Marijuana Use/Possession		Other Drug Offenses		Total	
	USAREUR	Army	USAREUR	Army	USAREUR	Army
1973	NA	23.72	NA	7.85	NA	31.57
1974	38.24	32.50	18.27	8.22	56.51	40.72
1975	28.77	28.63	19.49	8.43	48.26	37.06
1976	28.75	32.58	10.93	6.10	39.68	38.68
1977	26.49	28.83	9.03	5.36	35.52	34.19
1978	27.32	28.19	10.66	5.32	37.98	33.51
1979	22.69	27.32	12.61	6.46	35.30	33.78
1980	20.38	26.38	8.47	5.40	28.85	31.78
1981	32.01	31.04	7.14	5.10	39.15	36.14
1982	29.58	24.49	8.74	5.27	38.32	29.76

Source: Office of Army Law Enforcement, Office of the Deputy
Chief of Staff for Personnel, Washington, D.C.

Table 5.2. Frequency of Drug Use Among Officers By Race (Percent)

	Blacks			Whites		
	Frequent*	Infrequent**	Never	Frequent	Infrequent	Never
Marijuana	2.0	11.3	68.4	1.9	13.2	68.3
PCP	.8	1.5	94.0	.3	1.9	95.4
Mandrax	.8	1.7	95.5	.3	2.3	95.4
Uppers	.9	2.0	94.0	.4	5.4	89.5
Downers	.5	1.1	95.0	.3	3.4	93.3
LSD	.8	.9	96.5	.1	2.9	93.3
Opiates	.5	.2	97.7	.1	1.0	97.5
Cocaine	.5	2.0	89.9	.4	2.8	92.3

* Represents use three or more times per week.
** Represents use less often than three times per week.

Note: The table includes data on current usage and excludes certain
answer categories such as "Have tried experimentally once or
twice," and "Have used, but not in the last year." Hence, the
row totals for blacks and whites do not add to 100%. Data for
Hispanics, Asians, and other ethnic groups are also not included.

Source: Constructed from USAREUR Personnel Opinion Survey, Winter
1982. Data supplied by Office of Deputy Chief of Staff,
Personnel; Headquarters, United States Army, Europe;
Heidelberg, Germany.

Table 5.3. Frequency of Drug Use Among Enlisted Personnel By Race (Percent)

	Blacks			Whites		
	Frequent*	Infrequent**	Never	Frequent	Infrequent	Never
Marijuana	6.1	16.6	56.4	14.5	30.2	34.8
PCP	1.8	3.6	89.5	1.6	7.7	83.2
Mandrax	2.0	2.8	91.8	1.5	10.4	79.3
Uppers	1.8	5.9	88.1	1.9	21.6	65.9
Downers	1.1	3.4	92.0	1.3	12.9	75.6
LSD	1.2	2.4	93.8	1.1	15.3	74.8
Opiates	1.6	2.0	94.7	1.1	4.5	90.2
Cocaine	1.4	7.8	83.2	1.4	17.7	69.3

* Represents use three or more times per week.
** Represents use less often than three times per week.

Note: The table includes data on current usage and excludes certain
answer categories such as "Have tried experimentally once or
twice," and "Have used, but not in the last year." Hence, the
row totals for blacks and whites do not add to 100%. Data for
Hispanics, Asians, and other ethnic groups are also not included.

Source: Constructed from USAREUR Personnel Opinion Survey, Winter
1982. Data supplied by Office of Deputy Chief of Staff,
Personnel; Headquarters, United States Army, Europe;
Heidelberg, Germany.

Table 5.4. Frequency of Alcohol Consumption in the Last Year, By Rank and Race (Percent)

	Officers		Enlisted	
	Blacks	Whites	Blacks	Whites
None	11.7	6.9	10.7	5.2
Frequent[1]	20.8	27.9	21.9	40.1
Infrequent[2]	67.6	65.2	67.6	54.7

1. Represents consumption three or more days per week.
2. Represents consumption two or fewer days per week to once a month.

Source: Constructed from USAREUR Personnel Opinion Survey, Winter 1982. Data supplied by Office of Deputy Chief of Staff, Personnel; Headquarters, United States Army, Europe; Heidelberg, Germany.

Table 5.5. Number of Drinks Taken on a Day Alcohol is Consumed, By Rank and Race (Percent)

	Officers		Enlisted	
	Blacks	Whites	Blacks	Whites
Never Drink	16.2	11.4	16.2	9.6
Excessive[1]	11.5	14.7	16.7	41.0
Moderate[2]	72.2	73.9	67.1	49.4

1. Represents five or more drinks taken in one day.
2. Represents four or fewer drinks taken in one day.

Source: Constructed from USAREUR Personnel Opinion Survey, Winter 1982. Data supplied by Office of Deputy Chief of Staff, Personnel; Headquarters, United States Army, Europe; Heidelberg, Germany.

Table 5.6. Perceptions of Army Response to Alcohol Abuse, By Rank and Race (Percent)

Statement: "The Army is concerned with alcohol abuse and is trying to do something about it."

	Officers		Enlisted	
	Blacks	Whites	Blacks	Whites
Agree	77.7	71.6	67.7	57.4
Disagree	8.7	15.7	10.2	15.8
Don't Know/Neither	13.4	12.8	22.1	26.9

Source: Constructed from USAREUR Personnel Opinion Survey, Winter 1982. Data supplied by Office of Deputy Chief of Staff, Personnel; Headquarters, United States Army, Europe; Heidelberg, Germany.

Table 5.7. Clients Enrolled in the Army's Alcohol and Drug
Abuse Control Program, Europe and Elsewhere, By Grade,
1978-1982

	Calendar Year	Alcohol	Drugs	Total
Europe - Officers	78	23	0	23
Europe - Enlisted	78	4,667	6,046	10,713
All Others - Officers	78	98	2	100
All Others - Enlisted	78	8,388	2,771	11,159
Europe - Officers	79	32	1	33
Europe - Enlisted	79	5,992	3,799	9,791
All Others - Officers	79	113	8	121
All Others - Enlisted	79	9,013	2,457	11,470
Europe - Officers	80	38	1	39
Europe - Enlisted	80	7,601	2,926	10,527
All Others - Officers	80	116	8	124
All Others - Enlisted	80	10,564	2,780	13,344
Europe - Officers	81	56	2	58
Europe - Enlisted	81	9,338	2,519	11,857
All Others - Officers	81	170	15	185
All Others - Enlisted	81	11,970	2,958	14,928
Europe - Officers	82	68	4	72
Europe - Enlisted	82	10,204	5,448	15,652
All Others - Officers	82	220	22	242
All Others - Enlisted	82	14,905	6,701	21,606

Source: U.S. Army Alcohol and Drug Abuse Program and Technical
Activity, Falls Church, Virginia.

6

Crime and Indiscipline

The U.S. military's problems in West Germany with crime and indiscipline have proven to be almost, but not quite, as intractable as the drug problem. As I described in my earlier work, the Vietnam spin-off phenomenon brought about an escalation of crime and indiscipline in Europe that bordered on a regime of terror beginning in the late 1960s.[1] The situation continued unabated, indeed tended to worsen somewhat, in the first few years of the 1970s. Not until U.S. participation in the Vietnam War ended were the commanders in West Germany able to bring the problems under greater control. Beginning in about 1973, a veritable outcry by the media and political leaders in the Federal Republic, a high level of concern in the U.S. Congress, new programs devised by the Pentagon, and a new, more sensitive, yet tougher U.S. military regime in West Germany, presided over by General Davison, came together as a series of confluent factors to bring greater order and discipline to the U.S. forces stationed in the FRG. Since that time, the indiscipline problem, like the drug problem, has tended to wax and wane. In contrast to the drug problem, however, general patterns of increase and decrease are less discernible and hence more difficult to describe in reference to crime and indiscipline, as these categories cover such a large number of offenses, ranging from failure to carry out a simple task to rape and murder.

In very general terms, crime and indiscipline decreased in incidence from approximately 1974 until approximately 1978. In the late 1970s, however, a decided increase occurred in indiscipline in general, coupled with an uneven pattern of increases and decreases from 1978 through 1983. The reasons for these patterns are not entirely clear, though they certainly relate to the quality and character of the forces brought about by the AVF regime, to broader patterns of crime discernible in U.S. society, and to increasing morale problems caused by decaying physical facilities. Such factors are discussed in greater detail toward the end of this chapter.

Patterns in the 1970s

Some interesting features of the indiscipline problem are revealed by following the coverage in the West German press. In the early 1970s the press devoted great attention to criminality among U.S. forces, not only because the problems were highly visible, but because much of the criminality spilled beyond the borders of the U.S. bases, creating conditions of fear in German populations located near those bases. The race riots on U.S. bases also interested West German reporters because of the opportunity they provided to study the social dynamics of U.S. society close at hand. Though some of the reporting was sensationalist, the great bulk of it tended to be sober, analytical, and sympathetic. Nevertheless, during this period the West German press warned U.S. military authorities time and time again, that if stronger measures were not taken to bring the problems under control, respect for the U.S. forces would sooner or later evaporate.

By 1974, the incidence of race riots on U.S. bases in the Federal Republic had declined considerably. The mood of rebellion among the troops had softened to the extent that strikes, sit-ins, and milder forms of disobedience had replaced the earlier, belligerent eruptions. The changing tenor of the times is illustrated by a court case in Wuerzburg in early 1974. Two enlisted men, who had converted to the Sikh religion while on leave in London, refused orders to remove their turbans and shave their full beards when they returned to duty in West Germany. Though they were sentenced by a military court to three months in prison, the sentences were suspended and they were transferred to a unit at Fort Riley, Kansas, to serve a period of probation. No riots occurred, and no demonstrations were held on their behalf when they were taken to the military airport clean shaven and without turbans, a refreshing change from what might have happened a few years earlier.[2] The case seemed to demonstrate that though soldiers still felt free to defy military regulations in unconventional ways, the days were ending when such cases would lead to major outbreaks of hostility against military authority.

Later the same year a group of soldiers in Berlin protested in various ways for a period of four months against the army's prohibition of long hair and beards. In November, the protest escalated to a twenty-four-hour strike against a military order to transfer a troublesome black soldier out of Berlin. With the support of the members of one other company, both white and black, the protestors presented a list of demands to military authorities, which included an immediate congressional investigation, a right to veto all proposed transfers, more privacy in living quarters, the right to lock rooms, and the election of a morale council and a race relations council. Following the strike, the protestors refused to come to attention at first formation one morning, whereupon the officers dismissed the formation, but the protestors resumed their normal duties. The core group of protestors included only twenty-seven soldiers, and they were unable to expand the protest to a mass movement or provoke a riot, as they clearly had hoped to do. By agreeing to consider the demands seriously, the commanders were able to defuse the situation easily, again demonstrating how things had changed from the early 1970s.[3] It is interesting to note that the list of demands included an immediate congressional investigation. Protestors had evidently learned that violent action in the military could achieve very little, but that nothing frightened military authorities so much as a congressional investigation.

By 1974, the West German press felt that the general situation showed improvement. The *Stuttgarter Zeitung* was able to report that "the discipline of U.S. troops is still affected by the fact that the general crime rate, as well as the rate of crimes against property and violent confrontations among the troops stationed in Germany, are higher than in the army as a whole. At least, however, in reference to discipline one can note that, together with a decline in drug usage, there has been a corresponding decline in black-white racial conflict."[4] In February, General Davison testified before Congress that racial discrimination by West Germans against black soldiers as well as racial tensions within the military units stationed in the Federal Republic had declined considerably in the past few months. Interestingly, General Davison also felt that special praise was due the minister-president of the state of Rhineland-Pfalz, at that time Helmut Kohl, who had undertaken special efforts beyond the call of duty to try to improve the living conditions of military families.[5] In 1974, few would have believed that a decade later, Helmut Kohl would hold the post of federal chancellor.

In the spring of 1975 the *International Herald Tribune* undertook one of its periodic investigations into the state of affairs in the army in Europe. Its findings help to bolster the conclusion that the general state of morale, and with it the situation regarding crime and indiscipline, had improved materially since the early 1970s.

The U.S. Army in Europe is making headway against its Vietnam-era problems of drugs, racism, and drift. Although the drug and racial problems have been brought under control in the last two years, experts at the Army's headquarters here (in Heidelberg) concede that they are far from solved. They add that the problems not only are likely to remain for a long time, but also that the 185,000 men stationed in Europe are finding formidable new ones. In the barracks, a once-turbulent scene has been calmed by racial seminars, drug clinics and a cooler type of GI, who volunteered and was not drafted.

But a recent wave of disciplinary discharges and courts-martial has shown that some of the new enlisted men are still reluctant to accept the strict authority and rules of the old Army, which many officers consider necessary to build military spirit. . . .

Today's GIs in Germany complain mostly about "Mickey Mouse" regulations, overly rigid company commanders, lack of money and the fact that the Army did not supply them with the type of job promised at the recruiting station. They say that they do not have much faith in the official drug and race programs, but acknowledge that the situation is better than it was. They believe that the number of racially incited brawls and beatings in barracks and bars has declined, that there is less overt racism by officers and that fewer obvious drug addicts are seen in the barracks.

While their resistance to the "regs" is growing, the level of organized dissent is not. There were 10 underground GI newspapers in Germany a few years ago. Only two are left. Even when soldiers get together on an issue they usually choose to protest by a petition or strike instead of something more violent.[6]

In June of 1975 General Davison was replaced by General George S. Blanchard as commander in chief of the U.S. Army, Europe. Blanchard was considered to have the same activist, program-oriented approach as Davison to the army's military and social problems. In early 1976, however, differing views of the discipline situation in West Germany at the top levels of the command led to the abrupt removal of Lieutenant General Robert Fair from command of the 50,000-soldier Fifth Corps, one of the two corps comprising the Seventh Army in the Federal Republic. It was unusual indeed that such a high-ranking (three-star) and relatively young (fifty-two) general would be replaced less than five months after he assumed one of the army's most prized field commands. The Department of the Army first announced routinely in Washington on January 5, 1976, that General Fair had "requested retirement for personal reasons." A few days later, following press queries, army headquarters in Heidelberg put out another statement acknowledging that General Fair had in fact been replaced because of differences with General Blanchard. Those differences involved "Gen. Fair's mode of operation, [and] the relationship was such that it became inappropriate for Lt. Gen. Fair to continue as commanding general of V Corps."[7]

General Fair had a reputation as a stern disciplinarian. In his previous post as commanding general at Fort Hood, Texas, he had insisted that all soldiers with long hair have it cut short to regulation length. He demanded the highest standards of performance from his battalion commanders and insisted that all officers remain fully responsible for all aspects of performance and discipline in their units. He even had been the subject of a long, admiring article in *Playboy* magazine. He was known to take a dim view of what he considered the lax standards and inadequate discipline in the all-volunteer army. In Europe he had often expressed the view that, considering the military superiority of the Warsaw Pact, the U.S. Army in West Germany ought to be the epitome of readiness and discipline. He would not tolerate the slightest signs of sloppiness or lax discipline. As compared to the West German army, Fair believed that the U.S. Army was not a good match in either readiness or morale. Though he was controversial, few officers expressed a lack of respect for General Fair. According to a captain, he "never demanded from any of his soldiers more than he demanded from himself. But he would not tolerate the slightest bit of indiscipline."[8] According to another senior army officer, "If it's a case where the guy is incompetent, that's one thing. But if it's a case where he was just a tough commander, you are tampering with the whole system."[9]

Rumors circulated for days about the peculiar circumstances surrounding General Fair's removal. Some field officers believed that Fair was "essentially cut down behind the scenes by subordinates who did not like his style."[10] Whatever the real circumstances may have been, the case clearly demonstrates some of the changes that were taking place in the all-volunteer army in West Germany. At the same time that the situation with discipline was improving from what it had been a few years earlier, General Fair believed that the "spit and polish" organization the Seventh Army had once been ought to be rebuilt. The very nature of discipline had, however, changed materially in the regime of the all-volunteer army. Soldiers who resisted layers of regulations or refused to carry out orders could no longer be taken out behind the barracks building to get some good sense knocked into them by their company commander. They could simply threaten to walk out and never return, in which case the army would have a difficult time enforcing the contracts with the soldiers in the courts. Seminars, talkfests, and soldiers' rights organizations had effectively ended the days when commanders shouted orders and sternly disciplined any soldier who failed to carry them out to the letter. The older style of discipline had given way to new forms of communcation and new types of inducements and sanctions in the AVF, developments that General Fair felt were wholly negative. Without attempting to assign right and wrong in the Fair case, we may say that the nature of military discipline itself was in a state of ferment in the mid-1970s. Whether ferment equates with decline depends upon the values one assigns to moral and ethical standards within a military organization.

The Black Market Problems

Another aspect of the discipline problem in West Germany was prominently displayed in a series of articles in the newspaper *Stars and*

Stripes in October 1976. Practically everyone in military service in the FRG knew that illegal sales by GIs of goods from the military commissaries and post exchange (PX) stores had always been a thriving business. The extent of the black market was, however, displayed in shocking detail in the *Stars and Stripes* series and picked up, in turn, by the West German press. The precipitous decline in the exchange value of the dollar since 1973 had brought signs of poverty to the lower ranks of soldiers that U.S. forces had not experienced in West Germany previously. This phenomenon caused the black market trade to mushroom. West German customs officials estimated that the black market trade constituted a 10- to 20-million-dollar-a-year business. According to *Stars and Stripes*, a German raid in Frankfurt turned up 2,550 cartons of cigarettes in a GI's truck, and a raid in Heidelberg netted 4,000 bottles of whiskey and 5,000 cartons of cigarettes. Stereo sets worth $10,000 had been fenced during the previous six months by a resident of Frankfurt, and illegal trading in gas coupons diverted an estimated 118,000 gallons of gasoline.[11]

The routine violations of the rationing system revealed in the black market story demonstrated the ease with which military regulations could be widely flouted. According to the story as it appeared in the West German press, cashiers would simply forget to ask for or note sales on ration cards, and employees could easily get hold of stolen goods of all kinds. A GI in Berlin declared with obvious pride that "if you know enough customers, you can easily make 2000 marks a month with whiskey and cigarettes." West German police arrested a middleman in Frankfurt who in the previous six months had fenced stereo equipment worth 24,000 marks and gasoline coupons for 500,000 liters. West German customs authorities worried that the black market might expand to even greater dimensions when hefty new taxes on cigarettes and alcohol were scheduled to take effect on January 1, 1977.[12]

There are two ways in which one might consider the reports on the thriving black market in Germany. On the one hand, U.S. military authorities might have breathed a sigh of relief that the most sensational crime story of the time concerned illegal dealings on the black market rather than a violent crime wave on American bases—producing frightened German populations and immediate demands from German political leaders for swift action. On the other hand, the "softer" side of the indiscipline situation that the black market represents also has an insidious effect, creating distrust and negative feelings toward U.S. forces among the Germans. The black market in commissary and PX goods is, like drugs, a ubiquitous problem that military leaders can never bring under complete control. The market waxes and wanes in response to changes in the exchange rate of the dollar and the attention paid to the problem by military authorities. In late 1976, military leaders were forced to clamp down again, as they occasionally do, with new threats of severe penalties and new controls in the rationing system. The result was a considerable decline in the black market trade in the ensuing months. The market, however, never disappeared completely and continues to plague military authorities constantly, like a minor infection that never seems to clear up.

The general situation in reference to discipline and morale continued to improve in the middle to late 1970s. In the spring of 1977, the *International Herald Tribune* again assessed the situation and concluded that much improvement could be noted:

> Today there is a strong feeling that the morale problems have been reduced if not yet eliminated, partly because of growing awareness of Soviet strength. It is a volunteer Army now, and soldiers are more responsive to authority than draftees used to be. The casual, informal uniforms and long hair of the Vietnam era are gone. Drug use no longer appears rampant.
>
> Young enlisted men who used to look down on career soldiers do not snicker now when they salute with "Workhorse, sir," in the 11th Armored Cavalry Regiment whose shield is a black horse's head, or "Combat ready, sir," in the Eighth Infantry Division.
>
> Even the slang is different, less emotionally charged and less defiant. Career sergeants are called lifers less frequently: the strongest words of derision one hears are "turkey," for a loser, and "cheese-eater," one who curries favor.
>
> Both drug use and a related indicator of discipline, courts-martial, seem to have diminished dramatically in the last two years. There were 2,131 courts-martial in the year that ended June 30, compared with 3,803 the year before. Commanders concede, however, that the drug problem has not yet been overcome.[13]

Crime Increase in the Late 1970s
and the 1980s

In the late 1970s the incidence of crime and indiscipline in the U.S. military in the FRG began to increase once again. In May of 1979, in Erlangen, a series of three rapes of young German women by U.S. soldiers in a period of three weeks raised tensions between U.S. troops and West Germans to the highest level since the early 1970s. The West German police in Erlangen confirmed to the press that violent crime by U.S. soldiers had again risen during the previous months, with increasing cases of taxi drivers and people on the streets being threatened with knives. Following the third rape, the Erlangen police, fearing violence against U.S. forces in retaliation, requested a three-day restriction on troops leaving the barracks to allow things to cool down. The army declined the request, as usual, with the explanation that several thousand men should not be punished for the misdeeds of a few. The rape reports produced harsh reactions in the local newspapers, which described the attacks as of "great brutality." In an interview with the press, the mayor of Erlangen, Fritz Kindervater, expressed his alarm: "In the last four months or so, it is not so much the number of crimes and assaults, though it is higher than before, but that the crimes are more severe—burglary, robbery, and rape. . . . I get the impression that over the last two years, because of the all-volunteer army, the quality of the soldier has gone down. Some of them come across totally illiterate and without any internal leadership." The mayor hastened to add, however, that "this is no Americans-go-home movement. We know the necessity of defense and fully accept the presence of the U.S. here."[14]

A few weeks later, in July 1979, the violent-crime picture was highlighted by a decision of a military court in Fuerth to sentence a soldier to death, the first death sentence handed down by a U.S. military court in Germany in many years. The sentence, for the rape and brutal murder of the wife of a U.S. officer, would be subject to appeal to a higher federal court before being carried out. In commenting on the case, the West German press pointed out that the death sentence had not been carried out on a U.S. soldier since 1961 and that, should the sentence actually be carried out, it would have to be done in the United States, as the death penalty had been abolished in West Germany.[15] A second death sentence for murder was handed down by a military court in Bad Kreuznach in March 1982. This time the sentence was for the murder of a nineteen-year-old German girl by a U.S. soldier. Though the West German press had doubts about the wisdom or morality of the death sentence, there seemed little doubt that U.S. military courts were now willing to mete out the severest punishment in cases of murder by U.S. soldiers in the Federal Republic.[16]

The incidence of serious crime continued to increase in the early 1980s, giving analysts who remembered the abysmal conditions of the early 1970s an uncomfortable feeling of deja vu. In November 1981, *Stars and Stripes* sent out a team of reporters to research the situation. According to the *Stars and Stripes,* as reprinted in reports published by German newspapers, approximately 95,000 disciplinary punishments were handed out to service personnel stationed in West Germany in 1980—75,000 in the army and 20,000 in the air force. The figures are somewhat suspect, because they would indicate that 34% of the total army personnel and 66% of the total air force personnel in West Germany had been subject to disciplinary action in 1980. Despite probable exaggeration in the figures, the newspaper found wide agreement among officers and law-enforcement personnel that serious criminality was indeed on the rise. The reports also found that although punishments for thievery remained in first place, commanders were concerned about the rising incidence of more violent crimes, such as serious fights resulting in injuries, crimes committed by gangs in Mafia-style (such as the collection of protection money), homosexual rapes, and muggings.[17]

There seems little doubt that the general findings of Stars and Stripes are correct, though they are not borne out by the official statistics of the army and the air force. More complex and unclear, however, are the reasons for the increase of serious crime in the early 1980s. Crime, like other social problems, seems to occur in cycles or waves, which theories are unable to explain satisfactorily. We might suspect that the constant decay of the U.S. military's physical facilities in West Germany, or at least greater consciousness of the deteriorating facilities, breeds the conditions for periodic outbreaks of serious crime. Another explanation may lie in the quality of recruits the military services received. Test scores on the Armed Forces Qualification Test, the primary test used by the forces for establishing comparative mental categories, were lower for new recruits in the 1976–1980 period than at any time since the beginning of the all-volunteer force in 1973. These scores, as displayed in Table 6.1, show that the army was getting a much smaller proportion of above-average scorers and a much larger proportion of below-average scorers during that period. The percentage of those scoring in the lowest category eligible for military service, Category IV, was abnormally high. We might surmise that higher percentages of recruits from the lower mental categories might mean soldiers more prone to commit crimes when confronted with serious or prolonged stress. Such an assumtion is strengthened by the interviews with commanders recorded by the Stars and Stripes reporters. Richard Scheff, the highest military judge of the Fifth Corps, was disturbed by evidence that even the slightest irritations among soldiers at that time could lead to slug-outs and knife fights. Increasing alcoholism, he thought, was also a contributing factor.[18]

Other kinds of explanations were offered by different observers. Some commanders believed that racial tensions were getting worse again, and that differences between northern and southern soldiers were more pronounced and severe than they had been previously. In the analysis of the Stars and Stripes reporters, one circumstance in particular was seen as contributing heavily to the increasing crime problem: a declining presence of officers and higher-ranking NCOs (noncommissioned officers) in the barracks at night after duty hours. The percentage of soldiers in the all-volunteer force who were married was much higher than that in the draft army, and these soldiers often left the base to go home to wives and children in the evening. The worst outbreaks of violence seemed to occur among young single soldiers, who had little respect for the lower-ranking NCOs or other soldiers left in charge when the married NCOs and officers went home. Military judges recommended that a strengthened presence of officers and experienced NCOs in the barracks at night was essential; otherwise there was a danger that military discipline might collapse altogether.[19]

The services' own statistics on crime and indiscipline are displayed in Tables 6.2 through 6.4. The army provided data from 1973 through 1982; the air force supplied only 1979 through 1983 data because of a switch in progress from manual record-keeping to computer files. The picture presented in these tables corroborates in general the portrait gained from press reports, though in a less dramatic fashion. The column for total courts-martial in USAREUR shows that court cases decreased sharply from 1974 to 1978, then rose sharply in 1979 and 1980 and again in 1981 and 1982. Article 15 refers to a section of the Uniform Code of Military Justice that accords an officer the ability to hand out administrative punishments to personnel who have disobeyed rules, failed to carry out orders, or in other ways infringed military regulations. Guilt is implied, though not proven, whenever a soldier accepts the punishment. The soldier can, however, refuse punishment and demand a court-martial— a trial in a military court where guilt must be proven by applicable standards of military law. Commanders, of course, prefer to use Article 15 administrative punishments whenever possible to avoid spending time in gathering evidence and testifying in court. Thus, the rate of courts-martial is much lower than the rate of Article 15 punishments for every year shown in Table 6.2. The Article 15 column for USAREUR shows that the punishment rate declined from 1974 to 1977, then rose again in the years 1978 to 1982, though in a zig-zag fashion from year to year.

The air force data (Tables 6.3 and 6.4) leave many questions unanswered. They are given in numbers rather than rates or percentages, that translate into extremely small percentages, considering that approximately 27,000 to 32,000 air force personnel were stationed in West Germany during the years 1979 to 1983. Without further explanation, questions about the reliability of the data cannot be answered. We can assume, from various types of evidence, that the air force had a much smaller problem with crime and indiscipline in general than the army did, similar in scale to the problem of drug abuse (discussed in Chapter 5). We must also assume, however, that the air force data do not reflect the actual extent of punishments administered, and that the record-keeping and recording systems of the army and air force are vastly different. The tables show only punishments carried out, either through court-martial or Article 15 administrative punishment, not the actual incidence of crime or indiscipline. It is probably safe to assume, though the punishment rate reflects the crime rate in a general way, that the actual incidence of crime is much higher than the punishment rate, in the military as in civilian life, as the perpetrators of many crimes are never apprehended or evidence to prove guilt may be lacking.

Crime Among Blacks in the Military

One question that deserves scrutiny is whether there is a correlation between crime rates and the disproportionate percentage of black personnel in the military services in West Germany: Is the crime situation worse because of a high percentage of black service personnel? The question is highly charged and highly sensitive, and any attempt to answer it will offend the sensibilities of racial groups and other constituencies in the military one way or another. In the first place, no conclusive answers can be derived, and blacks are quick to point out that the question itself is inherently flawed, as we might just as legitimately ask, is crime worse because of a high percentage of lower-class or other categories of whites? The data presented in Tables 6.5 to 6.8 may yield some clues. Table 6.5 shows trends in two categories of discipline—unauthorized absence and designated deserter—for black and white males and females for the years 1978 to 1981. The rate of unauthorized absence for black males was consistently higher than for white males each year, though the rate for black females was lower than that for white females. The rate of desertion was higher for whites, both male and female, than for blacks each year. Hence, there was more unauthorized absence among black males, but more desertion among whites, both male and female. No very clear trend is evident.

A clearer picture emerged from the data for crime rates of army personnel, by race, for the years 1978–1980 (Table 6.6). Blacks accounted for a disproportionate percentage of serious crime in all three categories: crimes of violence, crimes against property, and drug offenses. The data are for the entire army, not only for army forces in the Federal Republic, and we do not know whether the data for USAREUR would be much different. It is probably safe to assume, however, that the situation in Germany does not differ substantially from the army as a whole in terms of racial statistics on crime. Table 6.7 shows that from 1977 to 1979 blacks represented a disproportionate percentage of prisoners in the army prison system by a fairly wide margin. The army points out, however, that blacks represent a smaller proportion of prisoners in military prisons than in civilian prisons. According to a 1982 study on blacks in the military,

In 1979 the proportion of black Army prisoners was 1.6 times the proportion of blacks in the Army; on the other hand, the proportion of blacks in the Federal Bureau of Prisons was almost four times the proportion of blacks in the national population.

It has been suggested that the overrepresentation of blacks in the Army's prison system is indirectly related to other disparities in black representation. The Southern Christian Leadership Conference in 1978 laid the blame for black overrepresentation in Army penal facilities on inequities in the criminal justice system—specifically the unrepresentatively low percentage of black officers (6.1 percent) and the predominance of prejudiced white officers from the South. Officers make the initial decisions to deal with problems through minor punishment, court-martial, or early discharge. Administrative discretion thus plays a large part in the initial corrective action—and the decisions are mostly made by white officers. For example, blacks are greatly underrepresented not only in the officer corps, but throughout the entire justice system. In 1978 only one of the Army's forty-six trial court judges was black (and one female), only 4 percent of the Army's lawyers were black, and only 13 percent of the Army's military police were black.[20]

Table 6.8 displays data on discharges from military service by race and branch of service for the fiscal year 1980. Army blacks had a higher rate of dishonorable and bad-conduct discharges than whites and a corresponding lower rate of honorable discharges than whites, though by small margins. The margins are more even for personnel discharged by the air force. Again the data are servicewide, not only for Europe-based personnel.

Though blacks accounted for a disproportionate amount of crime in the armed forces in general, we cannot conclude that the crime problem exists primarily *because* of a high percentage of blacks in the armed forces. Nor can we conclude that the crime problem would be reduced if the ratio of blacks to whites were reduced. In the case of West Germany, it must be remembered that the forces had declining rates of crime in the period from 1974 to 1978, precisely the period when the proportion of blacks in military service was rising rapidly under the new regime of the all-volunteer force. The increase was most dramatic in the army: The proportion of black enlisted personnel jumped from 18.4% in 1973 to 29.2% in 1978. If blacks are the primary cause of crime in the armed forces, then crime rates should have risen dramatically in the army during the period 1974 to 1978. Instead, this was the period when serious crime declined.

There is no doubt that higher rates of crime among blacks is a matter of great concern for the armed forces, especially the army. But it is unfair and unsound to accept race as the primary variable in the crime problem. In West Germany rates of crime were at an all-time high in the early 1970s, before the proportion of blacks in the services began to rise dramatically. The problems at that time had more to do with the spin-off conditions brought about in the forces in Europe by the Vietnam War than anything else. Lack of experienced officers and NCOs, revolt against the involvement in Vietnam, youth rebellion, declining morale, and a host of other factors account for the miserable condition of the forces in West Germany during this period. The declining incidence of crime and indiscipline from 1974 to 1978 should be accounted as a success for the military in coming to grips with the worst problems, improving the readiness and morale of the troops, and otherwise rebuilding the forces as a credible forward defense.

The Problem of Military Authority

The resurgence of crime and indiscipline problems in the early 1980s is certainly cause for concern, though by 1984 there were definite signs that the general situation was improving. A major question, of course, is whether under the regime of the AVF the military has lost the disciplinary tools it once possessed. Many military commanders, from second lieutenants to colonels, tend to think so. When commanders were interviewed on this subject, a general consensus seemed to emerge that the AVF is inherently weaker in terms of discipline than a draft army. Whenever discipline is tightened up, the lower enlisted ranks can easily threaten to leave when their tour of duty is up, or they can threaten desertion without fear of long prison terms. As one commander put it, "This is a gentleman's army of volunteers. We have nowhere near the disciplinary tools we need and which we had fifteen years ago. Whenever we decide to really clamp down and clean up a mess, as with drugs or other rules infractions, we are threatened with a revolt. We'll give you a more disciplined army and far less crime, if you will give us the tools we need as commanders."[21]

Many commanders also feel that rulings of the nation's highest courts, especially in the early 1970s, have to some extent undermined disciplinary authority in military service. The idea of soldiers' rights has been strengthened by court rulilngs as well as by the nature of the AVF. Views differ sharply, however, on the meaning of this development. Many analysts applaud the idea of military law based on a strong sense of soldiers' rights, as this makes military service more like civilian life and gives the United States the most enlightened military forces in the world. Others point out, however, that though an enlightened military is an altogether worthy goal, we must recognize the inherent difference between the rigor of military life and the freer spirit of civilian life. Few would deny that the idea of soldiers' rights is positive and enlightened. But many commanders would also argue that there is a price that must be paid for every increment added to the list of soldiers' rights that are inviolable by commanders. That price is a loss of the kind of authority and discipline that are essential to keeping the military a finely tuned machine.

The crux of the matter is that the U.S. military establishment is an undemocratic, authoritarian island that must exist within a democratic, free society. The tension between the military's need for authority and unquestioned obedience and society's need for inviolable individual rights can never be fully resolved. And the balance between the rights of military personnel and the authority of the commanders constantly shifts as society's values change. It is a balance that also must be readjusted in reference to the changing mission of the military, the goals that the military is expected to accomplish, as these are redefined from time to time, and the changing role of the military within the larger society. There is a minimum level of authority to command, which must be present in order for a military establishment to function. The more profound question is where that level rests and how it is to be defined.

In comparison with the West German military, with its much lower level of crime and indiscipline, the U.S. military appears to be soft and undisciplined. Enormous cultural differences must be taken into account if such a comparison is to have any validity, and that is not the real subject of this discussion. Whether U.S. forces in Germany tolerate or are plagued with rates of crime far higher than they ought to be depends upon the value one assigns to order within the military establishment. In one sense, any amount of indiscipline is too much, as indiscipline always sabotages the ability to engage in war, the ultimate mission of a military force. But the military is also a part of the larger society from which it is drawn, and it cannot be expected to be totally free from the problems of that society, including the problem of criminality. What the military could do to reduce this problem is far from clear, as resources to control crime and indiscipline must be subtracted from equipment, training, facilities, and other needs.

Crime and West German Perceptions

Two levels of analysis here ought to be clearly distinguished. The first level is concerned with crime and indiscipline as it affects the morale and readiness of the forces. Such effects of indiscipline within the United States are not different from those of the forces stationed abroad. Indiscipline lowers morale and readiness to engage in combat wherever the troops are located. The second level concerns the effects of indiscipline on the sociological relationships between forces stationed abroad and the populations of the countries where the troops are located. It is in terms of local public perceptions abroad of the character and quality of the foreign forces that this level of analysis begins to take shape. Perceptions are derived from interaction between the forces and the local population and from an array of images created by the media, especially newspaper reports and television broadcasts. Because perceptions influence public policy, there is at least an indirect, and probably a direct, relationship between perceptions of the population–troops relationships and the quality of the bilateral political relationship between the governments of the two countries.

The political relationship between the Federal Republic of Germany and the United States is different than that between the United States and other NATO allies precisely because of the physical presence of a quarter of a million U.S. service personnel in the FRG. The tone and texture of the U.S.–West German political relationship is heavily influenced by West German public perceptions. To the extent that the Germans perceive negative effects in their society from the presence of the troops, public support for their continued presence erodes. A high level of crime and indiscipline among U.S. forces raises questions about the readiness of the troops to defend the country; it also causes West Germans to ask whether the domestic social consequences of imported crime and indiscipline outweigh the security purchased.

There can be little doubt that the perception of too much crime and indiscipline within the U.S. forces has undermined respect for those forces in West German public opinion during the last fifteen years. How much respect has been lost, or what the effect of the loss has been, cannot be calculated with any certainty. It is not very accurately revealed even by public opinion polls, though they reveal related aspects of the problem (see Chapter 3). The viability of the continued stationing of U.S. forces in the Federal Republic depends, in the final analysis, on positive perceptions among the majority of West Germans—that the forces serve vital security needs and that their presence in the FRG is acceptable in sociological terms. No West German government would be able, over the long term, to continue a policy of security based on the stationing of a vast number of foreign troops if and when the presence of those troops became unacceptable to the people. This is why discipline and order are of crucial importance to U.S. forces stationed in West Germany.

Notes

1. See Daniel J. Nelson, *A History of U.S. Military Forces in Germany* (Boulder, Colo.: Westview Press, 1987), chapter 4.

2. *Süddeutsche Zeitung*, January 4, 1974.

3. Presse- und Informationsamt der Bundesregierung, Pressemeldung, PPP (Background paper for use of newspaper reporters), November 26, 1974; *International Herald Tribune*, November 27, 1974.

4. *Stuttgarter Zeitung*, February 26, 1974.

5. Ibid.

6. *International Herald Tribune*, April 23, 1975.

7. Ibid., January 15, 1976.

8. *Münchener Merkur*, January 15, 1976.

9. *International Herald Tribune*, January 15, 1976.

10. Ibid.

11. *Stars and Stripes*, October 5, 1976; *Guardian* (Manchester), October 20, 1976.

12. *Stern*, November 4, 1976.

13. *International Herald Tribune*, April 20, 1977.

14. Ibid., May 31, 1979.

15. *Süddeutsche Zeitung*, July 5, 1979.

16. *Frankfurter Allgemeine*, March 24, 1982; *Allgemeine Zeitung* (Mainz), March 27, 1982.

17. *Westfälische Nachrichten* (Essen), November 18, 1981.

18. *Westfälische Nachrichten* (Essen), November 18, 1981; *Münchener Merkur*, November 19, 1981.

19. *Westfälische Nachrichten*, November 18, 1981.

20. Martin Binkin and Mark J. Eitelberg (with Alvin Schexnider and Marvin M. Smith), *Blacks and the Military* (Washington, D.C.: The Brookings Institution, 1982), p. 54.

21. Author's interview with a lieutenant colonel stationed in West Germany, August 1982.

Table 6.1. Trend in AFQT Scores for Army Enlisted Accessions (Percent)

Fiscal Year	AFQT Categories			
	Above Avg (I,II,IIIA)	IIIB	IV	Total
Draft Period*				
1964	56	25	19	100
1968	51	21	38	100
1972	56	26	18	100
AVF Period				
1974	52	30	18	100
1977**	35	24	41	100
1980**	27	23	50	100
1981	39	30	31	100
1982	53	28	19	100
(9 Months)				

*Includes draftees and volunteers.
**Renormed scores.

Source: Military Manpower Task Force: A Report to the President
on the Status and Prospects of the All-Volunteer Force,
Department of Defense, October 1982.

Table 6.2. Indiscipline Indicators US Army Europe (USAREUR) and
Armywide, 1973-1982 (Rate per 1,000)

	Crimes of Violence		Crimes Against Property		Marijuana Use/Possession		Other Drug Offenses	
CY	USAREUR	Army	USAREUR	Army	USAREUR	Army	USAREUR	Army
73	NA	7.95	NA	86.68	NA	23.72	NA	7.85
74	9.21	8.25	79.90	89.77	38.24	32.50	18.27	8.22
75	10.12	7.96	80.64	88.67	28.77	28.63	19.49	8.43
76	8.15	6.82	76.56	85.04	28.75	32.58	10.93	6.10
77	9.15	6.26	70.85	79.29	26.49	28.83	9.03	5.36
78	8.19	5.84	64.06	72.83	27.32	28.19	10.66	5.32
79	8.75	6.15	68.97	74.11	22.69	27.32	12.61	6.46
80	8.67	6.38	69.62	78.19	20.38	26.38	8.47	5.40
81	8.66	5.79	67.01	72.45	32.01	31.04	7.14	5.10
82	7.50	4.87	59.14	65.10	29.58	24.49	8.74	5.27

	AWOL		Desertion		Total Courts-martial*		Article 15	
CY	USAREUR	Army	USAREUR	Army FY	USAREUR	Army	USAREUR	Army
73	77.1	104.7	15.9	51.4 73	20.49	26.56	239.9	221.61
74	40.5	75.2	7.8	32.8 74	24.57	27.65	239.3	220.32
75	27.5	54.6	5.3	19.6 75	18.10	20.57	203.0	214.03
76	17.1	45.0	3.9	13.6 76	13.20	13.26	182.3	202.88
77	16.4	45.3	3.6	16.4 77	10.46	10.34	169.0	214.08
78	20.6	39.5	4.2	16.2 78	9.46	9.89	182.5	200.39
79	20.2	38.1	5.3	16.3 79	11.81	9.89	174.5	193.02
80	16.5	42.0	7.0	19.1 80	11.53	12.06	160.6	196.87
81	15.9	33.5	5.7	14.7 81	14.02	13.71	176.0	196.97
82	12.7	26.4	4.6	10.0 82	14.96	12.49	167.1	177.60

NA=Not Available

*Source: U.S. Army Legal Services Agency.

Source: Office of Army Law Enforcement, Office of the Deputy
Chief of Staff for Personnel, Washington, D.C.

Table 6.3. Air Force in Germany: Punishments for Indiscipline
By Category of Infraction and Grade, 1979 and 1980

	Confrontation/ Failure to Repair		AWOL/ Desertion		Violation of Regulation		Larceny		Assault	
	Off	End	Off	End	Off	End	Off	End	Off	End
1979	0	4	0	6	1	12	0	17	0	1
1980	0	7	0	8	0	28	0	42	0	7
Total	0	11	0	14	0	40	0	59	0	8

	Drunk/ Disorderly		Drugs		Bad Checks		Other	
	Off	End	Off	End	Off	End	Off	End
1979	0	4	2	204	0	27	6	6
1980	0	5	2	241	0	29	0	14
Total	0	9	4	445	0	56	6	20

Note: Data for these years are for cases brought to courts-martial
only, and do not include Article 15 administrative punishments.
Data comprises Air Force installations at Bitburg, Hahn,
Hessish-Oldendorf, Lindsey, Ramstein, Rhein-Main, Sembach,
Spandahlem, Berlin, and Zweibrücken. Data for 1979 do not
include Berlin.

Source: From data supplied by Office of the Judge Advocate General,
Headquarters, United States Air Force, Washington, D.C.

Table 6.4. Air Force in Germany: Punishments for Indiscipline by Category of Infraction, Grade, and Type of Punishment, 1981-1983

	Failure to Repair		AWOL/ Desertion		Confrontation/ Violation of Regulation		Larceny		Assault	
	Off	End	Off	End	Off	End	Off	End	Off	End
1981										
Courts-Martial	0	10	0	15	1	26	5	24	1	17
Article 15's	0	736	1	53	3	578	0	133	0	126
Total	0	746	1	68	4	604	5	157	1	143
1982										
Courts-Martial	0	11	1	14	0	34	1	45	0	21
Article 15's	0	751	0	54	7	603	0	83	1	144
Total	0	762	1	68	7	637	1	128	1	166
1983										
Courts-Martial	0	0	0	3	0	2	0	6	0	4
Article 15's	0	170	0	6	0	161	0	35	0	34
Total	0	170	0	9	0	163	0	41	0	38
Total Courts-Martial	0	21	1	32	1	62	6	75	1	42
Total Article 15's	0	1657	1	113	10	1342	0	251	1	304
Grand Total	0	1678	2	145	11	1404	6	326	2	326

	Drunk/ Disorderly		Drugs		Bad Checks		Other	
	Off	End	Off	End	Off	End	Off	End
1981								
Courts-Martial	0	23	6	331	0	56	2	7
Article 15's	16	889	0	557	2	59	1	137
Total	16	912	6	888	2	115	3	144
1982								
Courts-Martial	0	7	3	233	0	48	2	9
Article 15's	19	851	0	540	0	43	1	106
Total	19	858	3	673	0	91	3	115
1983								
Courts-Martial	0	4	0	91	0	11	0	4
Article 15's	2	209	0	109	0	27	2	29
Total	2	213	0	200	0	38	2	33
Total Courts-Martial	0	34	9	655	0	115	4	20
Total Article 15's	37	1949	0	1206	2	129	4	272
Grand Total	37	1983	9	1861	2	244	8	292

Note: The data for 1983 are for the first three months of the year (January-March).

Source: From data supplied by Office of the Judge Advocate General, Headquarters, United States Air Force, Washington, D.C.

Table 6.5. Trends in Disciplinary Incidents in the Armed Forces, by
Race and Sex, Fiscal Years 1978-1981
(Number of persons per thousand average monthly strength)

Type of disciplinary incident and sex	1978 Black	White	1979 Black	White	1980 Black	White	1981 Black	White
Unauthorized absence								
Male	42.6	33.3	40.4	32.3	46.0	34.9	39.4	31.5
Female	10.7	11.4	11.4	13.5	13.5	16.6	11.6	12.9
Designated deserter								
Male	13.5	17.4	14.4	18.0	15.6	18.2	12.4	15.5
Female	3.4	4.9	3.2	5.4	4.0	8.0	3.1	6.2

Source: Martin Binkin et al., Blacks and the Military
(Washington, D.C.: The Brookings Institution, 1982), p. 52.

Table 6.6. Crime Rates of Army Personnel by Race, Fiscal Years
1978-1980 (Rate per 1,000)

Category	1978 White	Black	1979 White	Black	1980 White	Black
Crimes of violence[1]	2.8	12.7	2.8	11.7	3.1	11.8
Crimes against property[2]	10.1	17.6	9.9	18.9	12.8	22.1
Drug offenses[3]	36.6	54.6	34.7	56.7	35.9	54.2

1. Includes murder, rape, aggravated assault, and robbery.
2. Includes burglary, larceny, auto theft, and housebreaking.
3. Includes use, possession, sale, and trafficking.

Source: Martin Binkin et al., Blacks and the Military
(Washington, D.C.: The Brookings Institution, 1982), p. 53.

Table 6.7. Blacks as Percentage of Enlisted Personnel and
Army Prison Population, 1977-1979

	Blacks as percent of	
Fiscal year	Enlisted Personnel	Prison Population
1977	26.4	51.0
1978	29.2	51.3
1979	32.2	51.2

Source: Martin Binkin et al., Blacks and the Military
(Washington, D.C.: The Brookings Institution, 1982), p. 53.

Table 6.8. Distribution of Enlisted Personnel Discharged from the
Armed Forces, by Character of Service, Race, and Branch
of Service, Fiscal Year 1980 (Percent)

A. Army
B. Navy
C. Marine Corps
D. Air Force
E. All services

W=White
B=Black

Character of Service	A		B		C		D		E	
	W	B	W	B	W	B	W	B	W	B
Honorable	92.01	90.77	91.37	89.84	91.91	89.03	94.91	94.08	92.61	91.07
General	3.32	4.72	5.25	7.03	3.90	6.62	4.46	5.16	4.17	5.21
Other than honorable	4.28	3.73	2.75	2.46	3.23	3.14	0.54	0.61	2.80	3.02
Bad conduct	0.33	0.59	0.62	0.64	0.71	0.82	0.09	0.14	0.37	0.54
Dishonorable	0.06	0.19	0.01	0.03	0.04	0.13	2*		0.01	0.03	0.14
Unknown	0.00	0.00	0.00	0.00	0.21	0.26	0.00	0.00	0.02	0.02

Numbers:
  Army/White: 157,016
  Army/Black: 68,847
  Navy/White: 103,079
  Navy/Black: 11,301
  Marine Corps/White: 38,165
  Marine Corps/Black: 9,668
  Air Force/White: 107,111
  Air Force/Black: 18,055
  All services/White: 405,371
  All services/Black: 107,871

Note: Tabulations include enlisted personnel who were "discharged" for
purposes of immediate reenlistment and those who entered officer
programs.

* Records show that two white enlistees in the Air Force were
discharged by court-martial under dishonorable conditions.

Source: Martin Binkin et al., Blacks and the Military
(Washington, D.C.: The Brookings Institution, 1982), p. 170.

7

Race Relations

Race relations in the armed forces of the United States is a subject of enduring concern and analysis. Since the establishment of thoroughly integrated military forces in the mid-1950s, race relations in the forces have alternated between varying degrees of animosity and harmony, more or less in tandem with the quality of race relations in U.S. society.[1] Nevertheless, certain peculiar characteristics of race relations in the U.S. military have been well documented. Sociologist Charles Moskos and others have demonstrated convincingly that race relations in the military forces are smoother, more egalitarian, and in general more harmonious than in U.S. society as a whole.[2] Service in the armed forces has become an important avenue of status and social mobility for thousands of black young people. Not only are black service personnel more likely to "find a home" in the armed services than their white counterparts, but blacks are also more likely to internalize a more favorable view of military life than whites.[3] The Department of Defense asserts with justifiable pride that it is the largest equal opportunity employer in the world.

Despite the accomplishment of the military in achieving a higher level of racial integration than most other major U.S. institutions, large problems remain in the area of race relations. A pattern of mutual exclusivity prevails in social relations during off-duty hours, racial slurs are common occurrences both on duty and off duty, and incidents of racial brawling, though sporadic and isolated in recent years, occur with some frequency on practically all military bases, at home and abroad.[4] Racial integration as official military policy translates into racial mixing in most situations on duty, whereas social situations off duty often remain characterized by de facto segregation. On larger military bases where two NCO clubs exist, one of the clubs usually becomes unofficially designated as the black club.[5] Complaints of official and unofficial discrimination are commonplace among black personnel, especially among the lower enlisted ranks. White personnel, at the same time, complain that blacks are often accorded preferential treatment.

Research studies on racial issues in the last decade have tended to focus on black participation in the military in terms of the racial composition of U.S. armed forces, the recruitment and retention of blacks, unit cohesion and force readiness, the benefits and burdens of black participation in relation to national security goals, and the future implications of ethnodemographic trends for the nation's national security.[6] Relatively less attention has been paid to the qualitative aspects of race relations in the military.[7] Even more striking is the relatively little work that has been done so far in reference to the study of race relations in U.S. military forces stationed abroad.[8] Race relations in U.S. forces stationed in Germany are closely observed by the West German media, and the character and quality of race relations are of prime importance in the perceptions West Germans form of the credibility of the U.S. military presence.

This history of race relations in the U.S. army in Germany over the last two decades shows some fairly substantial swings between periods of bitter acrimony and periods of harmony or quietude. In the late 1960s and early 1970s a substantial deterioration of race relations occurred as a result of the spin-off syndrome of the Vietnam War.[9] Inevitably, many of the massive morale problems of the army in Vietnam subsequently appeared among U.S. forces stationed in Germany. From the mid-1970s to approximately 1978 the pattern of race relations improved, even as the proportions of minority personnel in the forces continued to increase steadily under the regime of the all-volunteer force. New programs and courses aimed at increasing racial sensitivity and improving relations had a salutary effect.[10] Nevertheless, the turmoil of the late 1960s and early 1970s left a lasting imprint, which later efforts have never been able to erase completely. The period of 1978–1982 saw a moderate increase once again in the incidence of racial flare-ups and demonstrations. Relations between the races deteriorated as the purchasing power of the dollar plunged, creating competition between blacks and whites for affordable living quarters, entertainment, drugs and alcohol, and other amenities of life in a foreign country. After 1982, race relations seem to have improved once again, perhaps markedly. Fewer racial incidents have occurred than at any time since 1978, or perhaps even since the late 1950s.[11] In the mid-1980s race relations appear to be far better than they were ten or fifteen years ago, though the situation remains far from optimum. The strain that pervades the general atmosphere forms a disconcerting setting for the tapestry of human relations in the forces.

This chapter presents a portrait of race relations based on recent data collected by USAREUR headquarters in Heidelberg. Though the portrait is in many ways incomplete, the available data do nevertheless allow us to draw some meaningful conclusions. What I have not tried to do is to compare the character or quality of race relations in the forces stationed in West Germany to the quality of race relations in forces stationed in other foreign locations, in the United States, or to the quality of race relations in the U.S. armed forces as a whole. Though such an inquiry would be highly beneficial to a comparative understanding of race relations in the military, it must form the subject of another inquiry using additional data. Here, we will attempt only to make some limited assessments of the quality of race relations in U.S. forces in West Germany, as perceived by enlisted personnel and officers, and to draw some conclusions as to the impact of race relations upon the long-term viability of the U.S. military presence there.

Survey Data on Race Relations

We may construct an overview of the state of race relations in the early 1980s by analyzing the data in Tables 7.1 to 7.6. The tables record responses to questions included in the personnel opinion survey conducted by USAREUR headquarters in Heidelberg in the winter of 1982. (See Chapter 5.) Seven questions in the survey elicited opinion on issues related to race relations; six of these questions were used to construct the tables.[12] Though questions on other aspects of race relations would have been useful, responses to these six at least allow the construction of a general picture.

The six questions contained between five and nine response categories. An analysis of this data would require more space than is available here, and I attempted to collapse the response categories in a reasonable manner according to two simple criteria: few enough categories to allow for analysis of the general phenomenon in overview, but sufficient categories to allow for meaningful analysis of the full spectrum of opinion on the issue. Hence, Tables 7.1 to 7.6 contain either three or four response categories. For example, the original wording of the question in the survey shown in Table 7.2 was "How often do racial expressions such as racial name calling, racial slurs, or other offensive remarks occur in your unit during *duty* hours?" Six responses were possible: (1) Racial expressions never take place; (2) racial expressions hardly ever happen; (3) racial expressions happen occasionally; (4) racial expressions are fairly common; (5) racial expressions happen all the time; (6) I don't know. I collapsed these into the four categories that appear in the table. The question in Table 7.6 asked only for agreement or disagreement to a narrative statement. Possible responses were: strongly agree, agree, neither agree nor disagree, disagree, strongly disagree, I don't know. Again, I collapsed these into three simpler categories.

Racial Mixing Off Duty

Table 7.1 records impressions of racial conditions during off-duty hours—more specifically, the extent to which racial mixing occurs in social situations off duty. Among both officers and enlisted personnel, blacks and whites tended to record similar impressions about the extent of racial mixing. The responses indicate some racial mixing, but probably not as extensive as it ought to be for truly healthy race relations. Fortunately, only very small percentages of both racial groups said that there was no mixing at all. Higher percentages of officers than troops said that most people mixed off duty, whereas higher percentages of troops said that only some people mixed but most did not. There is a tendency, of course, for officers to rate all factors concerning morale more positively than do the troops. Also, officers and troops do not spend much time together during off-duty hours, with the consequence that officers are sometimes less than optimally informed about the social life of the troops. The more reliable data concerning race relations are probably derived from the troops. For example, 50% of white officers said that most people mixed, as opposed to only 39.5% of white enlisted personnel. Only 30% of white officers said that most people did not mix, as compared to 39.6% of white enlisted personnel. The same pattern held true for the responses of black officers and black enlisted personnel. Among enlisted personnel, approximately 40% of both racial groups said that most people mixed, but a lower percentage of blacks said that some people mixed, but most did not. It is interesting that fewer blacks than whites believed that there was little racial mixing. Among officers, whites were more inclined to believe in extensive racial mixing than were blacks.

The conclusion that emerges from these data is that racial mixing in social situations after duty hours is not extensive in the army in Germany. Though some racial mixing occurs, and though many soldiers have friends of both races, by and large white and black soldiers tend to socialize with members of their own race.[13] It would be an easy matter to castigate the army for failing to reach a higher level of racial integration in its social order. Such criticism would, however, miss the mark. The army reflects the society from which it is drawn. A situation of de facto racial separation is a common occurrence in many major U.S. institutions, including universities and corporations. The army probably succeeds as well as other institutions in creating a milieu of social integration, and in some ways it may be even more successful. Nevertheless, there is still a long way to go in achieving a truly integrated social order in army units in West Germany.

Racial Epithets and Name Calling

Soldiers were asked how often "racial expressions such as racial name calling, racial slurs, or other offensive remarks" occurred on duty (Table 7.2) and off duty (Table 7.3). During duty hours the officers were much less conscious of offensive racial expressions than the enlisted personnel, which confirms the pattern of lower awareness (or higher optimism) among officers seen in previous data. Only 13.6% of black officers and 9.7% of white officers said that offensive racial expressions occurred commonly or all the time, whereas much higher percentages of enlisted personnel—26.3% of blacks and 21.3% of whites—said that such expressions were common. White officers appeared to be the least aware of the problem, if the responses of the enlisted personnel are valid. A majority of 52.1% of white officers believed that racial expressions never or hardly ever happened. Apparently many white officers disregard or choose to ignore unpleasant utterances. Black personnel, as might be expected, were much more conscious of offensive racial expressions than whites. Higher percentages of blacks, both officers and troops, said that racial slurs were common; higher percentages of whites, officers and troops, said that such expressions were rare or never happened. If we add the percentages for the occurrence of racial expressions "occasionally" and "common or all the time," we find that a majority of both black and white enlisted personnel admitted that racial expressions happen with some frequency during duty hours. This is a situation that does not lead to optimism about race relations.

Data on the occurrence of racial expressions during off-duty hours are seen in Table 7.3. The general pattern is similar to that during duty hours. Some differences, however, ought to be noted. Most significantly, the percentage of those who said that racial slurs occurred "hardly" or "never" falls in all categories, for officers and enlisted personnel, blacks and whites, indicating that the incidence of racial name-calling is probably higher during off-duty than during duty hours. Blacks and whites differed in their perceptions of the situation. Blacks, both officers and troops, did not believe that the situation was worse off duty than on duty. If we add the percentages for "common or all the time" and "occasionally," we see that slightly lower percentages of blacks recorded the occurrence of offensive expressions during off-duty hours than during duty hours in Table 7.2. Whites, both officers and troops, recorded a higher incidence of name calling off duty. Officers showed the greatest differences in their pattern of responses to the questions in Tables 7.3 and 7.2. The percentages of black and white officers who said that racial expressions occurred "hardly" or "never" were less for off-duty hours than for duty hours.

More significant is the fact that the percentage of officers who said "don't know" went up dramatically for off-duty hours—30.6% of black officers and 32.9% of white officers admitted that they did not know what the situation was during off-duty hours, though both groups were less confident that racial slurs occurred hardly ever or never.

The fact of the matter is that racial name-calling and slurs are fairly common occurrences among U.S. forces in West Germany. There is no hiding from this ugly truth. Though the quality of race relations in U.S. society is far from what could and should be achieved, the frequency of racial name-calling in the military forces in West Germany is a situation that warrants major concern. Military leaders must make every effort to sensitize soldiers to the importance of better race relations, though educational and behavioral backgrounds of army recruits may limit what can be achieved.

Programs to Improve Race Relations

In the mid-1970s military leaders instituted several new programs aimed at improving race relations. An orientation program on the subject was required for all new arrivals in West Germany, and periodic race relations classes and seminars were to be held in each company or unit.[14] In any organization new initiatives sometimes succeed, sometimes fail, and sometimes produce unintended effects that supplement or detract from the original goals. In the military, as in other organizations, various commanders instituted the programs in very different ways. Depending upon their values and estimates of the seriousness of racial problems, some commanders invested great effort in the new programs, and others merely went through the required motions with a minimum investment of enthusiasm or energy. By and large, the programs seem to have been moderately successful. Whether they justify the time and effort subtracted from other military duties remains a matter of lively debate.

The data in Tables 7.4 to 7.6 may give us some idea of the perceived results of the army's efforts in the area of race relations. Table 7.4 contains data on the perceived frequency of unit-level equal opportunity/race relations classes in companies or work units. The data suggest two generalizations: First, officers thought that race relations classes were held more frequently than enlisted personnel; second, the percentages who said they didn't know were fairly high for every group. The data indicate either considerable confusion as to how often classes are actually held or considerable variation in frequency from unit to unit. In any case, only small percentages of either officers or troops claimed that race relations classes were held frequently—defined as once every two months or more often—though higher percentages of officers than troops and higher percentages of blacks than whites believed that classes were held frequently. White enlisted personnel showed the lowest percentage saying that classes were held frequently (13.1%). However, higher percentages of blacks also said that race relations classes were never held. This result is puzzling. The most that may be said is that blacks are probably more sensitive to whether classes are or are not being held, whereas whites pay less attention. If we add the percentages for the categories "infrequently" and "never," we find that half or more of the respondents in all categories said that classes were held infrequently if at all. This result, coupled with the high percentages who said they didn't know, indicates that race relations classes in many units are held on a sporadic basis and are probably neglected at times when other military concerns seem more pressing.

More important than the frequency of these classes is the effect they have on generating cordial race relationships among military personnel. The army tends to place the major emphasis on the race relations orientation session all soldiers are required to attend when they first arrive in West Germany. The impact of the initial orientation is the subject of the data in Table 7.5. These results are either cheerful or dismal, depending upon what one wishes to emphasize. First, attendance is less mandatory than appears on the surface, as indicated by the percentages of personnel who said they did not attend the course, ranging from a low of 15% for white officers to a high of 24.5% for black enlisted personnel. No sanction is applied to anyone who, for whatever reasons, fails to attend the orientation session. Hence, though all personnel are instructed that attendance is mandatory, the word is out that nothing happens if a soldier doesn't make it, with the predictable result that about one-fifth of the arriving personnel do not attend the course.[15]

The impact of the course on blacks and whites seems to be quite different. Black personnel claimed, by substantially higher percentages, to have received more benefit from the course than white personnel. Military leaders may be dismayed that those who said that great benefit was derived from the orientation session did not constitute a majority for any group. Among blacks, 46.8% of officers and 43.4% of troops said that they derived "some or a lot" of benefit from the course. This contrasts to much lower percentages among whites—29.9% of officers and 27.3% of troops. The category of little benefit or none at all shows a mirror image, with higher percentages of whites than blacks choosing these responses. Among blacks, 36.9% of officers and 32% of troops said they derived little or no benefit. Most unfortunate is that a majority of whites chose these responses—55% of officers and 52.4% of troops.

Evaluation of the data in Table 7.5 is exceedingly difficult. On the one hand, it is most unfortunate that white personnel, who probably need it most, derived the least benefit from the race relations orientation course. On the other hand, the course does have concrete beneficial effects, as seen by the ample percentages of both whites and blacks who claimed to have received some or much benefit from it. Any course in such a sensitive area of human affiars is bound to have mixed results. Education in human understanding and cultural awareness is, as any educator knows, a hazardous enterprise. Percentages just short of a majority for blacks and approaching a third for whites register substantial benefit from the course. Not even the best-designed course in the world would be able to reach everyone. The statistics may be read as evidence that the military's investment in improving race relations has been eminently worthwhile.

Equal Opportunity

The question in Table 7.6 attempted to probe the commitment of military leaders to the principle of equal opportunity. If we examine the U.S. defense establishment as a whole, the assertion seems warranted that few other public organizations have attempted to implement equal opportunity as thoroughly as the armed forces have. Indeed, as we mentioned, the Department of Defense claims, with some credibility, to be the largest equal opportunity employer in the world. Real progress in reference to equal opportunity depends, of course, on a real commitment to the principle by all persons in positions of authority. The data in Table 7.6 shows perceptions military personnel in West Germany have of the commitment to equal opportunity. Two conclusions emerge: Officers were more convinced than enlisted personnel that the commitment to equal opportunity is real, and whites were more convinced than blacks. Among officers, majorities of both blacks and whites believed that their supervisors were committed to the Equal Opportunity Program; only small percentages believed that their supervisors were not committed to the program. Among enlisted personnel, smaller percentages believed in the supervisors' commitment, and larger percentages perceived a lack of commitment. The difference in responses according to race is significant. Lower percentages of blacks, both officers and troops, believed that their supervisors were committed to the Equal Opportunity Program, and higher percentages of blacks than whites perceived a lack of commitment. It should be noted, however, that a significant percentage of each group declined to register an opinion or claimed not to know. Especially among enlisted personnel, high percentages could not or would not register an opinion. Despite this, the data indicate that the principle of equal opportunity has had an impact upon the perceptions of most military personnel in West Germany. Majorities of the officers and significant percentages of the enlisted personnel believed that their supervisors are committed to the Equal Opportunity Program. U.S. forces in West Germany should be accorded appropriate credit for this achievement.

It is not easy to summarize the data in Tables 7.1 to 7.6. The conclusion seems warranted, however, that race relations in the army in West Germany were as healthy in 1982 as they have been anytime in recent years and much healthier than they were a decade earlier. Racial mixing in social situations was not extensive, but there also seemed to be no open hostility or animosity between the races. The frequent occccurrence of racial slurs and racial name-calling is an ominous situation that ought to be a matter of prime concern to the entire chain of command, as the line between racial epithets and racial animosity is extremely thin. Racial hostility may in fact lie not far beneath the surface and outbreaks might have to be reckoned with whenever this hostility is aggravated by other unpleasant conditions such as decreased purchasing power, deteriorating living conditions, or rapid changes in the demography of the forces.[16] There can be little doubt that racial harmony has been amplified by the orientation programs and the periodic classes in race relations sponsored by USAREUR in Germany. The principle of equal opportunity is perceived by most military personnel to have had a vital impact.

West German Perceptions

The Germans possess a lively curiosity about race relations in the U.S. forces in their midst. Such curiosity translates into newspaper articles or editorial opinion mainly at times when racial tensions become visible because of strikes, riots, or racial brawls. In more normal times the West German press is content to assume a more disinterested analytical attitude. Racial turmoil in the late 1960s and early 1970s left an indelible imprint on the West German collective memory. The press at the time was highly critical of the racial mess in U.S. forces, as it had every right to be. The situation was a kind of consciousness-raising experience for the Germans in general and for press commentators in particular. Since that time the German press has always been more aware of and inquiring about the character and quality of race relations in the U.S. military.[17] In the late 1970s and early 1980s, the press commented extensively upon race relations as an issue related to the poverty experienced by military personnel because of the weak dollar. The Germans did not fail to notice that the poverty seemed to afflict black military personnel more generally and more severely than it did white personnel. When the dollar gained strength after 1982 and conditions of poverty were less evident, the press expressed less interest in race relations once again.

In terms of the sociopolitical relationship between West Germans and U.S. military personnel, the quality of race relations in the U.S. forces is extremely important. The West Germans form their most vivid impressions of U.S. society through contacts with U.S. military personnel. Few things are more damaging to the image of the U.S. military than malevolent relations among the races. More important, however, racial turmoil reduces the credibility of U.S. forces. If the Americans are unable to keep peace among the racial components of their military forces stationed in the Federal Republic, then how well will these forces be able to defend the country if aggression should occur? Racial turmoil diminishes perceptions of the high level of readiness and overall capability of U.S. forces. It also serves to aggravate the problem of German discrimination against U.S. military personnel. Hence, few things are more vital to the long-term viability of the U.S. presence than conditions of racial harmony. Civilian and military leaders in the Pentagon are well aware of this, as are the senior U.S. commanders in the FRG. In the mid-1980s, race relations are generally stable and nonconflictive, much better than they were a decade ago but still not of the quality that could and should be achieved. Social integration is not extensive, and racial name calling remains a major problem. Under the placid surface lie fundamental problems that could cause serious outbreaks of racial violence in the future. Programs aimed at increasing racial sensitivity and racial harmony must therefore remain a matter of priority in the Department of Defense and at USAREUR headquarters.

Notes

1. The history of black participation in the U.S. armed forces has been well documented in a number of excellent studies. Of particular importance is the seminal work of Samuel A. Stouffer et al., *The American Soldier: Adjustment During Army Life* (Princeton, N.J.: Princeton University Press, 1949), vol. 1, especially Chapter 10, "Negro Soldiers," pp. 486–599. Other important studies include Gerald W. Patton, *War and Race: The Black Officer in the American Military, 1915–1941* (Westport, Conn.: Greenwood Press, 1981); Jay David and Elaine Crane, *The Black Soldier: From the American Revolution to Vietnam* (New York: William Morrow & Co., 1971); David G. Mandelbaum, *Soldier Groups and Negro Soldiers* (Berkeley: University of California Press, 1952); Richard J. Stillman, II, *Integration of the Negro in the U.S. Armed Forces*, Praeger Special Studies in U.S. Economic and Social Development (New York: Praeger Publishers, 1968); J. D. Foner, *Blacks and the Military in American History* (New York: Praeger Publishers, 1974); A. Barbeau and F. Henri, *The Unknown Soldiers* (Philadelphia: Temple University Press, 1974); U. Lee, *The Employment of Negro Troops in World War II* (Washington, D.C.: Office of the Chief of Military History, U.S. Army, 1966); R. Dalfiume, *Desegregation of the U.S. Armed Forces: Fighting on Two*

Fronts, 1939–1953 (Kansas City: University of Missouri Press, 1969); Lorenzo J. Greene, "The Negro in the Armed Forces of the United States, 1619–1783," *Negro History Bulletin* 14, no. 6 (1951), pp. 123–127.

2. Moskos concluded that "military life is characterized by an interracial equalitarianism of a quantity and of a kind that is seldom found in other major institutions of American society." See Charles C. Moskos, Jr., *The American Enlisted Man: The Rank and File in Today's Military* (New York: Russell Sage Foundation, 1970), p. 121. Moskos' conclusion is substantiated by the findings in Martin Binkin and Mark J. Eitelberg (with Alvin J. Schexnider and Marvin M. Smith), *Blacks and the Military* (Washington, D.C.: The Brookings Institution, 1982), p. 155.

3. Moskos, Jr., *The American Enlisted Man*, pp. 117–118.

4. See ibid., pp. 122–123; also Binkin et al., *Blacks and the Military*, pp. 101–108. For an analysis of problems in military race relations since the establishment of integrated forces in the mid-1950s, see Warren L. Young, *Minorities and the Military: A Cross-National Study in World Perspective* (Westport, Conn.: Greenwood Press, 1982), especially Chapter 5, "United States," pp. 191–243; David and Crane, *The Black Soldier*; Department of Defense, *The Negro in the Armed Forces* (Washington, D.C.: Office of the Assistant Secretary of Defense for Manpower and Reserve Affairs, 15 September 1971, and 31 December 1972); Stillman, *Integration of the Negro in the U.S. Armed Forces*; Richard O. Hope, *Racial Strife in the U.S. Military: Toward the Elimination of Discrimination* (New York: Praeger Publishers, 1979); P. Nordlie et al., *Measuring Changes in Institutional Racial Discrimination in the Army*, Technical Paper 270 (Washington, D.C.: Army Research Institute for the Behavioral Sciences, 1975); Morris J. MacGregor and Bernard C. Nalty, eds., *Blacks in the United States Armed Forces: Basic Documents* (Wilmington, Del.: Scholarly Resources, Inc., 1977), 13 vols.; Morris Janowitz and Charles C. Moskos, Jr., "Racial composition in the All-Volunteer Force: Policy Alternatives," *Armed Forces and Society* 1, no. 1 (November 1974), pp. 109–123; Alvin J. Schexnider and John Sibley Butler, "Race and the All-Volunteer System: A Reply to Janowitz and Moskos," *Armed Forces and Society* 2, no. 3 (May 1976), pp. 421–432; Charles C. Moskos, Jr., John Sibley Butler, Alan Ned Sabrosky, and Alvin J. Schexnider, "Symposium: Race and the United States Military," *Armed Forces and Society* 6, no. 4 (Summer 1980), pp. 586–613; John Sibley Butler, "Assessing Black Enlisted Participation in the Army," *Social Problems* 23 (1976), pp. 558–566; John Sibley Butler, "Inequality in the Military," *American Sociological Review* 4 (1976), pp. 807–818; Kathleen Maas Weigert, "Stratification, Ideology, and Opportunity Beliefs Among Black Soldiers," *Public Opinion Quarterly* 38, no. 1 (1974), pp. 57–68; John Sibley Butler and Kenneth L. Wilson, "The American Soldier Revisited: Race Relations and the Military," *Social Science Quarterly* 59, no. 3 (December 1978), pp. 451–467.

5. Moskos, Jr., *The American Enlisted Man*, p. 123.

6. See, for instance, Moskos, Jr., et al., "Symposium: Race and the United States Military," and the major work published in the last decade, Binkin et al., *Blacks and the Military*.

7. The major exception is perhaps Hope, *Racial Strife in the U.S. Military*. It is relevant to note that an important recent study of sociological relationships

among enlisted ranks in the U.S. Army devotes almost no discussion to racial issues. See Larry H. Ingraham, *The Boys in the Barracks: Observations on American Military Life* (Philadelphia: Institute for the Study of Human Issues, 1984).

8. The major exception is Moskos, Jr., *The American Enlisted Man*, Chapter 5, "Racial Relations in the Armed Forces." The subsections entitled, "The Black Soldier Overseas," pp. 124–127, and "Race at Home and War Abroad," pp. 127–133, must be considered the authoritative work in the area and probably the standard by which other work should be measured.

9. See Moskos, Jr., *The American Enlisted Man*, pp. 128–130. A more detailed history of race relations in U.S. forces in West Germany may be found in Daniel J. Nelson, *A History of U.S. Military Forces in Germany* (Boulder, Colo.: Westview Press, 1987), Chapters 4 and 5.

10. See Hope, *Racial Strife in the U.S. Military*, Chapters 4 and 5.

11. Data are not yet available to substantiate this point. The conclusion is, however, substantiated by a few formal interviews and many informal discussions I have had with company commanders in West Germany since 1982 and by various press reports.

12. For the sake of brevity one survey question was deleted in this discussion, as its content overlapped another. The question deleted asked for agreement or disagreement with the statement "After duty hours, most soldiers in this unit are seen only with other soldiers who are of the same social/ethnic group." I chose to use the question referred to in Table 7.1; its precise wording was, "Which of the following statements best describes racial conditions in your unit *off-duty?*" The collapsed response categories are shown in the table.

13. These findings broadly corroborate the earlier findings of Moskos in *The American Enlisted Man*, pp. 122–123 and 124–127. Moskos noted that "the pattern of racial relations observed among soldiers in the United States—integration in the military setting and racial exclusivism off-duty—prevails in overseas settings as well" (p. 125). Moskos found also that "the pattern of off-duty separation is most pronounced in Japan and Germany, and somewhat less so in Korea . . ." (p. 125).

14. For more detailed information on the military's new programs in the area of race relations, see Hope, *Racial Strife in the U.S. Military*, especially Chapters 3 and 4, pp. 37–59.

15. This finding emerged rather distinctly from informal interviews the author conducted with officers and enlisted personnel at several army bases in West Germany in the summer of 1982.

16. The author's interviews with officers in the summer of 1982 revealed an underlying uneasiness over the state of race relations and a generalized, if mild, fear that underneath the placid surface were unhealthy undercurrents that might sometime erupt into open racial animosity.

17. A study of West German press coverage of U.S. forces in the FRG appears in Nelson, *A History of U.S. Military Forces in Germany*, Chapters 4 and 5.

Table 7.1. Unit Racial Condition Off Duty, By Rank and Race (Percent)

	Officers		Enlisted	
	Blacks	Whites	Blacks	Whites
No Mixing	5.3	3.7	6.5	7.3
Some Mix, Most Don't	32.1	30.0	35.7	39.6
Most People Mix	45.8	50.0	40.5	39.5
No Opinion	16.9	16.3	17.3	13.6

Source: Constructed from USAREUR Personnel Opinion Survey, Winter
1982. Data supplied by Office of Deputy Chief of Staff,
Personnel; Headquarters, United States Army, Europe;
Heidelberg, Germany.

Table 7.2. Occurrence of Racial Expressions During Duty Hours, By
Rank and Race (Percent)

	Officers		Enlisted	
	Blacks	Whites	Blacks	Whites
Common or All the Time	13.6	9.7	26.3	21.3
Occasionally	32.2	24.3	23.7	29.8
Hardly/Never	36.4	52.1	29.4	35.7
Don't Know	17.8	13.9	20.7	13.2

Source: Constructed from USAREUR Personnel Opinion Survey, Winter
1982. Data supplied by Office of Deputy Chief of Staff,
Personnel; Headquarters, United States Army, Europe;
Heidelberg, Germany.

Table 7.3. Occurrence of Racial Expressions During Off-Duty Hours,
By Rank and Race (Percent)

	Officers		Enlisted	
	Blacks	Whites	Blacks	Whites
Common or All the Time	14.1	1.5	21.6	23.9
Occasionally	28.1	23.9	23.8	31.2
Hardly/Never	27.3	31.6	28.8	25.8
Don't Know	30.6	32.9	25.7	19.1

Source: Constructed from USAREUR Personnel Opinion Survey, Winter
1982. Data supplied by Office of Deputy Chief of Staff,
Personnel; Headquarters, United States Army, Europe;
Heidelberg, Germany.

Table 7.4. Frequency of Unit Level EO/RR Classes in Company or Work
            Unit, By Rank and Race (Percent)

	Officers		Enlisted	
	Blacks	Whites	Blacks	Whites
Frequently[1]	22.3	18.1	21.2	13.1
Infrequently[2]	29.5	40.5	21.4	23.0
Never	23.0	|6.9	28.0	26.9
Don't Know	25.1	24.5	29.4	37.0

1. Represents holding of classes once every two months or more often.
2. Represents holding of classes quarterly (four times a year) or less
   often.

Source: Constructed from USAREUR Personnel Opinion Survey, Winter
        1982. Data supplied by Office of Deputy Chief of Staff,
        Personnel; Headquarters, United States Army, Europe;
        Heidelberg, Germany.

Table 7.5. Benefit Received from Community Level Race Relations
            Orientation, By Race and Rank (Percent)

	Blacks		Whites	
	Officers	Enlisted	Officers	Enlisted
Some or a Lot	46.8	43.4	29.9	27.3
Little or None	36.9	32.0	55.0	52.4
Didn't Go	16.4	24.5	15.0	20.3

Source: Constructed from USAREUR Personnel Opinion Survey, Winter
        1982. Data supplied by Office of Deputy Chief of Staff,
        Personnel; Headquarters, United States Army, Europe;
        Heidelberg, Germany.

Table 7.6. Supervisor Support of Equal Opportunity Program, By Rank
            and Race (Percent)

Statement: "My supervisor supports and is committed to the
           Equal Opportunity (EO) Program."

	Officers		Enlisted	
	Blacks	Whites	Blacks	Whites
Agree	57.3	73.3	34.0	36.4
Disagree	12.6	6.3	23.9	17.5
Don't Know/Neither	30.1	20.4	42.1	46.1

Source: Constructed from USAREUR Personnel Opinion Survey, Winter
        1982. Data supplied by Office of Deputy Chief of Staff,
        Personnel; Headquarters, United States Army, Europe;
        Heidelberg, Germany.

8

Discrimination

Discrimination against U.S. soldiers in the Federal Republic of Germany is not a new problem. Since the early days of the U.S. occupation there have been West Germans who resented the presence of foreign soldiers and discriminated against them. In recent years, however, the incidence of discrimination has increased, and the problem has revealed a racial dimension that is more discernible than in the past. Prior to the precipitous decline in the dollar exchange rate in the 1970s, isolated incidents of discrimination against GIs were a minor problem that merited only scant attention by military authorities. Most service personnel seemed to have plenty of money to spend on the West German economy for entertainment and souvenirs, and GI dollars were an important source of income for West German businesspeople. In the 1950s and 1960s West German establishments with "Off Limits" signs were a rarity. No one worried much about them, as there were always many more establishments in the same vicinity that welcomed the patronage of GIs.

In the early 1970s, discrimination against service personnel increased, but the problem tended to be submerged by the other maladies that beset the forces in West Germany at the time as a result of the Vietnam spin-off syndrome. U.S. commanders well understood that West German establishments might refuse service to GIs for a variety of reasons. The general belligerence of the period produced fear in businesspeople that their establishments might become a haven for radical groups, that racial strife within the U.S. forces might spill over into West German bars and restaurants, or that pent-up emotions might lead to major brawls with only the slightest provocation. Both U.S. military authorities and the West German press were preoccupied with problems far more serious than discrimination against GIs. The wave of crime and indiscipline, racial strife, the serious shortage of experienced officers and NCOs, as well as problems related to combat readiness—these were problems that made the discrimination issue appear to be a tempest in a teacup. Not until the mid-1970s, when discrimination began to increase noticeably and when a distinct racial component began to appear, did the problem become a matter of discussion in the West German press and a matter of serious concern for military leaders. By the late 1970s and early 1980s, discrimination against American GIs was a major topic of discussion not only in the West German press, but in the U.S. press and the Congress as well.

Varieties of Discrimination

Discrimination against service personnel manifested itself in many forms, some blatant and others more subtle. In a number of cities taxi drivers refused to pick up GIs.[1] Apartments, otherwise freely available to Germans, could not be rented by U.S. military families. In Ansbach, a popular youth center lowered its maximum age for admittance to eighteen in 1981, a move interpreted by military authorities as an effort to exclude U.S. soldiers.[2] Most nettlesome, however, were problems of discrimination in public establishments such as restaurants, bars, discotheques, and clubs. A few examples, drawn from hundreds described in the extensive press coverage, illustrate various aspects of the problem. In Fulda, in 1976,

> Claudius Müller opened the green door to the disco-bar Pony Club where he works and revealed the sign that makes thousands of U.S. soldiers wonder what they are doing here. "This Club is Off Limits to American Personnel," the notice says. "No Club-Card Available—Per Order of the Management." Not far away, at the Hotel Lenz, Staff Sgt. Anthony Love-Gonzales of Atlanta tried to have dinner with his wife, who is a dark Puerto Rican, and the doorman told him that "it will be an hour before I can get a table." As they were leaving, the doorman admitted three German couples with no waiting.[3]

In the fall of 1981, Colonel G. H. Heath, chief of the Human Resources Development Division at USAREUR headquarters in Heidelberg, confirmed that the army maintained a list of establishments known to refuse admittance to U.S. soldiers. The list contained the names of 140 establishments, up from 90 two months previously.[4] One might claim, of course, that 140 out of 206,000 gastronomical establishments in the country[5] represented an infinitesimal percentage and hence a very small problem. Geographically, however, the establishments were concentrated in southern Germany and were clustered in the thirty-three communities where there was a large U.S. military presence. In addition, the list contained only the names of those establishments known to refuse service to American soldiers consistently as a matter of policy. It did not include hundreds more that might discriminate only intermittently. As the military explained, it was common practice for some establishments to admit U.S. soldiers on Tuesday or Wednesday evenings when there were otherwise few patrons, but to refuse admittance on weekend evenings when business was good.[6]

The varieties of discrimination were legion, as documented in the press. Some establishments simply posted a guard at the door with instructions to refuse admittance to U.S. soldiers. Other establishments might admit soldiers but then refuse to serve them, leaving them at empty tables for long embarrassing moments. Some establishments might advise that the restaurant or bar was fully booked or unable to accept additional customers, and some might insist on a dress code that would exclude service personnel, but not others, without coat and tie or formal dress. One favorite mechanism was the demand for a club card for entry, which might cost as much as 500 marks. There were even cases in which the soldier produced the 500 marks only to be told that the club cards were temporarily sold out.[7]

There can be little doubt that an increase in the incidence of discrimination against American soldiers constitutes a morale problem of some gravity for U.S. forces stationed in the Federal Republic. In the words of Lieutenant Colonel Lawrence Knotts, an army spokesman at Heidelberg headquarters, "The morale of the soldiers were very definitely suffers. Naturally they are frustrated and full of anger. And when they return [to the U.S.] they take back with them extremely negative perceptions." The sentiment of twenty-three-year-old Markel Muller might be considered restrained, after he was refused service in five locales in one evening in Aschaffenburg. "I'm expected to die for the Germans, and they won't even serve me a beer."[8]

Inevitably, the anger and frustration of U.S. soldiers caused retaliatory outbursts. In 1981 and 1982, a series of incidents occurred in which angry GIs threw bricks through the windows of establishments known for their discriminatory policies. In an ugly incident in May 1982, a group of GIs, in a fit of fury, wrenched the urinals from the walls of the men's restroom after they had been required to pay an admission charge to a bar where Germans were admitted free.[9] In a more restrained move, a white legal officer, with the support of military authorities, filed suit in court against a discotheque owner in Wuerzburg, who had refused him admission in the company of a black African student. Though the city court of original jurisdiction levied a fine of 4,500 marks on the discotheque owner, the sentence was overturned by a higher court. The soldier then appealed to the Bavarian Supreme Court, which in 1984 ruled in his favor and reinstated the fine.[10] U.S. military authorities feared a rash of further serious incidents unless there were some clear demonstration that discrimination against GIs was being rooted out.

Nature of the Discrimination Problem

The phenomenon of discrimination is difficult to analyze, because the primary target remains unclear. Those who practice discrimination in West Germany probably have some sort of grudge or ill feelings toward GIs in general. Many service personnel, including high-ranking officers, have experienced discrimination in one form or another. But there is no doubt that black soldiers are more sensitive to discrimination than are their white counterparts. The army tends to downplay the racial side of the discrimination problem. According to Colonel Heath, "We believe simply that blacks are the easiest to identify as Americans."[11] There definitely is, however, a racial component to the discrimination. Though there are many establishments that exclude all military personnel, others are particularly or even exclusively discriminatory to black personnel. Certainly it is no accident that discrimination against GIs tended to increase during the period when the percentage of black enlisted soldiers in the forces in Germany increased dramatically, from approximately 12.6% in 1972 to 31.4% in 1983. Hence, any discussion of discrimination leads us inevitably to a discussion of race problems in West Germany, though the problem of discrimination is itself part of a larger phenomenon. Whether West Germany is an inherently racist society is a question we shall take up later.

The personnel opinion survey conducted by USAREUR in the winter of 1982 included a question about discrimination. A description of various methods of refusing entrance to or service in public establishments was followed by the question "Have you been the subject of the type of discrimination described above in the local civilian community in the last six months?" The results, displayed in Table 8.1, contain a number of surprises. In the first place, higher percentages of officers complained of discriminatory treatment than did enlisted personnel. This may reflect the fact that officers frequent public establishments in Germany more often than do enlisted personnel. They are also likely to seek admission to a greater variety of public places. Whereas enlisted troops are likely to frequent familiar taverns and discotheques near base, where they are confident they will be served, officers are likely to go out to dinner or meet friends for cocktails at a more diverse selection of places throughout the area.

Second, and perhaps even more surprising, higher percentages of whites, both officers and enlisted personnel, recorded discriminatory treatment than did blacks. Of white officers, 21% complained of discriminatory treatment three or more times in the previous six months as compared to only 14.8% of black officers. Likewise, 22.2% of white officers said they had suffered discrimination one or two times within the previous six months as compared to only 17.9% of black officers. The pattern was even more pronounced for enlisted personnel. Whereas 16.9% of white enlisted personnel claimed discriminatory treatment three or more times, only 5.5% of black enlisted personnel made the same claim; 20.1% of whites claimed discriminatory treatment one or two times as against only 9.6% of blacks.

If we add together the percentages for all frequencies of discrimination, we find that among black officers 32.7% said they had experienced some discrimination within the previous six months, whereas 67.3% said they had not; only 15.1% of black enlisted personnel said they had experienced discrimination, compared to 84.4% who said they had not. Much higher percentages of whites—43.2% of white officers and 37% of white enlisted personnel—complained of discriminatory treatment. Consequently, the data seem to indicate that the incidence of discrimination is higher for white service personnel than for blacks. This confirms the conclusion, discussed more fully later in this chapter, that it is inappropriate to view the Federal Republic of Germany as a blatantly more racist society than the United States.

At the same time, however, I would argue that the data in Table 8.1 mask or hide an element of racism which, in the opinion of many commanders and other observers, is indeed embedded within the phenomenon of discrimination against U.S. service personnel in West Germany. It is quite possible, for instance, that white military personnel may interpret a wider spectrum of actions as implying discrimination, such as waiting a long time to be served, whereas blacks may be thinking more about overt acts clearly implying racism, such as being refused admission to a public establishment at the same time a white person is admitted. My argument is not that the data are wrong or false, but they they do not reveal all the dimensions of the wider phenomenon of discrimination. Many field commanders, equal opportunity officers, and other observers believe, on the basis of their own experience, that at least some element of racism is involved in the discrimination problem. It is probably no accident that the problem appears to have become worse during the years when the percentage of black service personnel in the forces in West Germany was rising. At the same time, however, the conclusion that the problem of discrimination arises from or is caused primarily by West German racism is entirely unwarranted.

The data in Table 8.1 also point out that discrimination against U.S. service personnel in West Germany is less extensive than press reports would lead us to believe. Approximately one-third of officers and troops said they had experienced discrimination within the previous six months, a figure that in any case is too high and about which there ought to be much concern. On the other hand, two-thirds of U.S. military personnel in West Germany recorded no discriminatory treatment at all.

The Causes of Discrimination

In searching for the causes of discrimination against U.S. military personnel, we must distinguish at least two separate categories of reasons: (1) the specific reasons, both explicit and implicit, of the particular persons who practice discrimination, especially the proprietors of eating and drinking establishments, and (2) the general reasons derived from an analysis of societal trends in West Germany and the United States and the changing texture of German-American relations over the years.

The specific reasons for discrimination by West German proprietors are rooted in usually vague emotions of prejudice or fear or a combination of both. But there is another side to the discrimination phenomenon that is too often overlooked by U.S. observers. The conduct in public places of U.S. service personnel in Germany is often so abominable that it is little wonder that certain establishments finally blacklist GIs. This is a fact of military life that even the army freely admits. As Colonel Heath put it, "Fear and uncertainty are part of the picture on the part of Germans, if we talk about increasing distance between Germans and Americans. They fear that fights will break out between rival groups [of GIs]; they fear irritation because of the language barrier; and they fear that with the Americans narcotic drugs will automatically be brought into the place."[12] In many cases the proprietors of restaurants, bars, or discotheques who hang "Off Limits" signs on their doors are those whose establishments have been torn apart, sometimes repeatedly, by brawls among American GIs. The owner of a popular bar in Frankfurt not far from a U.S. base avowed in 1982 that he liked Americans in general and that the last thing he ever wanted to do was close the place to military patronage. Three times, however, in the space of five months his bar had been reduced to shambles by brawling GIs. Repairs had cost thousands of marks, and over a period of several years he had been losing all his German customers. He felt finally that if he were to rescue what remained of his business he had no choice but to refuse service to all GIs.[13] Similar stories are told again and again by owners of establishments who bar GIs. Though no reliable statistics are available, the guess may not be far from wrong that a majority of proprietors who refuse service to U.S. military personnel have had severe problems through no fault of their own. Many other proprietors have instituted an off-limits-to-GIs policy out of fear that their establishments may be next on the list of places utterly devastated by unruly U.S. soldiers. Even casual tourists who visit bars heavily frequented by GIs are likely to witness enough disgraceful incidents on any given evening to cause them to wonder why the proprietors did not long ago close the establishments to military personnel.

This is the side of the story American audiences need to be aware of, as it is vastly understated by the American media. The fear of drugs is an especially powerful motive for discrimination against GIs. If one looks at the statistics on drug abuse published by USAREUR, it ought not be surprising that many German proprietors assume that heavy military patronage means their establishments will gain a reputation as drug havens, a situation that any conscientious proprietor would wish to avoid, even at the cost of patent discrimination against U.S. soldiers. This situation must be faced by military leaders, by the U.S. public, and by Congress. GIs are often seen by West Germans, in part or in toto, as a hooligan element in their society, and there is abundant evidence that this impression has gained credence in recent years. A taxi driver, pointing to a U.S. military base, was quoted in the West German press: "Those are not soldiers. That is an undisciplined mass of bums."[14] Is there then discrimination against GIs in West Germany? Yes, indeed, though by the army's own count, there were, by late 1982, only 110 establishments in the entire country that practiced discrimination consistently, most near military bases. Does the fault lie mainly with the prejudice of small-minded Germans? The reader may draw his or her own conclusions.

Sociological Distance

The reasons for increasing discrimination against service personnel must be sought not only in the specific reasons of particular Germans who discriminate, but also in the wider, more complex sociological circumstances of the American military presence in Germany in recent years. From the mid-1950s until the late 1960s, the German population not only welcomed the U.S. military presence in general, but even the individual soldier carried a certain celebrity status as a protector of the country's security, member of the finest military establishment in the world, and friend from that fascinating country that served as West Germany's closest ally. In the late 1960s, with the deep controversy over the Vietnam War and the decline in the quality of U.S. forces in West Germany that resulted from the war, distance began to develop between the West Germans and the U.S. military. Rising crime and indiscipline in the early 1970s eroded the bedrock of respect the West Germans had long had for U.S. forces and produced, perhaps for the first time since the occupation, a certain animosity between Germans and U.S. military personnel. The switch in 1973 from military forces based on the draft to the all-volunteer force caused further confusion and a tendency on the part of the West Germans to question the credibility of the new forces. Hence, the sociological "distance" between West Germans and U.S. service personnel widened, rather than narrowed, during the decade of the 1970s, despite the military's success in reforming the force structure and instituting a higher level of discipline. A new wave of disciplinary problems in the early 1980s served only to increase the sense of estrangement.

This sociological distance has led to a kind of cultural isolation for U.S. service personnel that, though not new, is deeper and more profound than it has been at any time since the 1950s. The cultural isolation is greater for black service personnel than for their white counterparts, at a time when the percentage of blacks in the military in West Germany is far higher than it was a decade ago. Even the white soldiers of the AVF, however, are drawn from the lower socioeconomic strata of the U.S. population and are therefore less able to comprehend and appreciate the cultural differences between West Germany and the United States.[15] In contrast to the soldiers of the 1950s and 1960s, many of whom traveled around Germany extensively, learned some German, and made friends among the German population, soldiers in the 1980s are more likely to become "barracks rats," spending all their free time on base and rarely venturing out into a perceived hostile, foreign environment. The cultural barriers often seem to be impenetrable. As the *International Herald Tribune* described the situation in Fulda,

> It is difficult for the Americans to break out of the isolation of their whitewashed barracks, to cross the cultural barriers that separate black ghetto youths from the Catholic burghers of Fulda. . . . There are more subtle barriers, too. A young soldier may take his wife out for a night on the town in a pair of jeans and a loud sport shirt. Fulda's inhabitants are conservative and the Hotel Lenz, which GIs have complained about repeatedly, has a sign in German that says: "We Don't Require Medals Here but We Do Insist on Coat and Tie."[16]

The growing distance between Germans and U.S. service personnel has also been described in the West German press. According to an editorial in the *Stuttgarter Nachrichten,*

> Indeed these individual, very destructive acts of discrimination against human beings, who by their presence here render a decisive contribution to our security, are in reality the most extreme expression of an unhealthy distance, which separates German citizens from American soldiers. The

problem becomes clear to anyone who speaks with American soldiers. For the GI's Germany is a strange world, strange most particularly by virtue of the greater distance which [German] people observe in their interpersonal relationships. In America one comes into contact with others much more easily, though as a rule contacts are much more superficial. When, in addition, the language barrier is brought to bear, the American soldiers often withdraw into the ghettos of their barracks.[17]

The phenomenon of cultural isolation has been made more severe in recent years by increasing divergence in the value structures of youth populations in West Germany and the United States. West German youth in general lean somewhat more to the left in terms of contemporary cultural and social values than do their U.S. counterparts. Environmental concerns, objections to nuclear energy plants, and cynicism in regard to major social institutions are more pronounced among young people in the Federal Republic than in the United States. Camaraderie is less extensive than it was in the 1950s and 1960s. Even at major rock concerts, the once universal medium of communication, American youth in the FRG now tend to remain segregated from their more numerous German hosts, even when the performers are American. Young West Germans no longer imitate the dress codes, popular slang, or mannerisms of young Americans as they did years ago.

Lacking camaraderie and easy crossover, U.S. service personnel are naturally more conscious of their cultural isolation. This is accentuated by widespread German perceptions of AVF personnel as representing the lowest strata of the youth population of the United States, the "losers" who had nowhere else to go but into the military, an option deemed wholly undesirable by many German young people. AVF soldiers, often proud of their decision to join the ranks of the military forces, discover, to their dismay, that this decision commands scorn rather than respect from the majority of West Germans their age. According to *Die Welt:*

> The climate is not like it used to be, young people explain, since the U.S. army has consisted only of volunteers. Nowadays a young person in this country is very mistrustful of someone who voluntarily joined the army. This change plays a very great role in reality. The soldiers are on the average younger than previously. They belong mostly to the lower social strata. There are many more blacks, many more women. And they remain longer in Germany, as a rule three years. And many bring their families along, before they can actually afford it in terms of rank and salary.[18]

The problem of isolation is compounded by the language barrier. Among the lower ranks of enlisted personnel, few are able to speak any German at all; most never even give it a try. The most common German words uttered by soldiers tend to be *Fräulein* (girl), *Geld* (money), *Bier* (beer), and *ins Bett gehen* (go to bed). Without a rudimentary knowledge of common street German, GIs are afraid, often unnecessarily, to venture out into West German communities beyond the well-known military hangouts, thus making their sense of cultural isolation complete. In respect to language capability, German expectations appear to have changed somewhat in recent years. In the 1950s and 1960s, it was taken for granted that U.S. service personnel would be able to speak very little German. In those years, however, West German young people were anxious to learn English and to practice their schoolbook English with U.S. soldiers. That is no longer true. The increasing estrangement between German and American youth has also meant that English is no longer as popular among young West Germans as it once was.

In addition, the FRG's rise to the status of a great power and its search for respect and identity have created a situation in which West Germans often expect Americans, even military personnel, to make an attempt to learn some German and to communicate simple requests in the native language of their host country. The West German press is replete with comments that demonstrate a certain impatience with the inadequate language facility of U.S. military personnel. One example from the *Stuttgarter Zeitung:* "This is the reality for the lower ranks, as far as German-American relations are concerned: there are hardly any relations at all. Reasons: the language barriers, because—particularly since the U.S. Army has become an all-volunteer army—hardly a boy comes across the Atlantic who has heard a German word, except for 'sauerkraut,' or 'kindergarten,' or 'Hofbräuhaus.'"[19]

In this area, the U.S. military must begin to make a greater effort. It is of course true, as any commander will affirm, that the military mission is not to teach language and culture. The expense of language training and the time and resources diverted from other, more pressing needs tend to diminish the military's enthusiasm for language programs. Indeed, as military authorities point out, substantial language programs are available on most military bases for any soldier who wishes to enroll. These efforts by the military are to be commended. But there is also a need for the military to be much more sensitized to its diplomatic and representational functions in Germany, which in the long run are the foundation stones upon which the strictly military mission must rest. If discrimination against U.S. service personnel is to be diminished, if respect for the military establishment is to be gained, then much more attention must be paid to training in the areas of culture and language. More could be done to emphasize, before service personnel depart for the foreign assignment, that familiarity with German will be a major key to a successful period of assignment in the Federal Republic. Direct encouragement and incentives, such as pay bonuses or provision of free time, could be granted to service personnel who acquire a certain level of fluency in German. It cannot be overemphasized how much the image of the U.S. military in Germany could be improved if a large percentage of soldiers could speak rudimentary German. A new reservoir of respect from German peers could be tapped, and the fear of cultural isolation could be diminished substantially. Language being the key to culture, language training could also be a vehicle for acquiring greater cultural sensitivity. And cultural sensitivity may be, in the final analysis, a master element upon which the continuation of the U.S. military presence in Germany depends.

U.S. audiences also need to be made aware that to a very great extent the cultural isolation of enlisted personnel is self-imposed. There are over 6,000 German-American friendship clubs in West Germany that sponsor get-togethers, recreational activities, and invitations to German homes for U.S. service personnel. Some of these activities have withered in recent years for lack of American takers. The cultural milieu of the barracks rats is a function both of the quality of AVF recruits and of the lack of cultural initiative they bring with them to West Germany. But not all soldiers are barracks rats. Even among the eighteen- and nineteen-year-olds, many make it a point to learn some German, view the artworks in the local museum, investigate the architecture of the cathedral, walk in baroque gardens, and attend concerts of the symphony orchestra. The stories of many soldiers with that extra *savoir faire* attest to the fact that any soldier who wishes to make the effort may easily enough form sound new friendships with German young people and enjoy an exhilarating life in West Germany.

One example may suffice to illustrate the point. Roger, an eighteen-year-old soldier from Atlanta, was stationed at McNair Barracks in Berlin in the early 1980s. During his first month in Berlin he toured all parts of the city, joined a German-American friendship club, and enrolled in a German language class. Within a few weeks he had formed several good friendships with West Germans his age, both male and female. From that time on all his holidays were spent in German homes, and most of his off-duty hours were taken up with activities with German friends. He attended the opera, which he had never seen before, and developed a penchant for the performances of the Berlin Philharmonic. He joined the base theater group, invited his friends to the performances, and with his friends attended performances at all of Berlin's major theaters. He was invited to join a German bowling club, which met every Wednesday evening. During his first two years in Germany he toured several countries in Western Europe with a combination of German and American friends.

As might be expected, he loved Germany and thought that his assignment in Berlin had been the best thing that ever happened to him.[20]

Unfortunately, for every Roger, there are probably twenty or more barracks rats, who spend the bulk of their off-duty time in the barracks drinking and listening to music. The comments of the barracks rats in the local canteen at McNair might evoke from a listener a mixture of pity and contempt. They hate "stupid Berlin," one of the Western world's most exciting cities. The world of the opera, the symphony, the theater they will never experience, nor will they ever enjoy the companionship or sense of cultural exhilaration that could come from close friendships with young Germans. And they will never give it a try. Their world is that of crap games in the barracks with six-packs of beer. The only part of Berlin they know is the seedy Potsdamer Strasse with its multitude of red-light houses and lonely GI bars, where young punk Germans wait for a good fight—a human tragedy of major dimensions! Yet all the lectures in the world and all the exhortations of commanders will not enlarge the dimensions of their small, drab world. The wonder of Berlin is waiting, and there are many German young people who would be delighted to meet young Americans and become intercultural friends. But the sense of personal responsibility, indeed even the curiosity to experience another culture, is entirely lacking. The scenario is repeated in cities and towns all across southern Germany. One need not be in Berlin to enjoy West Germany. Even Fulda and Idar-Oberstein are loaded with old world charm and crowded with citizens who would welcome a U.S. soldier into their homes.

The changed economic circumstances of the U.S. military forces also contribute to the problem of discrimination. In previous decades the U.S. military presence was much more important to the German economy than it is today. With a healthy exchange rate of 4.20 West German marks to the dollar, GIs in the Federal Republic were for twenty-five years comparatively well off, with substantial amounts of money to spend on the local economy. With the simultaneous rise of German purchasing power and the fall of the dollar exchange rate during the intervening fifteen years, GI patronage and money are no longer needed and, in many cases, are counterbalanced by the perceived pernicious effects that military patronage might have on local establishments. The days when GIs handed out candy to German children and escorted beautiful young German women to the most expensive restaurants and clubs in town are now only a faded memory. There is no doubt that the increased poverty of GIs has heightened the sense of cultural isolation. Especially for married soldiers with children, spending a night on the town and dining in a local restaurant is out of reach except on special occasions. GI money is no longer important to most German businesspeople and this increases the tendency of proprietors to discriminate against U.S. service personnel.

It is not inappropriate to suggest that part of the poverty problem, like cultural isolation, is self-inflicted by GIs. The problem is exaggerated in many cases by poor budgeting practices. It is simply not necessary for service personnel to have lots of excess cash to enjoy certain sectors of the good life in West Germany. Free concerts in public parks, reduced admission prices at museums, and many interesting activities sponsored by German-American clubs are never taken advantage of by GIs who prefer to complain while guzzling beer at the local base club. There are small inns, country restaurants, and cozy *gaststätte* in every city and town in Germany where GIs with proper decorum would be welcome at any time. Though GI poverty has had a pernicious effect on morale, it is by no means a root cause of discrimination against service personnel in Germany, especially since the dramatic rise in the exchange rate of the dollar in 1983 and 1984.

The pacifist, anti-war movement in West Germany is yet another factor that has increased the distance between Germans and U.S. military personnel in recent years. Most particularly, the rise of the Green party since 1979 and the movement to block the stationing of Pershing II and Cruise missiles in the FRG have embittered relations between young Germans and U.S. soldiers. Anti-war sentiment thrives most particularly among the younger generation and creates a tone and an atmosphere of misunderstanding between U.S. GIs and their younger hosts. Whereas U.S. soldiers are likely to view their primary mission in West Germany as defense of the country against Soviet aggression, younger West Germans may well view the soldiers as the vanguard of U.S. war-mongering. According to the *Frankfurter Rundschau,* "The tensions between Bonn and Washington over nuclear weapons policy have served to increase the antipathy of West Germans toward U.S. soldiers. Many supporters of the anti-nuclear-weapons movement view the Americans as nothing more than an occupying power. . . . From such circumstances American GI's can only conclude that they are outcasts in a country which they must defend."[21] The problem of discrimination does not arise primarily from this antipathy, though it is probably exacerbated by it. The proprietors of most public establishments are older Germans, who are less likely to share the pacifist sentiments of their younger compatriots. Nevertheless, to the extent that the pacifist, anti-war movement in Germany does create a mood unfriendly or hostile to the U.S. military presence, it augments the problem of discrimination against GIs.

Finally, the German legal system does not contain the multiple remedies against discrimination that Americans have long taken for granted. The Basic Law of the Federal Repubic does contain blanket prohibitions against all forms of discrimination based on religion, age, sex, color, or national origin. German courts have been vigorous in their protection of citizens' rights. Nevertheless, the extensive case law built up over many years' time in reference to discrimination cases in the United States finds no counterpart in West Germany. The proprietor of any West German establishment has a nearly absolute right to refuse service to a particular customer for any reason whatever, unless it can clearly be shown that refusal of service was based on patent discrimination against a particular group on a basis forbidden by the Basic Law. The burden of proof rests with the plaintiff in civil law cases. The claim by a German proprietor that he had reason to believe that a particular customer would cause trouble or disturb the good order of his establishment, especially if the claim is coupled with a demonstration that the establishment had previously been disturbed by like persons, is usually enough for courts to rule in favor of the proprietor.[22] Hence, the few legal challenges U.S. military authorities have mounted against proprietors who discriminate against service personnel have been, for the most part, unavailing. This complicates the problem for U.S. authorities by augmenting impressions that discrimination against GIs is deeply rooted in German society and that U.S. authorities are powerless to do anything about it.

Efforts to Combat Discrimination

The discrimination issue poses an almost insoluble information policy problem for U.S. military headquarters in the FRG. If top command echelons indicate that off-post discrimination is widespread, it serves to convince soldiers that their perceptions of discrimination are valid, and morale is adversely affected. Furthermore, this adds fuel to the fire that U.S. news media have already built on the issue and adds to anti-German feelings in Congress. On the other hand, if GIs come to believe that their leaders are downplaying or ignoring a problem that affects them and their innermost feelings of self-esteem, the impact on troop morale may be even worse. If the attitude of headquarters is perceived as benign neglect, the effects upon troop morale could be devastating.[23] In addition, military leaders face a delicate diplomatic situation in taking up the problem with West German political leaders. These leaders are dismayed if they feel the problem is being blown out of proportion by the Americans. It is not, after all, a problem of widespread dimensions, and the Germans are highly sensitive to accusations of racism. At the same time, however, German leaders must be made to face up to the problem as it really exists and must understand the negative effects of discrimination upon the morale of U.S. troops. According to a spokesperson at army headquarters in Heidelberg,

There is very solid evidence that when the U.S. military community commander makes the reduction of discrimination a front burner issue and when local German political authorities are willing to expend some of their political clout to exert the pressure of moral suasion on local owners of public accommodations, the number of owner/operator designated off limit establishments can be reduced to a minimum. There is a sufficient number of success stories to make it appear that the problem can be controlled if all the players are willing to spend the time, the effort and the political price that it costs to get these places opened up and to remain open.[24]

The reaction of West German political leaders to the discrimination problem has been, on the whole, positive and forthright. Some German leaders tend to be defensive and attempt to rationalize the situation by pointing out that part of the problem is self-created by the poor behavior of U.S. troops. Even Chancellor Helmut Schmidt was quoted as having said, in the spring of 1982, that even though discrimination affected black soldiers much more than whites, "I do not believe, to be sure, that this is exclusively a German phenomenon."[25] The owner of a popular club in Frankfurt added his own analysis of the real causes of discrimination: "They have terrible race problems in the United States, and they export them to us in Germany."[26] Such defensiveness is understandable, if not excusable. People accused of nefarious behavior are likely to invent rationalizations and defenses as palliatives for their own consciences. These have not, however, been the typical reactions of German leaders. Especially at the local level, many leaders and citizens' groups have attempted to tackle the discrimination problem head on.

A few examples may serve to illustrate some of the steps that have been taken. In Bayreuth, a group of citizens, at the urging of a lieutenant colonel of the Bundeswehr, circulated a highly successful petition calling on all establishments to cease discrimination against U.S. military personnel. In Augsburg, the city administration joined forces with the local hotel and restaurant association and the local American military commander in taking action to end discrimination by individual proprietors. The city of Karlsruhe passed a new local ordinance making it illegal to refuse to serve military personnel in public establishments.[27] The case of Stuttgart deserves special mention because of the tireless efforts of the mayor, Manfred Rommel, to combat discrimination in all forms. Mayor Rommel, son of the famous "Desert Fox" of World War II fame, took it upon himself to visit personally every establishment in the city known to discriminate against military personnel. If personal persuasion was unavailing, he requested the sympathetic city council to revoke the licenses of offending establishments and threatened them with civil suits in court. His efforts brought dramatic results. The number of establishments that refused service to GIs dwindled considerably between 1980 and 1982.[28] In the spring of 1982 the newspaper *Stars and Stripes* awarded a special citation of merit to the highly respected mayor. According to a military spokesman, "Mayor Rommel stands out as a shining example of a man who was willing to commit his career and personal prestige to the cause of improving German-American relations. All of us consider him an excellent administrator and a good friend. He has done more than anyone else we know to cement a real friendship between Germans and American military personnel."[29]

The German Hotel and Restaurant Association (DEHOGA) has also been active in working against discrimination. The association strongly recommended to all its members in the summer of 1982 that no signs discouraging patronage by foreigners be posted in windows and that members actively discourage all forms of discrimination.[30] Even members of the German Federal Parliament have made unusual efforts to combat discrimination. When Peter-Kurt Wurzbach, CDU deputy and respected expert on defense, heard the news that two black U.S. soldiers had been asked to leave a restaurant in Aschaffenburg, he promptly invited the two soldiers to spend a weekend at his home. At the June 1982 memorial service to commemorate the June 17, 1953, uprising in East Germany, he seated the two young soldiers as guests of honor on the dais of the Bundestag assembly hall. Later the same day the soldiers were again seated as guests of honor at a memorial service at the zonal border near Ratzeburg. Mr. Wurzbach then accompanied the soldiers to several restaurants in Bonn and Schleswig-Holstein. As the men entered one small restaurant to drink a fast cup of coffee, they were given a spontaneous pat on the shoulder by an elderly German gentleman. "I just wanted to do what I could to correct the distorted picture these two soldiers had of the Federal Republic," Mr. Wurzbach said.[31]

As a counterpoint to those proprietors who discriminate, we ought not forget people like Rudi Franke, and there are many such people. In his cozy restaurant, the Winzerstube in Heidelberg-Kirchheim, GIs, black and white, young and old, are welcomed with open arms and accorded friendly service as a matter of house policy. If tipsy soldiers tend to imbibe too much or get overly raucous, Rudi intervenes in a firm, but fatherly manner. Asked why he encourages U.S. military personnel to patronize hs establishment, Rudi says,

> We dare not forget whom we have to thank in the first place for our contemporary standard of living and our security. Does no one remember the Marshal Plan, the reconstruction of our industry, and the humanitarian help that came from America? In an emergency we expect that the boys

from the USA will defend us. And they risk their lives for that. . . . We ought to set an example for the Americans through personal contacts.[32]

Stories of discrimination against Americans in Germany make eye-catching headlines and good copy. Stories about proprietors like Rudi Franke rarely get printed. According to a spokesperson at army headquarters,

> We need to try to convince the news media to publicize the success stories as well as the bad news, because it simply is not true that U.S. troops are unwelcome in Germany. There is a plethora of evidence from scientific opinion surveys that Germans like Americans and would deplore the departure of American troops from their country. It is important that this information be provided convincingly to our troops, and to opinion molders in the United States.[33]

Is West Germany a Racist Society?

We have discussed the major reasons for discrimination, societal and personal. Even though white U.S. military personal register a higher incidence of discrimination than blacks, we may still assume that blacks often perceive an invidious element of racism whenever they encounter West German discrimination, simply because of the racial difference between blacks and most Germans. We have seen that black soldiers suffer much more from discrimination than their white colleagues. All of this begs what is perhaps the master question: Is West Germany an inherently racist society, where black U.S. soldiers are bound to suffer from discrimination, no matter what official policy is? There are no pat answers, and "racist" is a term that easily lends itself to polemics by any group with an axe to grind. There is, however, much evidence to indicate that Germany is certainly no more racist than the United States, and probably less so. The Germans, as a people, are neither angels nor beasts. Like other nationalities, they are proud, at times arrogant, suspicious of too many foreigners, and protective of revered traditions and the "national way of life."

Studies of West German political culture indicate that the orientations and behavior patterns that support a healthy democracy, individualism, and social responsibility have taken firm root in the postwar period.[34] German reactions to the great influx of foreign workers in the 1970s have not been materially unlike reactions to the influx of Hispanics and Asians into the United States. Germans have never had much exposure to blacks. There is no significant African population in West Germany, and until recent years, blacks comprised a small minority of foreign troops stationed in the FRG. Unfamiliarity often breeds suspicion and distrust. West Germans have, however, built a society that is surprisingly tolerant and accepting of ethnic minorities. The weight of the tragic history of racial and ethnic genocide during the Third Reich has had profound effects on postwar generations. Germans seem to be more conscious than other West Europeans of attitudes that could be viewed by outsiders as small-minded or petty. The careful observer often gets the impression that most Germans work very hard to be, or at least to appear, tolerant and open-minded. The younger generations of West Germans, especially, make a great effort to be viewed by the rest of the world as liberal, informed, and egalitarian.

Public opinion studies reveal that most West Germans do not harbor negative attitudes about black U.S. soldiers. A review of three of the tables appended to Chapter 12 lends credence to this conclusion. Only 1% of those polled believed that a large number of black soldiers in the U.S. Army diminished the army's ability to defend the Federal Republic (see Table 12.2). An overwhelming majority of 87% rejected that view, and only 12% were undecided or declined to answer. The data in Table 12.3 show that only 4% of the respondents registered an objection to a black U.S. military family living in the apartment or house next door. A decisive 93% said that they would have no objection. The results were strikingly similar when the West Germans were asked if they would have any objection if a white U.S. military family moved into the apartment or house next door (Table 12.4). The data in the three tables, considered together, should dispel notions that rampant racism is the root of the discrimination problem against U.S. military personnel in the Federal Republic.

At the same time, however, the problem of discrimination against U.S. service personnel in Germany is real, and it is true that blacks in particular are sometimes singled out as the subjects of such discrimination. It is possible, though unlikely, that racist attitudes are more prevalent in West Germany than is revealed in the survey data. Most Germans have not had much personal contact with black soldiers, and most are quite cognizant of the riots that occurred in black sections of U.S. cities in the 1960s. Discrimination is obnoxious behavior whenever and wherever it happens, and it has a very deleterious effect upon the morale of U.S. troops, especially among blacks. Military authorities are correct in giving high priority to combatting discrimination in all cases and all forms in Germany and in putting pressure upon German authorities to do everything possible to eliminate the problem.

What must not be overlooked is that the problem has been blown all out of proportion by the U.S. media. A report by Dan Rather on the CBS Evening News in late May 1982 and an article in *Newsweek* in May

1982, entitled "The American Outcasts," have led U.S. audiences to believe that most U.S. service personnel suffer from rampant discrimination in Germany all the time. This portrait simply does not square with the facts. It has the effect also of raising the level of anti-German sentiment in the Congress and lends impetus to the movement in Congress to withdraw U.S. troops.

The other side of the story must be emphasized to U.S. audiences. Discrimination against service personnel is sporadic, concentrated in certain places where there is a huge U.S. military presence and practiced by a small minority of German establishments. West Germans overwhelmingly approve of the presence of U.S. troops, and most Germans welcome contact and friendship with U.S. soldiers. When discrimination does occur, it is occasioned by the profound cultural insensitivity and obnoxious behavior of U.S. troops as much as it is by the small-mindedness of hateful or racist Germans.

Notes

1. See, for instance, the *International Herald Tribune*, March 30, 1976.
2. *Die Welt*, November 13, 1981.
3. *International Herald Tribune*, March 30, 1976.
4. *Die Welt*, November 13, 1981.
5. *Frankfurter Allgemeine*, July 8, 1982.
6. *Mannheimer Morgen*, April 27, 1982.
7. *Die Welt*, November 13, 1981; *Mannheimer Morgen*, April 27, 1982.
8. *Welt am Sonntag*, June 13, 1982.
9. *Frankfurter Rundschau*, May 27, 1982.
10. *The Week in Germany*, vol. 15, no. 7 (February 17, 1984), p. 5.
11. *Die Welt*, November 13, 1981.
12. *Ibid.*
13. Interview with German proprietor, Frankfurt, September 1982.
14. *Neue Rhein Ruhr Zeitung* (Essen/Köln), August 12, 1982.
15. According to Moskos, " . . . the army is not only attracting a disproportionate number of minorities, but also an unrepresentative segment of white youth who, if anything, are even more uncharacteristic of the broader mix than are our minority soldiers." Charles C. Moskos, Jr., "Making the All-Volunteer Force Work," in William J. Taylor, Jr., Eric T. Olson, and Richard A. Schrader, eds., *Defense Manpower Planning: Issues for the 1980s* (Elmsford, New York: Pergamon Press, 1981), p. 229.
16. *International Herald Tribune*, March 30, 1976.
17. *Stuttgarter Nachrichten*, July 31, 1982.
18. *Die Welt*, November 13, 1981.
19. *Stuttgarter Zeitung*, August 2, 1980.
20. Extracted from one of many interviews with soldiers in Berlin in 1980.
21. *Frankfurter Rundschau*, May 27, 1982.

22. See, for instance, cases described in *Welt am Sonntag* (Hamburg/Essen), June 13, 1982; and *Rheinische Post* (Düsseldorf), July 15, 1982.

23. Interview with Benton G. Moeller, political affairs analyst, Wartime Host Nation Support Unit, USAREUR headquarters, Heidelberg, September 7, 1982.

24. Ibid.

25. *Frankfurter Rundschau,* May 27, 1982.

26. Ibid.

27. *Südwest Presse* (Ulm), September 12, 1980.

28. *Mannheimer Morgen,* April 27, 1982.

29. Interview with Dr. Robert C. Larson, United States Forces Liaison Officer for Baden-Württemberg, Stuttgart, September 19, 1982.

30. *Rheinische Post* (Düsseldorf), July 15, 1982.

31. *Hamburger Abendblatt,* June 19, 1982.

32. *Neue Rhein Ruhr Zeitung* (Essen/Köln), August 10, 1982.

33. Interview with Benton G. Moeller, September 7, 1982.

34. See, for instance, Kendall L. Baker, Russell J. Dalton, and Kai Hildebrandt, *Germany Transformed: Political Culture and the New Politics* (Cambridge, Mass.: Harvard University Press, 1981); David Childs and Jeffrey Johnson, *West Germany: Politics and Society* (New York: St. Martin's Press, 1981).

Table 8.1. Subject of Discrimination Within the Last Six Months,
           By Rank and Race (Percent)

	Officers		Enlisted	
	Blacks	Whites	Blacks	Whites
3 or More Times	14.8	21.0	5.5	16.9
1-2 Times	17.9	22.2	9.6	20.1
None	67.3	56.8	84.8	63.0

Source: Constructed from USAREUR Personnel Opinion Survey, Winter
        1982. Data supplied by Office of Deputy Chief of Staff,
        Personnel; Headquarters, United States Army, Europe;
        Heidelberg, Germany.

9

Terrorism

In the mid-1980s, U.S. military forces stationed in West Germany were again the target of several brutal terrorist attacks. On August 8, 1985, a car bomb exploded outside the headquarters building at the Rhein-Main Air Base, killing two Americans and wounding twenty people, both Americans and West Germans.[1] The incident was the most serious attack on a U.S. installation since the bombing of Ramstein Air Base in 1981, when twenty-two people were wounded. A few days after the Rhein-Main attack, the Red Army Faction claimed responsibility in a letter sent to the Frankfurt office of the British news agency Reuters.[2] Equally chilling was the terrorist attack on the La Belle Club, a discotheque popular among U.S. military personnel in West Berlin, on April 5, 1986. The explosion killed a U.S. soldier and a Turkish woman and left two hundred and thirty others burned and wounded. A Jordanian arrested on suspicion of involvement in the West Berlin bombing had, according to West German government representatives, clear ties to the Qaddafi regime in Libya.[3]

A History of Terrorist Attacks in West Germany

U.S. forces in West Germany have been subject to terrorist attacks repeatedly over the last decade and a half. Our purpose here is not to probe the complex causes and effects of terrorism, a subject treated in a burgeoning, steadily more sophisticated literature in recent years. Rather, what we seek to do here is to review the history of terrorist attacks in the Federal Republic since the early 1970s and to understand how terrorism affects the morale of U.S. forces and hence the texture of U.S.-German politico-military relations.

Isolated attacks against U.S. military installations and personnel by disgruntled West Germans have been occurring for many years. Most of these incidents were, however, mild by contemporary standards and did not result in loss of life or substantial property damage. Even in the 1950s and 1960s, automobiles of U.S. military personnel were occasionally vandalized, fires were set within or near military installations, bricks were thrown through windows, or minor explosions were detonated. These incidents were infrequent, not part of a systematic pattern, and not threatening enough to cause security precautions to be increased. It was not until the early 1970s that terrorism became a coordinated, systematic phenomenon and a real threat to the safety and well-being of U.S. forces.

Terrorism became a subject of major concern in West Germany with the rise in the early 1970s of radical, violent groups, whose purpose was to disrupt the social fabric of the country, destabilize its political institutions, and interrupt the alliance relationship between the FRG and the United States. The best known and most dangerous of the terrorist groups was the infamous Baader-Meinhof gang, named after its two major leaders, Andreas Baader and Ulricke Meinhof. At its peak, in the mid-1970s, the group consisted of perhaps as many as several dozen hard-core terrorists, an outer ring of a hundred or so co-conspirators, and several hundred more sympathizers. The Baader-Meinhof gang and other terrorist groups had, as their first targets, mainly German political and opinion leaders, business magnates, and industrial plants symbolic of the military-industrial complex.

As their strategies developed and their methods were refined into more deadly instruments, the terrorists turned their fury also toward the U.S. military presence. The first major attack occurred in May of 1972 when three powerful bombs exploded at the headquarters of Fifth Corps in Frankfurt, the former I. G. Farben building. One high-ranking officer, Lieutenant Colonel Paul A. Bloomquist, was killed, and thirteen other people were seriously injured. Responsibility for the attack was claimed by the "Kommando Petra Schelm," a unit of the Red Army Faction, as an assault against U.S. imperialism and as retaliation for the U.S. bombing of North Vietnam. A short time later army headquarters in Heidelberg were bombed, killing three soldiers and seriously wounding six. The Baader-Meinhof group, a close ally of the Red Army Faction, claimed responsibility for the second attack. The ferocious attacks were orchestrated to demonstrate the muscle of the terrorist organizations. Both occurred at high-ranking headquarters installations, the second at the nerve center of the U.S. military complex in West Germany, bringing the message that the terrorists were prepared to strike with ferocity at the very centers of the military organization.[4]

Less dramatic incidents of terrorism continued in 1973 and 1974, though during this period terrorist activity seemed to be aimed more at West German than U.S. targets. Three cities seemed especially to be centers of terrorist organization and activity: Frankfurt, Heidelberg, and Berlin. Frankfurt served as a center of ceaseless pamphleteering against the so-called evils and atrocities of U.S. imperialism. In February 1974,

German police searched a suspected terrorist house in Berlin and found hand grenades, mines, and automatic weapons, together with a list of names of U.S. generals as targets of assassination and detailed maps of U.S. military buildings in Berlin.[5] In March 1974, the West German press printed an interview with U.S. military representatives that expressed fear that "at any time direct aggression could be expected against American installations and personnel." The report also alleged that U.S. military leaders were planning to set up new special units to combat West German terrorists.[6] Following lively discussions in the press over whether such units adhered to prevailing NATO treaties or whether they might lead to illegal abuses against either Germans or Americans resident in West Germany, the report was strongly denied by the West German government.[7] A few months later, however, in June and again in November, spokespeople at military headquarters in Heidelberg admitted that the army conducted ongoing surveillance against radical U.S. organizations throughout West Germany and in West Berlin. U.S. military authorities feared collusion between German terrorist groups and U.S. radical groups based in West Germany. Obviously, the U.S. military could not conduct any surveillance against Germans; hence, they were restricted to surveillance of Americans. The surveillance measures were defended as fully within constitutional guidelines and as absolutely necessary for the security of U.S. forces in Germany.[8]

The issue of surveillance became more nettlesome when court suits were filed against military authorities by leftist U.S. groups based in West Germany. The suit that attracted the greatest attention was filed by the Lawyers Military Defense Committee, an affiliate of the American Civil Liberties Union and one of the many leftist groups based in the politically active city of Heidelberg. The suit, brought on behalf of twenty U.S. citizens, claimed that the army since 1972 had maintained illegal surveillance, including wiretaps, over many Americans resident in West Germany. The civilians in the case were organizers of an array of antiwar activities and were clearly committed opponents of the U.S. military establishment. In March 1976, a U.S. district judge in Washington ruled that the army must obtain a court warrant before wiretapping U.S. civilians abroad and opened the way for attorneys of the plaintiffs to obtain depositions from high officers alleged to have authorized the surveillance.[9] Though the ruling clearly protected the rights of Americans to protest and dissent, it had the effect of weakening the military's effort to gain information about or infiltrate radical American groups that might aid or abet West German terrorist groups in attacking military targets.

The next major terrorist attack occurred in June 1976, the fourth anniversary of the arrest of Andreas Baader, while the much-heralded Stammheimer court proceedings were still in progress against persons accused of the first major attack four years earlier. Two powerful bombs exploded once again at Fifth Corps headquarters in Frankfurt, one in the service and shopping area where large crowds usually gathered, the other in the Terrace Officers Club, 100 meters behind the main headquarters building. Thirteen Americans and one German suffered serious injuries in the explosions, which were heard three kilometers away at the studios of Hesse Radio. Simultaneously a bomb went off in Hamburg in an unsuccessful attempt to assassinate a judge who had meted out long prison sentences against convicted Baader-Meinhof terrorists.[10] A few months later, in December 1976, a bomb explosion totally demolished the Officers Club at the sprawling Rhein-Main Air Base near Frankfurt. Miraculously only three Americans were injured, none seriously.[11]

During the following three years, from 1976 to 1979, the U.S. military managed to foil or preclude spectacular terrorist attacks. Increased security precautions at all military installations in West Germany made terrorist attacks more difficult to plan and execute. Nevertheless, in 1979 terrorists attempted unsuccessfully to assassinate General Alexander Haig, NATO Supreme Commander, when a bomb was detonated under a bridge in Casteau, Belgium, as the general was being driven across. Haig's life was spared by a misfiring of only a few seconds.

By the late 1970s and early 1980s, many people assumed that terrorism was on the wane in West Germany. The unceasing efforts of the West German police and security organs seemed to have broken the back of the major terrorist groups and to have brought the problem under control. Many of the most-wanted terrorists had been incarcerated, and large-scale terrorist attacks had become few and far between. Despite great progress, however, military authorities learned in 1981 that the smaller, rump terrorist groups could still wreak major havoc. Ten violent incidents against U.S. forces occurred in the first nine months of 1981, five in a three-week period beginning in late August. On August 31, a huge bomb exploded at the headquarters of the U.S. Air Forces Europe at Ramstein Air Base. Twenty U.S. service personnel and two West German civilian workers were seriously injured, and property damage was immense. A short time later a second, unexploded bomb was discovered inside the headquarters building, apparently knocked into the building by the force of the first explosion. The Red Army Faction claimed responsibility.[12]

Two weeks later, on September 15, 1981, a spectacular attempt was made to assassinate General Frederick J. Kroesen, commander in chief of USAREUR and commander of the Central Army Group (CENTAG) in NATO. The ambush attack occurred in the early morning hours as General Kroesen, with his wife and adjutant, was being driven into Heidelberg on the highway alongside the Neckar River from his home east of the city. The terrorists fired two rocket-propelled antitank missiles and a volley of bullets at the armor-plated Mercedes sedan. The projectiles came from about 200 yards away, halfway up a wooded hillside, where police later found equipment used in the attack, sleeping bags, food, a radio transmitter and a Soviet-made, RPG-7V antitank rocket launcher. One of the missiles pierced the car's trunk, blasting the lid up and shattering the rear window. The second missile dug a foot-deep hole a couple of yards to the car's rear. Miraculously, Kroesen and his wife suffered only scratches, and the adjutant and the driver, a plainclothes West German police officer, were unharmed.[13] "They have declared war on us," General Kroesen said at a brief news conference three hours after the attack. "First Ramstein, and now this," added another officer.[14] In a letter to the *Frankfurter Rundschau*, the Red Army Faction claimed responsibility and urged further attacks on "the centers, bases and strategists of the American military machine." The letter described Kroesen as one of the generals who "really controls the imperialist policy from Western Europe to the Gulf because he decides the deployment and the means of the confrontation."[15] The day after the attack on General Kroesen, terrorists planted two bombs on a rail spur line used to supply the Rhein-Main Air Base. The explosive devices were discovered about a mile from the base and were defused by police.

Terrorist attacks continued sporadically, though none were as daring as the Ramstein and Heidelberg attacks. In the first eight months of 1982 army officials counted thirty-six terrorist attacks on U.S. army targets. The pace of attacks increased in the final months of the year. Numerous bombings and arson attacks occurred in the Frankfurt area, causing thousands of dollars of damage to cars and buildings. In late October, terrorists damaged twenty-three cars owned by service personnel in Karlsruhe and spray-painted the words "U.S. Pig" on a wall.[16] Despite the arrest in November of three leaders of the Red Army Faction, three terrorist attacks were mounted in the week of December 10–17, all car-bombing incidents undertaken by the so-called "Revolutionary Cells," a group of loosely organized units that appeared to be a spin-off of the Red Army Faction. According to West German Interior Minister Friedrich Zimmermann, "It could be that we are dealing with a new kind of violence."[17] Terrorist attacks declined somewhat in 1983, 1984, and the first half of 1985. Though bombings of cars and buildings continued sporadically, with major property damage suffered several times, there were no further lives lost in terrorist incidents until the car-bomb attack at Rhein-Main Air Base in August 1985.

A matter of special concern for military authorities in recent years has been the protection of tactical nuclear weapons sites from terrorist attacks. In the fall of 1982 the director of physical security for the Defense Nuclear Agency, Colonel C. R. Linton, confirmed that military authorities had received intelligence information indicating that terrorists in Europe might be planning to break into an undisclosed number of sites where nuclear artillery shells and other tactical weapons were stored. The Pentagon's five-year Defense Guidance Plan reflected the concern, saying, "The existing program and efforts to improve the security of nuclear weapons sites overseas must be sharply accelerated."[18] The Defense Nuclear Agency completed a 3-million-dollar test site at Fort McClellan, Alabama, in 1983, where military police and other troops trained to guard storage sites could be tested under realistic conditions, including live demolitions. Officials of the agency expressed fear that, in addition to the enormous physical threat the theft of a nuclear weapon would represent, such an event would cause political embarrassment to the United States and to foreign governments in whose countries nuclear weapons were based.[19]

Terrorist Goals

Terrorists, unlike those who practice discrimination against GIs, operate from a definite ideological base, however vague or ill defined it might be, and aim to achieve definite goals. Their chief goal, it may be said, is to undermine the authority and legitimacy of the state, the prevailing system of values, the major social and economic institutions, and the sense of social order. Some terrorists kill and maim to experience the sheer thrill of violence or prove their mettle; others believe that the capitalist economic order and the military-industrial complex must be smashed. In terms of alliance relations, terrorism aimed at U.S. forces or military installations is calculated to undermine the viability of the U.S. military presence in West Germany and hence the integrity of the U.S.–West German political relationship. The aim of terrorism is to strike fear into people's hearts and minds and to weaken resolve to the extent that social relations can be restructured according to the design of the terrorists. If the German population becomes fearful enough, it will be inclined eventually to demand the removal of U.S. forces from the FRG, moving the country in the direction of neutralism. If the fear of the Americans can be escalated to high levels, they will eventually tire of working in a dangerous and hostile environment and return home. The credibility of the NATO guarantee will thereby vanish.

Have the terrorists succeeded, or will they be able to make progress toward accomplishing their goals over the long term? The question leads us back to the central issue of morale and to the effects of terrorism upon the morale of U.S. forces stationed in West Germany. The issue is exceedingly complex, and there are no easy answers. There is good evidence, however, that the effects of terrorism upon those subjected to it are not unilinear. As with other phenomena, the results are a mixed bag of diverse and somewhat contradictory consequences, of both positive and negative results.

Terrorists aim, of course, to affect the living and working conditions of people by inducing an atmosphere of threat that makes necessary new networks of security precautions. Increased security, in turn, creates a kind of "bunker mentality," a feeling of working within an alien, hostile environment under conditions of unrelenting stress and strain. In this endeavor terrorists do, of course, succeed to a certain extent. Existing security measures have to be increased and new ones invented to protect against further terrorism and loss of life. In recent years military authorities have tightened security within and around U.S. military installations massively. Identification cards are closely scrutinized, without exception, for all persons entering a military compound. In sensitive areas or areas where classified information is stored, body searches are required for those entering and exiting the premises. Twenty-four-hour guard detachments have been posted around many buildings. Even the parking lots and living areas of military personnel have to be carefully guarded much of the time. Not only does this kind of security consume scarce resources, it imparts to everyone a sense of living or working in a dangerous environment. In discussing the new security precautions in a television interview, Defense Secretary Caspar Weinberger said:

> It's a very unpleasant, difficult thing to do because these posts are necessarily open, and one of the hallmarks of our activities in Europe and with NATO has been to maintain the best possible relationships with the civilian population. When we have instances of this kind and have to take increased security, it increases the strains all around. What we don't want is to let these attempts succeed in either reducing our commitment to NATO or in exacerbating any problems with the civilian population. So far they haven't approached that.[20]

Increased security precautions are inconvenient and often controversial. Some people are convinced they are not really necessary, and others deeply resent the intrusions upon personal freedom they bring about. Most especially, when counterterrorist units are set up to gather intelligence information on the aims and targets of terrorist groups, questions of unconstitutional intrusions into personal privacy are bound to be raised by groups that zealously protect civil liberties. A lively debate occurred in the West German press in the spring of 1981 following reports that the United States planned to send to West Germany special antiterrorist task forces, which until then had operated only in the Panama Canal Zone and other sensitive areas. Though the specific purpose of the task forces was reported to be guarding nuclear installations, the task forces were said to have been trained in Florida in tactics for combatting urban guerrillas and to have studied the strategies and methods of the Red Army Faction and the Revolutionary Cells. They were also said to be particularly interested in keeping tabs on militant U.S. groups that were trying to stir up turmoil among the troops. Leftist-oriented civil rights groups naturally used the reports as a platform to disseminate the idea that U.S. activities in West Germany were progressively turning the country into an armed garrison and threatening the liberty and peaceful order of the country.[21] Certain West German officials, in turn, questioned the implication that security for U.S. forces could no longer be guaranteed by the West Germans themselves, as had heretofore been the case. The *Badische Zeitung* in Freiburg commented:

> As Defense Secretary Weinberger has indicated, the Americans do not intend to rely only upon the protection of German authorities, but to undertake strengthened security measures themselves. This is, to be sure, not a return to the occupation era. But it is indeed a return by Washington to the possibilities contained in the [NATO] troop treaties and hence a noticeable change in the climate between Americans and Germans, which already has cooled down quite a bit. The bomb throwers of the RAF are the ones to whom credit is due, if the idea of "alllied reservations" has taken on a new, negative meaning.[22]

The editorial addresses the issue directly. The effort to combat terrorism inevitably introduces new stresses and strains into the political relationship between the United States and West Germany.

Tightened security measures also increase the physical separation and hence the psychological distance between the West Germans and U.S. forces. The terrorists' aim is to force the Americans further and further into isolated ghettos and to induce fear in the Americans' minds that they are operating in a hostile environment. To the extent that the terrorists are able to convince Americans that most Germans harbor some sympathies with the goals of the terrorists, relationships become ever more acrid. The terrorists have only partially succeeded in this endeavor. Military headquarters at Heidelberg and Ramstein have devoted great efforts to inform U.S. personnel that the overwhelming majority of Germans abhor both the terrorists and their goals. Public opinion polls showing strong support for the presence of U.S. forces have been widely disseminated in the military media. The available evidence seems to indicate that, despite a trend toward cooler relations between Germans and U.S. military personnel, most U.S. personnel realize that the terrorists represent a tiny band of fanatics, whose insidious work is an abomination to most West Germans.

The Effect of Terrorism on Military Families

The effect of terrorism upon military families has increasingly become a subject of concern on the part of U.S. military leaders and community service organizations in West Germany. Military families are required to cope with several kinds of pressure not common to civilian families. These include frequent separations; regular relocations to different communities; subordination of family life to the dictum that "the military mission comes first"; fears of loss due to death, injury, or capture; and feelings of isolation from those in civilian communities. As Richard I. Ridenour, chief psychiatrist at the San Diego Naval Hospital expressed it, "Although the families of police officers, physicians or corporate executives may know one or two of these stresses, there may be no other major group that confronts all of them."[23] The best social science research shows, however, that family problems such as alcoholism, drug abuse, family violence, and mental illness are no more common among military families than in the U.S. population at large.[24] According to Dr. Ridenour, despite the stresses a military family faces, "there are no studies that show the military family is sicker or more pathological."[25] A study published in the *American Journal of Psychiatry* in 1981 found that the children of military parents were even less likely to have psychoses than were children from nonmilitary families.

Though the majority of families in military life appear to be healthy and resilient, we find, as in other settings, a certain proportion of unhealthy families who are unable to cope with the unusual stresses and strains.[26] Terrorism is likely to have very different effects upon two types of military families. According to Kaslow, healthy military families "are flexible and adaptable, have good problem-solving skills, a high level of trust and a lot of mutuality and respect." They also benefit from a strongly shared sense of duty, patriotism, and pride "and feel part of a world that has meaning and a system of values."[27] For these families, the threat of terrorism is yet another challenge that must be faced in course of living and working abroad. If anything, the terrorist threat is likely to draw the family closer together and instill in each family member, children included, a heightened sense of mission and shared responsibility. For less-healthy military families, however, the threat of terrorism represents another stress factor that may aggravate already severe problems leading eventually to family disintegration. These families either need special help from the Army Community Service Program, which has strong programs in West Germany as well as in the United States, or they ought to be returned to the United States. The Army Community Service Program was revised in 1978 and updated again in 1983. In West Germany the program has incorporated the terrorist threat into its counseling programs. Military families are instructed in various ways to prepare for the threat and the reality of a terrorist act that might affect them directly or indirectly.

Though no reliable figures on the subject have been collected, there is no evidence that the terrorist threat in West Germany has caused an appreciable number of family removals to the United States or in other ways caused an increased frequency or range of family problems. There can be no doubt that some soldiers, both officers and enlisted men, have hesitated or decided not to bring their families to West Germany because of the possibility of terrorism. How many families have reached such a decision cannot be known. Military commanders report, however, that most soldiers do not mention terrorism as a major factor in the decisions they make about bringing their families to West Germany or leaving them in the United States. Likewise, in the case of familly departures to the United States, military commanders say that factors other than the terrorist threat usually appear to be the dominant reasons.

We may conclude that, though West German terrorists have certainly made life more difficult for U.S. military families, they have not yet even come close to achieving their wider goal of forcing a mass exodus from West Germany of the families of U.S. military personnel. By and large, these families conduct their affairs in West Germany on a routine, "business as usual" basis, though with feelings of increased isolation from the wider West German community and with a somewhat heightened sense of possible danger. Whether or not American families can continue to live and work in West Germany with any sense of normality depends largely upon the West German government's ability to keep the incidence of major terrorist strikes infrequent and sporadic. The larger threat looms, of course, that an increased incidence of major terrorism might create conditions of panic that could aggravate family problems for less-healthy military families or even eventually cause a substantial exodus of military dependents. Such a panic would have the effect of weakening the viability of the U.S. military presence over time. Given the cycles of terrorist activity in West Germany over the years, however, with its repeated surges and recessions, it is unlikely that terrorism will be the undoing of U.S. military family life in the Federal Republic anytime in the near future.

Positive Effects on Morale

Terrorism is apt to backfire in an environment of stable sociopolitical values and stable institutions. In West Germany, terrorism has been a notable failure in its attempt to destabilize the country's political and social life. German security organizations have successfully ferreted out and arrested the majority of hard-core terrorists and have reduced once-powerful terrorist groups to smaller, more fragmented rump groups. Because of the excesses and violent rhetoric of the terrorist groups, public opinion seems to have turned against terrorism as a means of change. As it relates to the morale of U.S. troops, terrorism has also backfired, in that it has had unintended positive effects that at least counterbalance if not overshadow its negative effects. In the mid-1980s, the morale of the troops seemed to be higher than at any time during the decade of the 1970s. It cannot be known with any certainty, of course, the extent to which a reaction to terrorism accounts for the improvement in morale. But there is a general consensus among company commanders that the terrorist threat has indeed been one significant factor.

The "bunker mentality" has had the effect of increasing unit cohesion. Soldiers faced with a threat of random violence in the surrounding external environment draw together more closely in an effort to cope with the threat. Indeed, there seems to have developed a vibrant new esprit de corps among military personnel in West Germany, not unrelated to the terrorist threat. Many commanders have consciously used the threat of terrorism as a means of challenging the troops to show their true mettle. By patiently informing the troops that violent terrorism is abhored by the majority of West Germans, commanders have been able to arouse their deeper emotions. If anything, terrorism has probably stiffened the resolve of both commanders and troops to accomplish the job they were sent to Germany to do. Commanders report that discipline improves and resolve stiffens during periods when the threat of terrorist attacks is greatest.

Terrorism and the U.S. Media

The terrorists seem to enjoy somewhat more success when it comes to influencing U.S. public opinion and opinion in Congress. The treatment of the problem in the American media leaves much to be desired. In 1981, coverage of events in West Germany was extensive not only because of the dramatic terrorist attacks at Ramstein and Heidelberg, but because of massive demonstrations in Bonn in the fall and a large demonstration staged in West Berlin at the time of Secretary of State Alexander Haig's visit to the city in the summer. Though the demonstration in Bonn mainly concerned nuclear weapons and environmental matters, it had a distinctly anti-U.S. and a particularly anti-Reagan edge. The demonstration against U.S. foreign policy in Berlin also seemed to be infused with a strong spirit of anti-Americanism, or so it seemed, at least, to the U.S. media. Terrorism and demonstrations against U.S. foreign policy seemed to many commentators to constitute a strong case for the existence of blatant and growing anti-Americanism.

The West German press, ever sensitive to U.S. media treatment of terrorism and demonstrations, has been highly critical of that coverage. According to the *Hessische Allgemeine*, "They [Americans] are informed by their newspapers, as though a tidal wave of letters to newspapers and anti-American demonstrations were gaining strength daily."[28] The Mannheim newspaper deplored the coverage of Secretary Haig's visit: "Typical of the precariousness, with which the changing mood in America progresses, was also the coverage of the demonstrations in West Berlin on the occasion of the Haig visit. In many radio and television reports [commentators] spoke blithely of 'anti-American excesses.' Television programs showed in addition wild scenes of confrontation between brawling youth and police."[29]

An even more disparaging critique of U.S. media coverage was offered by the *Frankfurter Neue Presse*:

> [According to coverage in the American media] the Federal Republic is in danger of falling into the neighborhood of those exotic countries in which terrorist acts, if not the daily diet, are at least so frequent that anti-Americanism is a widely diffused tendency. Such an image of Germany would be quite new in America. To a great extent this derives, to be sure, from the manner in which television, radio, and provincial newspapers report about events abroad: if at all, then only briefly and incidentally when the USA is not directly involved, but prominently and in detail when—as at the present time in the Federal Republic and West Berlin—America is involved. . . . The series of anti-American demonstrations and assaults is perfectly adapted to give nourishment to the constant inclination toward isolationism in the USA. . . . The Americans pay much more attention to their own problems than those of other countries. Moreover, the voices of those who plead for a greater distance from the European allies have been getting louder for some time now. They do not yet, by any means, control public opinion, but even three or four years ago they were hardly heard at all. . . . General Kroesen warned on American television about "over-reaction." But in the Senate and Congress isolationism may well gain ground.[30]

Despite a possible tendency toward oversensitivity, the German press is justified in such criticism. The U.S. press and television, especially in 1981, constructed a picture of widely diffused anti-American sentiment in West Germany, which runs contrary to the facts and to any portrait constructed more scientifically by public opinion research. It is true that political and social relations between West Germany and the United States have cooled on a number of fronts in the 1980s, but to label this as "anti-Americanism" is an inexcusable misnomer. The effects of this slanted media coverage of events in West Germany upon U.S. public opinion are extremely unfortunate. To the extent that Americans believe dramatized reports about widespread anti-Americanism in West Germany, public support for the alliance relationship and the continued U.S. military presence there is eroded.

Even more serious are the effects of this kind of coverage upon the mood in Congress. It not only exacerbates the tendency to view West Germany as an unreliable ally and inconstant friend, but also adds grist to the initiatives to withdraw U.S. troops. Many representatives and senators are notoriously uninformed as to the real meaning of events and trends in West Germany as it is. American media coverage serves mainly to fan the flames of anti-Germanism and hence to undermine the most strategically important relationship in the Altantic Alliance.

Conclusion

We may conclude then, that in terms of the maintenance of a sound political relationship between the United States and West Germany, the phenomenon of terrorism has many more pernicious than positive effects, both because of the coverage given it in American media and the general feeling of malaise induced by terrorism in any and all situations. The U.S. military presence in Germany is naturally an inviting target for terrorists. And the more frequently terrorists are able to stage dramatic assaults against military targets, the more likely it is that Americans, both in and out of government, will form negative images of West Germans and come to the conclusion that American lives should not be sacrificed for the defense of a hostile country. In terms of the morale of American forces stationed in Germany, however, terrorism has dual and somewhat contradictory effects. On the one hand, it has increased the level of fear and uncertainty, induced a bunker mentality, made necessary a heavier security apparatus, and increased the psychological distance between American personnel and Germans. On the other hand, terrorism has stiffened the resolve of the forces to accomplish their mission, increased unit cohesion and the level of discipline, and has added an increment of esprit de corps to the élan of the U.S. military establishment in West Germany.

Notes

1. *New York Times*, August 9, 1985, p. 1.
2. *Atlanta Constitution*, August 15, 1985, p. 9-A.

3. *New York Times*, April 24, 1986, p. 6.

4. *Frankfurter Neue Presse*, June 2, 1976; *Army Times*, September 28, 1981.

5. *Frankfurter Allgemeine*, November 13, 1974.

6. *Frankfurter Neue Presse*, March 15, 1974.

7. Ibid., March 19, 1974; *Süddeutsche Zeitung*, March 19, 1974.

8. *Süddeutsche Zeitung*, June 14, 1974; *Frankfurter Allgemeine*, November 13, 1974.

9. *Christian Science Monitor*, April 9, 1976.

10. *Frankfurter Neue Presse*, June 2, 1976; *Allgemeine Zeitung* (Mainz), June 2, 1976; *Frankfurter Rundschau*, June 2, 1976.

11. *Frankfurter Rundschau*, December 2, 1976.

12. *Army Times*, September 28, 1981.

13. Ibid.

14. *Frankfurter Presse*, September 16, 1981.

15. *Army Times*, September 28, 1981.

16. *New York Times*, November 1, 1982, p. 3.

17. *The Week in Germany* (Weekly bulletin published by the German Information Service, New York) 13, no. 45 (December 17, 1982).

18. *New York Times*, October 24, 1982, p. 27.

19. Ibid.

20. *Army Times*, September 28, 1981, p. 4.

21. *Die Welt*, May 4, 1981; *Deutsche Tagespost*, May 13, 1981; *Hessische Allgemeine* (Kassel), September 16, 1981.

22. *Badische Zeitung* (Freiburg im Breisgau), September 16, 1981.

23. Quoted by Glenn Collins in "Strengths Found in Military Families," *New York Times*, April 22, 1985.

24. See Florence W. Kaslow and Richard I. Ridenour, *The Military Family* (New York: Guilford Press, 1985).

25. Quoted by Collins, "Strengths Found in Military Families."

26. See Richard Halloran, "Army Seeks to Help Families Cope With Extra Pressure of Military Life," *New York Times*, August 17, 1985.

27. Quoted by Collins, "Strengths Found in Military Families."

28. *Hessische Allgemeine* (Kassel), September 16, 1981.

29. *Mannheimer Morgen*, September 17, 1981.

30. *Frankfurter Neue Presse*, September 18, 1981.

10

Poverty Problems and Outmoded Facilities

The Decline of the Dollar

Signs of poverty first appeared among U.S. forces in Germany in the early 1970s, but did not become severe enough to constitute a major morale problem until the latter part of that decade. The link between the poverty phenomenon and the dollar-mark exchange rate is extremely close. Indeed, it may be asserted that the prolonged slide in the value of the dollar in international currency markets during the 1970s was the primary cause of the poverty that began to afflict U.S. forces stationed abroad. Given the differential performances of the German and American economies during the 1970s, the dollar's loss of purchasing power was especially pronounced in the case of the West German mark:

Year	Value of One Dollar in German Marks
1967	3.90
1970	3.63
1972	3.50
1975	2.50
1977 (August)	2.30
1978 (March)	2.01
1978 (October)	1.72
1978 (November)	1.87
1979 (June)	1.86
1980 (August)	1.74
1982 (June)	2.48
1983 (July)	2.56
1984 (August)	2.80

For a period of nearly twenty years, from the late 1940s until the late

1960s, the dollar was worth somewhere in the neighborhood of four German marks. With the end of the Bretton Woods system of fixed exchange rates and the introduction of floating exchange rates in 1973, the dollar began a period of precipitous decline that was not halted until the early 1980s. Even in the mid-1970s, however, when the dollar still fetched approximately two and a half marks, most U.S. military personnel could, with stringent budgeting, afford to live relatively comfortably in West Germany. The real troubles began in 1977, when the value of the dollar plunged 11% during the calendar year, with the most serious deterioration beginning in the fall. Between August 1977 and October 1978, the dollar's value plunged 26%, from 2.30 marks to 1.72 marks. In November 1978, the Carter administration announced a package of support measures to shore up the dollar's value in international currency markets. These helped a bit, bringing up the exchange rate in German marks to 1.87 within a few weeks. From November 1978 through the latter part of 1981, the dollar wavered between 1.70 and 1.96 marks. Recovery started slowly in late 1981 and proceeded rapidly after the spring of 1982. Hence, the worst period of poverty for U.S. forces extended from the spring of 1978 until the early months of 1982.

Media Coverage

Media in Germany and the United States began to display awareness of and interest in the problem in 1977. The *International Herald Tribune* ran its first feature article on poverty among Americans in the Federal Republic on August 3:

> The slide in the value of the dollar against the deutsche mark has lowered the standard of living for more than a half-million Americans living in West Germany and has hit hardest at low-ranking married soldiers who live outside U.S. government-paid housing.
>
> Spec. 4 Lawton Fuller, stationed at Nuremberg, is typical. Because of his rank and brief time in the service, he had to pay personally to bring his wife to Europe and is not entitled to live in a government-supplied apartment. He has to live "on the economy," paying rent in marks.
>
> Spec. Fuller said that the cost of his wife's transportation "took all the money we had saved, and then I had to borrow from the Red Cross to put food on the table."
>
> Spec. 4 Charles Botts said, "If we don't get to move into government quarters soon, I may have to send my family back to America."
>
> "Ninety-five percent of the time we can't afford to go to the movies," Spec. Botts said. "Usually, I have just enough money to get through the month." . . .

The Army is concerned by the effect on GI morale and worried about the possible effect on the number of soldiers willing to sign up for another tour of duty in West Germany. Bringing in replacements is costly. Also costly are the increases in payments to local contractors, suppliers and workers.[1]

Time magazine ran an article in December that detailed additional cases of hardship:

A few young G.I.s have written bad checks to keep their children in nursery schools while their wives look for jobs. Some have shipped their families back to the U.S. . . . Cases of financial distress have become increasingly common among the 224,000 U.S. soldiers and airmen in Germany. . . . In the first eleven months of this year, Kaiserslautern's Army Emergency Relief office made 326 interest-free loans totaling $95,467 to G.I. families.[2]

The West German press was quick to pick up on stories of poverty among U.S. GIs. A story in *Welt am Sonntag* in March 1978 captured some of the essence of the new situation surrounding GIs in West Germany:

"My real enemy is no longer the Russian," said U.S. Staff Sergeant Harold Coe, 36, in Giessen: "My enemy is poverty." The sergeant is one of the 217,000 American soldiers stationed in the Federal Republic. Their presence is the Germans' protection. They came as conquerors to this country after World War II. They all lived as minor kings: the Germans used to pick up their cigarette butts from the gutter. Now the plunge of the dollar has reversed the roles. Formerly the generous Americans helped the Germans get back on their feet with the Marshall Plan and Care packages. Now benevolent Germans send food parcels to American soldiers in severe distress.[3]

The Effects of Poverty

As the dark cloud of poverty thickened after 1978, military personnel at all ranks began to feel the effects. Those hardest hit, however, were enlisted personnel at the lowest ranks. Only personnel who were "command-sponsored"—had completed four years of military service in the army or two years in the air force—could bring their families to West Germany at government expense and were also eligible for government-owned or -rented housing. For those without these privileges, if they chose not to live in the barracks, all living expenses off base, including rent, were their own responsibility. That might not pose a particular problem if most of these personnel were single. In the all-volunteer army, however, approximately 30% of the youngest group at the lowest ranks (E1–E4) are married and over 50% of enlisted personnel as a whole (E1–E9) are married. A large percentage of married personnel bring their families to Germany, whether command-sponsored or not, in order to avoid the ordeal of prolonged separation. This means that approximately one-third of all U.S. military personnel in West Germany have their families with them.[4]

Even for enlisted personnel with a claim on government housing, the situation has for many years been totally insufficient. Long waiting lists exist for government-owned apartments in the compounds near military bases and for apartments farther away rented by the military from West German owners. In 1980, for instance, army headquarters reported that the army had available 52,000 off-base housing units, ranging from small studio apartments to four-bedroom apartments. However, 10,000 additional units were needed to meet the demand. If we add to this the demand for nongovernment housing on the West German economy, at least 55,000 additional housing units were needed. The Housing Referral Office reported that in 1979 there were 37,000 housing requests from army personnel and 22,000 requests from air force personnel. The army was able to accommodate only 78% of the requests, and the air force met 91% of the requests. The higher air force figure was accounted for by the fact that the percentage of high-ranking officers was higher in the air force than in the army, and these officers, able to afford the more expensive housing on the German economy, could be accommodated more readily. The army estimated in 1980 that 40% of the troops with families lived in government-owned housing (excluding single soldiers living in the barracks), and 60% lived in nonsubsidized housing on the German economy, almost a mirror image of the situation during the days of the draft army.[5] For those eligible for government housing, the waiting periods became so long that many were forced to look for nonsubsidized and much higher priced accommodations, thus increasing the poverty of those who otherwise might have been able to cope. In Hanau, for instance, in 1981 enlisted personnel had to wait an average of 73 weeks for a two-bedroom government apartment, and in Fulda junior officers had to wait 101 weeks for housing in a military compound.[6]

Military personnel who were command-sponsored could bring their families to West Germany at government expense and, in addition, received two important allowances: "hola," or housing allowance, plus "cola," or cost-of-living allowance, to compensate for higher costs of living in the Federal Republic. With the precipitous fall of the dollar in 1978, both hola and cola began to be woefully insufficient to make ends meet, despite periodic readjustments. Even higher-ranking officers in both services began to feel the pinch materially, in the sense that their living conditions in West Germany were far below what they could have afforded in the United States. The worst calamities, however, befell the non-command-sponsored service personnel, to whom neither hola nor cola was available. If these personnel attempted to bring their families, either dire poverty or total financial collapse was frequently the result. Case after case was described in the West German press:

> A "Specialist 4" lives on the Homburger Landstrasse in Frankfurt and has only five dollars per day to support a family of five persons. "Last winter we were really hungry," said the sergeant. The American residents of the 64 apartments in the BBK House in Kaiserslautern described their living conditions as follows: "Formerly prostitutes lived here, but then it wasn't good enough for them any more. Now we live here. It's a terrible place." . . . Of the 62,000 Americans who belong to the community called "K-town" (Kaiserslautern), 18,000 are at present looking for a place to live. . . . The result is as described by an officer at the HRO (Housing Referral Offfice): "In some areas of Germany the slums appear to be reserved only for the American soldiers, because otherwise no one would live there, not even the foreign workers who live in the Federal Republic."[7]

The poverty phenomenon coupled with the chronic shortage and high price of accommodations produced distressing results in the early 1980s. Thousands of GIs failed to meet rent payments to German landlords, creating severe acrimony between landlords and military personnel. This, in turn, aggravated the housing shortage, as many landlords refused to rent to U.S. military tenants who might be unable to keep up with the rent payments. According to one news report,

> Today American soldiers who try to find a German apartment meet with a great deal of mistrust. A rental agent in Frankfurt said, "When I suggest American G.I.'s to the owner of rental property, the first question is: 'But will they be able to pay the rent?' That's how much times have changed."[8]

Added to complaints of rent nonpayment was a steadily increasing stream of landlord complaints concerning property damage by U.S. military tenants. According to the Housing Referral Office at army headquarters in Heidelberg, 9,000 complaints were registered in 1978 against military tenants for rowdy behavior or property damage. The number increased by 700 in 1979.[9] The extent to which West German–American relations were soured by the poverty-induced housing crisis is vividly illustrated by the Gonsenheim Affair in 1981-1982. A total of 630 persons, 273 soldiers with their families, lived in two apartment towers owned by the Koch Company in the Gonsenheim section of Mainz. In October 1981, the firm mailed letters to all the American families demanding that they vacate their apartments "immediately or at the latest by June 30, 1982." According to the Koch Company, the Americans had caused property damage amounting to over 100,000 marks within the preceding year and had diminished the rental value of the property so substantially that the further rental of apartments to U.S. military personnel could not be contemplated. Given the outcry by the tenants and military authorities, the case subsequently led to a complex series of negotiations between the Koch firm, several ministries of the West German federal government, and American military authorities. In March 1982, military headquarters sent a construction unit to repair the damage to the apartments and grounds of the complex. Nevertheless, the Koch Company was able to accomplish its goal in the end, because of the complexities of the German legal system and the nature of the free market economy. The German government was only able to work out an arrangement for a phased eviction program extending over a period of three years.[10]

The deepening poverty of U.S. personnel during these years had many other manifestations. One visible evidence of the malaise could be seen in the demise of the once-universal symbol of American wealth and prowess: the automobile. In the 1980s, jokes could be heard everywhere in West Germany about the old-fashioned junk heaps being driven around the country by U.S. personnel, bearing the unmistakable green military license plates. Many Germans also complained that the old American cars were a traffic hazard and a threat to traffic safety. The contrast between the spiffy new sports cars driven by German young people and the rotted-out contraptions driven by GIs was rich in imagery:

> What happened to the days when American chewing gum, coffee, chocolate and whiskey were music to the ears of German citizens after the war? When G.I.'s made a big impression with their enormous chrome-plated motorized coaches? Today they park their old "used cars," which no young German motorist would find acceptable, in the parking lot next to the exhibition grounds near Robinson Barracks as a pictorial instruction of the differences between German and American life.[11]

Another manifestation of military poverty could be seen in the jobs accepted by the wives of American servicemen. There is nothing peculiar, of course, about working wives either in Germany or the United States. What was painful, indeed often humiliating, was that American spouses were required to accept the lowest-paying jobs in the labor market, jobs that were characteristically held by guest workers or illiterate, unskilled laborers. Lacking a working knowledge of the German language and marketable technical skills, many wives accepted jobs as workers on assembly lines or as maids. Again, the imagery was tinged with the pathos of a faded grandeur. In earlier times few military wives would have had to work at all. If they did, they would most likely have been found in managerial positions in various German-American organizations, in philanthropic foundations, or in fashionable department stores that catered to American trade. In the 1980s, however, poverty forced the young wives of enlisted men to find work wherever jobs might be available, most often as janitors, street cleaners, factory workers, or household maids. Some even resorted to prostitution. The case of Marilyn was one of many described in the German Press:

> Spotlights from the [American] army scene: Marilyn, in faded jeans and T-shirt, two large brown paper bags in her arms (with melons, baby food, cereal, ketchup and other things an American household needs) comes out of the "PX" at Robinson Barracks. She is 19 years old, just married, comes from the Bronx. Her husband has been in the army for a year. . . . Marilyn can go shopping only in the "PX" stores, where she receives for her dollars about twice as much as in the department stores downtown in the Königstrasse, which she has seen only from the outside. Contact with the Germans? Marilyn works as a maid, for a German lawyer and a retired couple.[12]

The growing demand for jobs by wives of U.S. servicemen has complicated West German–American relations in at least two major ways. First, the rise in the level of unemployment in the Federal Republic that accompanied the recession in the early 1980s put Americans in competition with both Germans and foreign workers for jobs in a shrinking labor market. According to the provisions of the NATO troop statute and other agreements, U.S. military personnel are granted the same legal status in West Germany as are citizens of Common Market countries. They do not need a special work permit or residence permit. Even though many military spouses competed for factory or service jobs that many Germans did not seek, the competition still caused strains in relations with those West Germans and foreign workers willing to take any available job to support their families. Second, the attempts by the army and the air force to find employment for spouses within the military establishment led to charges by German labor unions, primarily the OTV (Public Service, Transport, and Commercial Workers' Union), that German civilian workers were being illegally displaced by American workers. Angry exchanges in the press over the displacement issue became commonplace in the early 1980s, and lengthy negotiations between military authorities and representatives of the OTV failed to resolve the issue.

That poverty and unemployment are reinforcing aspects in a syndrome of malaise and hopelessness is no secret to social workers. In the case of military spouses seeking employment in Germany, two factors stand out as singularly important in placing them at the bottom end of the employment totem pole: lack of skills needed in the labor market and the language barrier. The situation was aptly described in *Die Welt*:

> Since the plunge of the dollar an increasing number of the wives of American soldiers seek employment in the Federal Republic. . . . But is it then true that many of them stand on assembly lines, work as cleaning women, or pursue the oldest profession in the world, as the rumors would have it?
>
> Reinhold Brennfleck, head of the labor office in Kaiserslautern, emphasizes two factors: "The U.S. military authorities have asked us to help. We are ready. But the difficulty is the language. We have here an unemployment rate of 4.7 percent, higher than average. 62 percent [of the unemployed] are women, mostly unskilled. And the great majority of the American wives are unskilled."[13]

Military authorities had limited options in dealing with the poverty crisis. Without specific authority from Congress to compensate military personnel stationed abroad for the diminished purchasing power of the dollar, all the Pentagon could do was to raise housing allowances and cost-of-living allowances within the budgetary limits set by existing legislation. Several raises in the allowances were granted in the late 1970s and early 1980s, but they were of little help to the lower enlisted ranks faced with a chronically shrinking dollar and escalating prices of German goods and services fueled by inflation in the German economy. Emergency relief offices were granted authority to make additional types of loans and loans in greater amounts to help soldiers and air force personnel avoid default in meeting rental payments and other obligations.

In April 1978, the army took the dramatic step of opening the troop mess halls to the families of soldiers in Germany. Previously, the mess halls had been off limits to wives and children except on special occasions such as Thanksgiving and Christmas. With mounting evidence that many military families were living below the poverty level and that in many households food suplies were inadequate to support balanced diets, the army was forced to take strong action. In the mess halls, adults and children over twelve were charged 90 cents for breakfast and $1.45 for lunch and dinner.[14] Laudable as the new food program was, its effects were not spread uniformly to all soldiers, and participation was actually lower than expected. Transportation turned out to be the major obstacle. Many families living substantial distances from the base mess halls were without transportation to get there, and others found the long trips more hazardous or disruptive than beneficial. Nevertheless, tens of thousands of service wives and children flocked to the mess halls to take advantage of simple but nourishing food at bargain prices.[15]

Deterioration of Military Facilities

Closely related to the personal poverty of GIs is the poverty of the U.S. military establishment itself in reference to the condition of its physical facilities in the Federal Republic of Germany. The seriousness of this problem, as a factor both of morale and combat readiness, cannot be exaggerated. Though the problem has existed for many years, its dimensions are more serious in the 1980s than at any time since World War II. The reasons for the dilapidated facilities arise from complex historical circumstances and from a series of unwise or postponed decisions by successive administrations and Congress over the past thirty years. The U.S. Army, after the war, moved into bases formerly occupied by the German Wehrmacht or Luftwaffe and into other public or private facilities commandeered by the occupation regime. Aside from Congress' reluctance to appropriate funds for renovation and modernization, the primary reason that necessary maintenance was never undertaken was the long-standing idea that the U.S. troops were in Germany only for a temporary period of time.

In the early years after the war, a majority of the members of Congress and major figures in the administration assumed that the troops would be withdrawn when the occupation period ended. Even in the early 1950s, when the decision was made to send additional troops to the Federal Republic to counter Soviet expansionism and possible Soviet aggression, the prevailing mindset for most policymakers was that the troops would remain temporarily until the Europeans were able to provide sufficient means for their own defense. The idea of temporariness never disappeared. It was underscored by the debates over the Mansfield initiatives to withdraw troops in the 1960s and 1970s, and it can be seen today in recurrent motions in Congress to bring the troops home. Though such hopes are based on the illusion that the defense of Europe might somehow be viable in the absence of U.S. troops there, the hopes have prevented Congress from appropriating the funds necessary to modernize existing facilities or build new ones.

The only completely new facility constructed for the U.S. military in the FRG has been the base built in the late 1970s at Garlstedt, for which no appropriations by Congress were involved. The Garlstedt facility was built by the German government in lieu of a new offset payment arrangement when the offset payments program was ended in 1976. The functional modernity of the facilities at Garlstedt contrasts sharply with the decaying, ramshackle quality of the accommodations at military bases elsewhere in the country. The passing years have exacted a heavy toll. Buildings that once adequately fulfilled minimum needs are now in an advanced state of deterioration.

The deplorable state of U.S. facilities has been chronicled extensively in the West German press. A feature article in *Die Welt* is typical of many that have appeared in recent years:

> One look at the depressing barracks buildings, which date from the period of the rapid construction of the *Wehrmacht* a half a century ago, exposes a condition of neglect, which a lieutenant referred to as simply "scandalous". The plaster is peeling, and moisture from the toilets and washrooms penetrates the walls. Inside, the sanitary facilities are in a state of collapse. Black mildew on the walls and in the corners, which defies even regular disinfecting with chlorine. In the course of the decades urine has penetrated deeply into the untiled walls.[16]

Other descriptions are equally graphic:

> As one enters the rotted-out barracks buildings hopes and dreams burst like soap bubbles. . . . In Bamberg a soldier shudders every morning at the entrance to the washroom, because the latrines are overflowing. For other soldiers in Kitzingen the sight of slowly rotting drain pipes, exposed electric cables or tattered screens is as common to everyday life as cursing the broken shower pipes. . . . Astronomical sums would be necessary, according to the estimates of experts at military headquarters in Heidelberg, to replace current facilities with new ones for soldiers and equipment in all major troop areas in Europe.[17]

Extensive press coverage has made the German population quite aware of the miserable physical condition of U.S. facilities. Before pressure can be brought to bear upon Congress to take steps to remedy the situation, however, public awareness in the United States must be raised substantially. American media have not devoted much attention to the problem, though major stories have appeared from time to time, as for example, an article in *Time* in the summer of 1981:

> At Budingen, a U.S. Army base near Frankfurt in West Germany, helicopter maintenance crews do much of their work under tents instead of in hangars. They use jerry-rigged lighting and, in cold weather, kerosene heaters that military regulations prohibit as safety hazards. Across the road, 36 armed M-60 tanks stand ready to go to war—if they can churn their way out of a vast mudhole that turns into a pond whenever it rains. At

Fliegerhorst barracks near Hanau, 15 miles south of Budingen, helicopter repair crews have taken over the base's only gymnasium. They repack drive shafts on the basketball court beneath a sign that reads NO DUNKING ALLOWED. At Rivers Barracks near Giessen, nearly 3,000 soldiers are crammed into what was a Wehrmacht military prison during World War II. "The tip-off is that the barbed-wire-fence topping points in, not out," says an officer stationed there.

There are more than 240,000 Americans in uniform in West Germany stationed at three dozen bases that are supposedly part of NATO's front-line defense. Yet the Pentagon's $20 billion facilities in that country are woefully obsolete and inadequate. The maintenance backlog for U.S. forces in West Germany has reached $1.3 billion. Soldiers live and work in conditions that could cause riots in U.S. prisons. The G.I.'s, fortunately, do not riot. They just quit the Army at the end of their tours.

. . . Morale would probably be bad anywhere that U.S. soldiers had to sleep 18 to a room, as some have had to do at Hanau, or where soldiers took their exercise in the middle of an active firing range, as at Ayres barracks near Butzbach. . . .

G.I.'s in West Germany frequently react to their hardship with gallows humor. A sign in a maintenance shop at McNair barracks near Frankfurt reads WE'VE DONE SO MUCH WITH SO LITTLE FOR SO LONG THAT NOW WE CAN DO ALMOST ANYTHING WITH NOTHING.[18]

The inadequacy of U.S. facilities is exacerbated by the surrounding affluence of West German society and by comparison with the newer, more luxuriant facilities of the West German army and air force. Whereas most U.S. facilities were originally constructed during the two world wars and requisitioned by the Americans in 1945, the German facilities were all constructed after 1955—architecturally pleasing, highly functional, and capable of expansion when needed. In addition, as the West Germans are in their homeland rather than stationed thousands of miles away, plans for renovation and modernization have been carried out on a regular basis. The German military, like most other major institutions, takes pride in the appearance and functionality of its physical surroundings. Consequently, the contrast between the physical plants of the two militaries has served to heighten the impression of second-class status on the part of the Americans. The contrast was aptly noted by *Time*:

But conditions seem especially intolerable in contrast to West German prosperity, both military and civilian. American facilities almost all predate World War II. Some are World War I cavalry stables. In comparison, the bases of West Germany's Bundeswehr were all built after the country was permitted to rearm in 1955 and are meticulously maintained. At Hardthöhe, for example, on the outskirts of Bonn, grass is closely cropped and bald spots are quickly reseeded. Some of the yellow brick barracks are only five years old, and they have Thermopane windows and new, automated heating systems.

G.I.'s wash their tanks outdoors with garden hoses, chipping off ice in winter, watching tanks settle three feet deep in mud in summer. "You won't ever see a single U.S. tank in West Germany that's truly clean," says SP/4 Kim Kosko of Smethport, Pa., who is based at Budingen. West German soldiers use outdoor motorized washracks in summer and heated buildings in winter for tank maintenance and cleaning.[19]

Combined Effects of Poverty and Deterioration on Morale

The combined effects of GI poverty and dilapidated physical facilities upon military morale in West Germany have been devastating. Again, it may be convenient to look first at the short-term and more tangible effects and then consider the more abstruse, intangible, long-term effects. One important tangible effect has been the lower rate of retention for military personnel stationed in Germany. Not only have troops and noncommissioned officers been loath to reenlist in the mist of deepening poverty and collapsing facilities; even many seasoned officers tended to become disillusioned and to opt out of military service at the end of their assignments. The Pentagon began to register serious concern about the problem in the spring of 1978, when the dollar began a protracted downward slide.

Other military sources said that the excessive cost of living in Germany caused by the dollar devaluation could affect the Army's efficiency by discouraging the better officers and noncommissioned officers from volunteering for duty in the country.

"Right now, Europe is seen as the most desirable tour of duty for a professional soldier," an officer said. "This is where the action is now. But if the word gets around that a man can't support a family over here, he won't come."[20]

The concern turned out to be well founded. Though reliable statistics are not available to document the situation, interviews with young soldiers, noncommissioned officers, and officers at the height of the poverty period confirm that the retention rate for all of these groups tended to plummet. *Time* noted an illustrative case in the early 1980s: "When the plum job of command sergeant major opened at scenic, historic Heidelberg, the first three men chosen left the military rather than take the assignment."[21] Lower retention rates are an obvious sign of malaise in a military establishment, especially one that depends upon volunteer recruits. Costs of recruitment to replace those who opt out of the service increase, and the experience level of the force is diminished. The loss of experienced noncommissioned officers is especially serious. As every recruit and many senior officers confirm, these are the people who conduct the day-to-day business of military life and keep an army ready to fight on a moment's notice. In West Germany, where the ability to meet Soviet aggression on short notice is the raison d'être of the U.S. military presence, the services can ill afford to be short of experienced noncoms, as the experiences of the Vietnam War vividly illustrated.

Poverty and inadequate facilities are also related to the level of crime and indiscipline. As noted in Chapter 6, problems of crime and indisciplline in West Germany, after a four-year hiatus from 1974 to 1978, tended to become more severe in the late 1970s and early 1980s. Given the severe personal burdens poverty places upon people, it is not surprising that the precipitous slide of the dollar tended to increase discipline problems on every front. In the Federal Republic, the combination of poverty with the sad state of physical facilities has been particularly potent. The stress of being barely able to make ends meet is difficult enough for young recruits with families; when such stress is added to the depressing conditions of the work facilities, the effect is a compounded sense of deprivation. Nevertheless, the situation improved when the dollar began to gain strength again in 1982; disciplinarv problems decreased, and the general level of morale tended to improve materially. The improvement has been maintained well into the mid-1980s.

Psychological Estrangement

The long-term intangible effects of poverty are perhaps more profound than the short-term effects. As with other factors of morale, the poverty syndrome has tended to increase the isolation of Americans and the sense of distance between the U.S. military community and the German population. Isolation and distance, in turn, have reduced the level of interchange and cultural understanding between Americans and Germans and, hence, have undermined to some extent the viability of the U.S. military presence by reducing German popular support. As the poverty crisis deepened in the late 1970s, military families tended to circulate less in West German communities and to withdraw to the safer, cheaper bastions of military bases. The increasing separation was noted by many commentaries in the West German press, as illustrated by the following example:

One of the most important results of the shrinking buying power and weakness of the [dollar] exchange rate: the separation between the American troops and the inhabitants of the guest country does not become less, but rather more. The trend to live and buy "all American" has become stronger. The soldiers now say, "My wife goes shopping almost exclusively at the commissary, the grocery store of the garrison. It has become too expensive for us to buy things in German stores."[22]

As the U.S. military community in the FRG becomes increasingly isolated in ghettos, less effort is made to understand the culture and the mindset of the country. Estrangement leads finally to alienation. The phenomenon is similar for the German population. Respect and affection for the ghettoized foreigners who prefer to live "all American" inevitably decrease.

The poverty phenomenon has also adversely affected the tone and texture of the German-American relationship. Both the image the Germans have of U.S. military personnel and the self-image American military personnel have of themselves have been diminished. The United States and West Germany are affluent societies with standards of living that are among the highest in the world. American military personnel are taught to think and believe that it is precisely their presence in Germany that guarantees the security of Europe and hence of the United States. When, however, U.S. soldiers and air force personnel must live like paupers in an affluent and ordered society, the image they have of themselves becomes distinctly negative. No one believes that the clock should be turned back to the days after World War II when American soldiers were the image of rich Uncle Sam in a poor, devastated country. But American military personnel also should not be reduced to the level of the poorest of the poor in the country they are protecting against Soviet aggression. Poverty is a particularly demoralizing form of humiliation. When American soldiers cannot afford to dine in German restaurants or purchase anything of value in German stores, when the wives of servicemen must work at the lowest-paid unskilled jobs in the labor market, when military families must live in slum accommodations unacceptable to most Germans and even to foreign workers from poorer countries, it should come as no surprise that morale plummets to the basement level. The self-image of second-class status in a wealthy country cannot support the first-rate effort required of a military superpower, because such a self-image is not congruent with the objective reality—that the military might of one of the world's major superpowers has been transposed abroad to guarantee the security of a smaller, weaker country.

Equally undermined by the poverty of the U.S. troops is the image Germans form of the American military presence. If the American presence is indeed the final guarantee of Germany's security, then that presence must be seen and felt to be something awesome, splendid, incapable of defeat. The Germans must have an indelible impression of the U.S. fighting machine as second to none, with combat readiness at top pitch and morale at the highest pinnacle. If, instead, they constantly see and read about the Americans as ghettoized foreigners who live in ramshackle accommodations and are unable to afford the rudiments of a decent standard of living, respect turns to pity and pity to disdain. The security guarantors ought at least be able to maintain themselves with some minimum of style and élan. There can be no doubt that some respect for the integrity of the U.S. military presence was lost during the years of chronic poverty. Equally certain is that the contrast between the degraded condition of the U.S. physical facilities and the robust condition of their own military plant is not lost upon the West Germans. With the passage of time, they cannot escape increasing feelings of doubt that the Americans might not be able, in the final analysis, to defend their country if real aggression occurred. Such doubt may, in fact, be a wellspring of latent impulses to end military dependency and veer toward some type of neutrality. At the very least, the misery of the Americans contributes to a loss of respect on the part of the West Germans.

Images are vital components of the morale equation. The poverty-induced low self-image of U.S. service personnel, coupled with their awareness that the West German image of them is becoming ever more negative, translates into a morale problem of major dimensions. And when morale reaches a low ebb, combat effectiveness declines. Expressions of concern about lowered combat effectiveness were legion during the worst years of poverty, from military sources and from civilian commentators alike. Some of them bear repeating here:

> . . . Army officers, U.S. diplomats and some West German officials are concerned that the fall of the dollar against the value of the deutsche mark is undercutting soldier morale so seriously that combat effectiveness could be reduced. . . .
> "There is concern now that if soldiers spend so much time worrying about how their families are making out, they will lose some of their combat effectiveness," one officer commented. In addition, diplomats are worried that Germans will lose confidence in the military's spirit and willingness to defend their country.[23]

> The condition of the [American] military, constantly at the edge of a minimum standard of life, has repercussions on the morale of the troops. For the Pentagon and the American generals in Europe the social question has become the central problem of leadership. It influences mood, readiness, and the quality of the army.[24]

> Conditions are so bad for American soldiers because of the decline of the dollar that the [German] federal government fears very negative consequences. Above all the deficient accommodations . . . will lead, in Bonn's

opinion, to negative impressions of military service and of the host country. And consequently the morale and capability of the G.I.'s will be destroyed.[25]

The consequence for U.S. forces in West Germany is not just low morale; there is a growing concern that they could not mobilize quickly enough to ward off a Warsaw Pact attack.[26]

Given the mission of the U.S. military in West Germany, combat effectiveness is perhaps the lead question related to fears of a decline in troop morale. To the extent that combat effectiveness is actually subverted by conditions of poverty, or even perceived as such by the West German population, the viability of the U.S. military presence is effectively undermined.

West German Initiatives

No real remedy to the poverty problem could be found until the dollar began to recover its exchange value in 1982. In the interim, however, there were many attempts by the West Germans, officially and unofficially, to help the Americans weather the worst of the crisis. In the spring of 1978, a U.S. colonel in Illesheim wrote a letter to 300 landlords and rental agents requesting assistance for the plight of U.S. soldiers. He pointed out that the morale of the troops would suffer badly if soldiers were forced to send their wives and children back to the United States. He asked that, wherever possible, landlords grant rent reductions to soldiers and stated that he would be most grateful for any assistance the Germans were able to render. The local newspaper followed up by printing an editorial and an official request from local authorities for rent reductions. The results were more than had been hoped for. According to one account, "At the present time successes are registered daily for the American installations in and around Ansbach, the division head-quarters for the 1st tank division. The latest result from Illesheim: 35 landlords have reduced the rents for the Americans, some as much as 20 percent."[27]

In Gersthofen, a military chaplain established a special account in a West German bank with the name "Helping Hand" to collect donations for the benefit of the poorest military families. When the account number was published in the local press, contributions poured in in unexpected amounts.[28] In Augsburg community leaders established a donation center at which a variety of gifts, ranging from old cars and clothing to cash donations, were received.[29] The Frankfurt issue of the newspaper *Bild* ran a lengthy article on the hardships faced by GIs, followed by an appeal to readers who wished to help, asking them to contact the local office

of the Army Community Service. "The response is overwhelming," Roger
Lehman, ACS director, told reporters. "We weren't in any way prepared
for the article." Mr. Lehman was quoted as saying that many people had
called and offered to write checks for 500 marks or 1,000 marks. "A
couple of times when I got back to the office I found an envelope with
50 marks or so included for the Americans." Other West Germans offered
to accompany the wives of GIs to the supermarket and pay for their
groceries.[30] In a few cases local commanders were unprepared for the
flood of charitable donations and other offers. According to military
regulations, gifts and offers to help were supposed to be approved through
appropriate channels before being accepted by GIs. When such donations
began to pour in in unexpected amounts, army headquarters had to put
together a special staff to devise new technical and administrative
procedures and to render advice to local commanders on how to handle
the charity program.

The generosity of the Germans was heartening to U.S. military authorities. Such generosity was, however, tempered by occasional rounds
of criticism in the West German press, which pointed out that the
Americans themselves were really responsible for the crisis. German
commentators were not hesitant to point out that the dollar's decline in
international currency markets was at least partially a result of the United
States' loss of competitiveness in the global economy. In addition to
criticizing U.S. international economic policy as shortsighted, West German
analysts took a dim view of Pentagon policies that inflicted the greatest
misery on military personnel at the lowest ranks.

> The apparently unforseen consequences of an all-volunteer army—very
> young soldiers with a low educational level—are made more severe in their
> effects by the weakness of the dollar and poverty. The ability to adjust to
> a new and strange environment sinks, and the isolation in military garrisons
> and compounds increases. . . .
> The error lies to some extent in the system of the all-volunteer army.
> It is divided into "sponsored" and "non-sponsored" soldiers, i.e. those who
> have a right to receive government subsidies for housing costs and costs
> of living, and those who do not have such a right. In the army one gains
> the right usually after four years of service, and in the air force after two
> years. In addition, the right to house one's family in government quarters
> is derived according to the same system.[31]

Occasionally criticism was drawn in even sharper terms:

> The army cares for its members according to a class pattern, which
> no longer fits well with contemporary society. The youngest people, who
> are inexperienced and unsure of themselves and who are afraid of contact

with Germans because of the lack of language facility, the army throws out onto the free rental market with tiny salaries, while the officers, who possess more experience and maturity, are given not only generous salaries, but also government quarters or housing subsidies and often even good paying jobs for their wives.[32]

In 1980 the Carter administration decided that substantial help was needed from the Federal Republic to remedy some of the worst effects of the poverty crisis. In November of that year, the so-called Stoessel Plan was presented to the West German government in Bonn by U.S. Ambassador Walter Stoessel. Though the major impetus of the plan had to do with German assistance for rapid U.S. troop deployments to Europe in times of emergency and with the master restationing plan, there were several points that concerned the housing shortage and the poverty crisis. Included were requests for apartment complexes constructed by the German government for the use of the U.S. military, low-interest construction loans from the German government, tax rebates for purchases in the FRG by American military personnel, and abolition of security payments to German landlords from military personnel.

The German government received what the press often referred to as "the American wish list" with characteristic courtesy, but with notable resistance nonetheless. Government representatives immediately pointed out that the new requests violated both the letter and the spirit of the original 1951 NATO Troop Statute and the 1959 amendments to the Troop Statute. The treaties specified that although the German government was obligated to provide all necessary real estate for NATO forces, the governments supplying the forces were fully responsible for all measures concerning the upkeep and social well-being of the forces. Military salaries, subsidies, housing, maintenance of facilities, and social programs were clearly the responsibility of the governments sending troop contingents.[33]

Clearly, the Bonn government wanted to avoid the assumption of new financial burdens for the upkeep of foreign forces, especially at a time when government budget deficits seemed to be reeling out of control. From the West German government's point of view, the precipitous decline in the value of the dollar could not be blamed on the Germans. Both GI poverty and the poor condition of U.S. physical facilities were the result of U.S. neglect, not attributable to acts of omission or commission by the Federal Republic. Nevertheless, given West Germany's vital interest in the continued presence of U.S. troops as the linchpin of the country's security, the government agreed to negotiate with the United States on the Stoessel proposals. The negotiations, as could be expected, were complex and difficult. What the Germans were willing to offer fell far short of what the Americans expected them to do. The American government was obviously handicapped by several disadvantages: the German propensity to stick by the letter of treaty provisions that were drafted in clear terms, leaving the United States with weak legal arguments; the credibility of the German argument that long-standing U.S. policies were at the root of the poverty crisis; and the general atmosphere of the discussions, which made it appear that the Americans were coming to the Germans hat-in-hand to receive whatever generosity they might be willing to render.

In contrast to the parallel negotiations on wartime host nation support, which resulted in a new treaty in 1982, the negotiations on other portions of the Stoessel proposal never reached a satisfactory conclusion in treaty form. The outcome was merely a series of promises by the Bonn government to take what little steps it could along the way to ease some of the worst manifestations of the poverty crisis. Bonn agreed to take up the matter with the German Conference of Mayors (Städtetag) in an effort to persuade municipalities to grant U.S. military personnel free use of or reduced rates for communal facilities such as swimming pools or municipal transportation networks, as was the rule for members of the West German armed forces. In response to the U.S. complaint that military personnel had to spend an average of 12% of their incomes for transportation, the German government agreed to publish new tariff provisions that would grant substantial fare reductions on all trains and buses operated by the German Federal Railways. Bonn also agreed to negotiate with the Länder governments on a plan whereby the Länder would grant low-interest loans to GIs in need. In addition, the Länder would make available to military personnel units in public housing complexes when no requests from German citizens were waiting to be filled.

Coupled with these promises the Bonn government stated repeatedly that in order to make real progress in overcoming the poverty crisis, the U.S. government would need to devise a plan to compensate military personnel in real terms for the higher costs, arising from the dollar's weakness, of living in the Federal Republic. This would mean the granting of substantial and meaningful cost-of-living and rent subsidies, similar to German government subsidies to German federal personnel serving in high-cost-of-living areas around the world.[34]

The Partial Recovery of the Dollar

Though the steps taken by the German government were helpful, they were not on a large enough scale to make much of a difference in the poverty situation. In addition, they required time to reach fruition and relied heavily on federal pressure on the Länder governments to take the most important concrete measures. Before many of the Länder governments were able to devise new legislation, the crisis began to ease as the dollar commenced its recovery in the spring of 1982. The unexpectedly strong performance of the dollar increased the buying power of military personnel considerably within a few months, thus rendering the efforts of the Länder governments moot.

By the summer of 1982 the worst of the poverty crisis appeared to be over. With the dollar at its highest value in marks since 1975, GIs, though far from affluent, at least felt that better times had arrived at long last. What remained quite clear, however, was that the relative luxury of the first two decades of the U.S. military presence in West Germany had vanished forever. Gone were the days when U.S. service personnel afforded comfortable accommodations anywhere they chose to reside, dined in the finest restaurants, and purchased leather goods, cameras, automobiles, and cuckoo-clocks with ease. A period of stringency had arrived that was likely to be permanent. Military personnel, though they might no longer have to suffer conditions of dire poverty, would always have to budget carefully and live modestly in order to survive in the Federal Republic. And though the dollar was a strong currency in 1983–1984, the cloud of poverty could descend again at any time if its value began to plunge in international currency markets. In the global regime of floating exchange rates, the value of the dollar is highly dependent upon the overall performance of the U.S. economy in the larger global economy and upon related factors, such as the growth of the U.S. money supply and interest rates in the United States. If confidence in the economic performance of the United States declines, the dollar might again go into a prolonged tailspin, bringing back the conditions of poverty that caused so much havoc in the late 1970s and early 1980s. Indeed, that very scenario seemed to be returning in 1987.

The easing of the poverty crisis also did nothing to ameliorate the more serious crisis caused by the shameful condition of the U.S. military's physical plant in Germany. In the final analysis, the rickety physical facilities may have a more lasting and profound effect upon troop morale than the temporary poverty caused by the dollar's weakness. The problem of the degraded physical plant is pervasive; it influences every aspect of the conditions of life and work in West Germany. It also has enormous dimensions and would require billions of dollars to correct. The Pentagon's master restationing plan, which would represent at least one plausible solution, will remain in limbo, unless and until Congress decides that the U.S. military presence in Germany requires a long-term commitment and needs to be adequately supported with sufficient facilities. Until such a commitment is made, American troop morale will continue to suffer under a crushing burden of official neglect.

Notes

1. *International Herald Tribune*, August 3, 1977.
2. *Time*, December 26, 1977.
3. *Welt am Sonntag*, March 12, 1978.
4. *Die Welt*, September 18, 1981.
5. *Saarbrücker Zeitung*, August 8, 1980.
6. *Time*, July 27, 1981, p. 14.
7. *Saarbrücker Zeitung*, August 8, 1980.
8. *Kölner Stadt-Anzeiger*, September 10, 1980.
9. *Stuttgarter Zeitung*, April 13, 1982.
10. Ibid.
11. Ibid., August 2, 1980.
12. Ibid.
13. *Die Welt*, November 4, 1978.
14. *International Herald Tribune*, April 13, 1978.
15. Ibid., August 19, 1978.
16. *Die Welt*, September 18, 1981.
17. *Ruhr-Nachrichten* (Dortmund), December 29, 1981.
18. *Time*, July 27, 1981, p. 14.
19. Ibid.
20. *International Herald Tribune*, March 8, 1978.
21. *Time*, July 27, 1981, p. 14.
22. *Saarbrücker Zeitung*, August 17, 1980.
23. *International Herald Tribune*, March 8, 1978.
24. *Frankfurter Allgemeine*, July 11, 1978.
25. *Wiesbadener Kurier*, July 25, 1980.
26. *Time*, July 27, 1981, p. 14.
27. *Westdeutsche Allgemeine* (Essen), March 2, 1978.
28. *Express* (Köln/Bonn), March 8, 1978.
29. *Die Welt*, November 4, 1978.
30. *International Herald Tribune*, November 11, 1978.
31. *Saarbrücker Zeitung*, August 8, 1980.
32. *Hannoversche Allgemeine*, September 13, 1980.
33. *Wiesbadener Kurier*, July 25, 1980; *Kieler Nachrichten*, August 29, 1980.
34. *Wiesbadener Kurier*, July 25, 1980; *Augsburger Allgemeine*, July 26, 1980; *Kieler Nachrichten*, August 29, 1980.

11

Reflections and Conclusions on Morale Factors

The Six Key Factors: A Review

Before reaching general conclusions in regard to the morale of American forces in Germany, it might be helpful to review the major findings in reference to the six key morale factors we have analyzed.

We have seen that problems with drug abuse increase and decrease from period to period reflecting such factors as the availability of various substances, youth styles and trends, and the effort expended by the military to control the problem. The problem is, however, persistent and intractable. Military authorities have never been able to conquer it and will not be likely to do so, as the problem in the military is simply an extension and a reflection of the wider phenomenon of pervasive drug abuse in U.S. society. Drug abuse rates are at all times higher than they ought to be, but it is unfair to blame the military for failing to control the problem adequately. Military authorities have, at times, resorted to near-draconian measures, and the problem remains a matter of high priority at military headquarters. Whenever drug abuse problems increase or receive increased attention by the media, the image of the American military in Germany suffers another setback. In general, it is fair to say that the persistent drug problem quite negatively affects the approval rating of the U.S. military in Germany by the German population.

Like the drug problem, the problems of crime and indiscipline wax and wane. The Germans are fully aware, however, that crime rates are substantially higher among U.S. forces than among the forces of any other NATO ally. The occasional periods of very high rates of indiscipline and serious crime—as from 1969 to 1973 and 1979 to 1982—have produced fear in German populations adjacent to U.S. military bases as well as lengthy, sensational stories in the West German press that have serious consequences for the image of the U.S. military in Germany. The military crime problem, like the drug problem, never disappears and cannot be expected to as long as the United States itself continues to have rates of serious crime far higher than those of any other industrialized society in the world. In recent years analysts of military affairs and military commanders have raised the question of whether, under the regime of the all-volunteer force, the military's tools for the control of crime have been seriously weakened. In addition, a series of U.S. judicial decisions and the development of a stronger sense of soldiers' rights have had the result of weakening the enforcement and order-keeping competence of military commanders. Whether these developments are, in the long run, desirable or undesirable is a matter of considerable dispute based on the perspectives of differing value systems. Given the nature and mission of a military force, however, it is not difficult to conclude that the rates of crime and indiscipline among U.S. forces in Germany are definitely higher than they ought to be. This circumstance, by creating negative images of American forces in the German mind, reduces the viability of the U.S. military presence.

Discrimination against American soldiers has existed in West Germany for many years. For the first quarter-century after World War II, however, the problem was not considered particularly serious, as discrimination tended to be infrequent and relatively mild. In recent years discrimination against U.S. military personnel has increased in both frequency and intensity. In addition, a distinct racial component has become more evident, in the opinion of many observers. Even though white military personnel claim discrimination from West Germans by higher percentages than black personnel, there is little doubt that black soldiers and air force personnel experience an injurious racial element in such discrimination not felt by whites. It is not correct to conclude, however, that discrimination against American military personnel is either endemic or widespread throughout West German society. Mass media, especially in the United States, have tended to exaggerate the story beyond all reasonable bounds. Survey data and other types of evidence do not indicate that Germany is a society in which racism and discrimination are rampant and deeply embedded. German political leaders at both the federal and state levels have confronted the problem with forthrightness and courage and have taken many important steps to reduce the incidence of discrimination. It is also true that German discrimination is caused in large part by the obnoxious behavior of American troops. In order to improve the behavior of the troops and reduce the level of behavior-induced discrimination, it is imperative that military authorities become more highly sensitized to the cultural and representational functions of the American presence in Germany. The purely military mission of American forces cannot be carried out if the cultural/political foundation upon which the American presence rests is eroded. Greater efforts in the areas of language training and cultural awareness must be made, if the viability of the American military presence is to be preserved.

Terrorism became a major problem for U.S. forces in the early 1970s. From 1975 to 1979 the problem appeared to be well under control. The years 1979 to 1981 brought a major escalation of terrorist activity, culminating in the spectacular terrorist attacks at Ramstein and Heidelberg in the fall of 1981. Terrorism has had mixed effects on the morale of U.S. troops. It has increased the physical separation and hence the psychological distance between Germans and Americans because of heightened suspicion and additional layers of security measures. But in somewhat contrary fashion, terrorism has also served to increase the troops' sense of commitment to duty and the level of unit cohesion. Commanders have reported a greater sense of esprit de corps at times when the terrorist threat has been greatest. The terrorists have made almost no progress in achieving their major goals, which are to drive American forces into a totally ghettoized existence and to undermine German confidence in the ability of these forces to defend the country. The coverage of terrorism by the mass media in the United States, by exaggerating the nature and scale of the problem, has had negative effects upon both public and congressional opinion. To the extent that American publics are mistakenly led to believe that American forces operate within a vast sea of terrorists who have many sympathetic German supporters, the stage is set for the development of greater distance in the German-American political relationship.

The first signs of poverty among American forces in Germany appeared in the early 1970s. The worst period of hardship, however, was the four-year period from the spring of 1978 to the spring of 1982, when the dollar's exchange rate remained consistently well below the two-mark level. Severe poverty had a devastating effect upon the morale of U.S. forces at all levels, although hardest hit were the younger, married, enlisted personnel who were not entitled to the benefits of command-sponsored status. The short-term, more tangible effects of poverty included lower rates of retention, leading to shortages of experienced noncommissioned officers and commissioned officers, high rates of turnover, and thus a lower level of experience for the forces as a whole. The problems of crime and indiscipline were also aggravated by the poverty syndrome. The long-term, less tangible effects of poverty included: negative images, both the West German image and the self-image of U.S. troops; increased isolation of U.S. military personnel from the German population; and concern that low levels of morale would diminish the combat effectiveness of American forces. Closely related is the degraded condition of American physical facilities in Germany. The highly negative effects that the outmoded facilities have upon morale at all levels can scarcely be exaggerated. The condition of the physical plant is now so serious that the ability of U.S. forces to continue to operate with such facilities is open to question. If a solution is not forthcoming in the near future, the viability of the U.S. military presence in West Germany is certain to be seriously undermined.

These generalizations would seem to constitute a portrait of U.S. military morale in West Germany so negative as to leave little room for optimism. Separate studies of each factor of morale provide heavy doses of discouraging information. Excessive pessimism is, however, unwarranted. It is important to remember that the various factors are so closely related that the effects of each one are hardly separable from the effects of the others. Moreover, in reference to each individual morale factor, there is also cause for satisfaction. Though rates of drug abuse are perhaps always higher than they should be, the services have on several occasions been successful in bringing them down dramatically in short periods of time. Similar successes have been reported in bringing down rates of crime and indiscipline. The problems in the air force are much less severe than in the army, but even the army has enjoyed periods when drug abuse and crime were not major problems and were kept at levels far below those prevalent in U.S. society as a whole. Though discrimination has devastating results on a personal level wherever and whenever it occurs, it is not so widespread in West Germany as to constitute an insoluble dilemma for military authorities.

There is room for encouragement also in the success U.S. military and German leaders have had in combatting discrimination in a sizeable number of localities. West German terrorists have largely failed in the realization of any of their major goals, and the increased security precautions instituted by military leaders, though inconvenient, have not had the effect of placing military communities within the confines of sealed ghettos. The poverty crisis, after inflicting four years of hardship and suffering upon thousands of GIs and their families, finally eased up in the spring of 1982. Even in reference to the most intractable problem of all, outmoded physical facilities, the construction of the beautiful and functional large new base at Garlstedt in the late 1970s gives rise to hopes that formulas can be devised to build additional new bases in the years ahead.

The Cumulative Effect: Psychological Distance

If there is a recurrent theme that seems to be woven into all the morale factors, separately and collectively, it is the phenomenon of increasing distance that has characterized the relationship between the U.S. military and the German civilian population in the last decade and a half. This theme is apparent especially during periods of heavy drug abuse, periods of high rates of crime and indiscipline, periods of racial struggle, periods of greater discrimination by Germans against military personnel, periods when the terrorist threat escalates, and periods of severe poverty for American personnel. In each case the troubles experienced by American forces translate into a higher level of isolation of the forces from a supportive German environment and into greater social and psychological distance between American forces and the German civilian population. Some problems derive in large part from circumstances attributable to the Americans. Periods of heavy drug abuse and rampant criminality have badly tarnished the image of American forces in the German mind. Increased estrangement is but a logical and expected outcome. On the other hand, some of the problems are more attributable to the Germans, such as the increased terrorist threat and higher levels of discrimination.

The trend toward increased estrangement is unfortunate. If one thinks back to the "good old days" of the 1950s and 1960s, when American soldiers lived well in Germany and seemed to enjoy the respect and admiration of almost all Germans, one might conclude that the relationship had gone sour in the intervening years. The "good old days," however, were never that blissful, and it is important not to overidolize the better years of the relationship. Even during the heyday of good relations, there was always a substantial though minority group of Germans who opposed the large-scale U.S. military presence. It is important to realize also that a certain amount of distance would have developed in the relationship even if the U.S. forces had not developed severe problems. The political relationships among close allies are not unlike relationships within families. Rivalries, competition, hurt feelings, status adjustments, and misunderstandings occur from time to time despite the best intentions of all parties.

Shifts in the structure of world politics and in the basic nature of the alliance relationship would have altered the politicomilitary relationship between West Germany and the United States with the passage of time in any case. The Federal Republic of Germany would not have been content to remain in a condition of permanent subservience to unquestioned U.S. hegemony. There is a natural rhythm and flow to the events that have taken place. With generous U.S. assistance, West Germany has quite naturally developed from adolescence to adulthood both economically and politically. As the country began to flex its diplomatic muscles in the 1960s and 1970s, it was inevitable that greater distance would characterize the relationship. The FRG reemerged as a major participant in world politics, the European Community gained economic clout, and the United States simultaneously lost ground as a political, military, and economic superpower; it was only natural that the erstwhile big brother–little brother relationship between the two countries would undergo drastic change. Hence, the alliance relationship would have become more difficult to manage even if the morale problems of the U.S. forces had not appeared.

At the same time, however, it is true that the problems we have outlined widened the distance considerably beyond what it otherwise would have been. One is struck by the extent to which the West Germans' respect for U.S. forces diminished due to intractable problems on the U.S. side. The estrangement arising from these problems need not and should not have taken place. The assignment of responsibility is a hazardous enterprise at best, as it cannot be pinpointed with any degree of accuracy. At the very least, however, it is appropriate to cite the failures of leadership in the Department of Defense and the Congress. In reference to the drug problem and the crime problem, we may legitimately ask why military leaders permitted these problems to escalate to such oversized dimensions in the first place. Why were military leaders for too long a time oblivious to the damage these problems were doing to the relationship between the military forces and the West German population? Why were strategies to cope with these problems devised so belatedly?

The Question of Responsibility

It is easy to criticize the military leaders in the Pentagon. Their failures are apparent for anyone to see. At the same time, however, one gets the impression that the nation's military leaders, both in the United States and in Germany, were struggling with herculean problems not of their own making. The massive drug and crime problems were not invented by military commanders; though the commanders may not have come to grips with the problems soon enough or effectively enough, the problems themselves represent simply an overflow into the military of problems endemic in U.S. society itself. The senior U.S. military leaders in Germany, in both the army and the air force, seem to be highly sensitive to the substantive problems that beset the forces. They have attempted to combat discrimination against U.S. service personnel with energy and dedication. During the worst of the poverty crisis they intervened forthrightly with the limited tools at their disposal, such as opening the mess halls to the spouses and children of service personnel.

The real insensitivity rests at the higher levels of the civilian leadership in the Pentagon. The constant problem for the senior commanders at Heidelberg, Ramstein, and Stuttgart is to get through to the Pentagon's civilian leadership in Washington the message that problems with troop morale in West Germany demand attention and imaginative responses. The fascination of the Pentagon's leaders with technology and weapons programs at the expense of the mundane day-to-day living conditions of the enlisted troops results in endemic inattention and insensitivity to morale problems of U.S. troops stationed abroad.

More fundamentally, however, criticism ought to be directed at the political body that establishes the policies and appropriates the funds for all U.S. military operations, namely, the Congress. In the first place, relatively few members of either the House or the Senate possess any familiarity with conditions affecting morale in the nation's armed forces. The giant cat-and-mouse game played out constantly between the administration and Congress, whereby Congress searches for ways to cut what is considered an overly fat defense budget zealously protected by the executive branch, is a process that directs attention almost exclusively to big-ticket weapons programs and funding for major military programs. As the members of Congress grandstand to their publics by purporting to stand tough on the defense budget, it is the low-ranking soldiers in the field who are totally forgotten. Congress appears to be responsive occasionally by holding highly publicized hearings on specific military problems such as the drug problem, the crime problem, or poverty. Headlines are made on the evening news with sensational revelations concerning drug abuse or rampant mafia-style crime in the military. But after a number of congressmen have made headlines with statements to the effect that drastic steps must be taken to reform the military immediately, nothing really happens, beyond a report that concludes that military leaders should take strong new measures. The problem then promptly fades into the recesses of congressional concern. The case of the severe poverty crisis among the U.S. military in Europe is instructive. What military commanders needed was authority and funds to compensate U.S. personnel in real terms for the hardships caused by the dollar's loss of purchasing power. Congress responded with nothing at all.

A careful review of morale factors among U.S. forces in West Germany leads us to the conclusion that the everyday needs of soldiers and air force personnel stationed abroad is a subject for which Congress has very little time or interest indeed. This has been the situation for the last twenty years. Congressional interest is focused on matters of grand strategy, weapons programs, interservice rivalry, and overall force levels. Actual conditions in the barracks and matters concerning the social and physical welfare of the troops are subjects of low priority. Congress could have and should have created various support systems for military authorities to use in remedying the negative aspects of each factor of morale we have discussed. The record shows, to the contrary, that

Congress did nothing, except hold hearings from which various members could gain political mileage. In the case of West Germany, Congress has never really made up its mind whether the troops are there to stay over the long term or whether they are not. The threat of troop withdrawals has for many years been a convenient weapon used by Congress to force the Germans to acquiesce to congressional wishes. The refusal of Congress to face facts in reference to decaying military facilities in Germany is a tragedy of major dimensions. The pernicious effect of the degraded facilities upon troop morale compromises even the combat effectiveness of the forces. Yet Congress refuses to acknowledge the problem, let alone do anything about it. The conclusion is inescapable that, in the final analysis, the responsibility for the health and well-being of U.S. forces in West Germany rests primarily with the Congress. That Congress does not accept this responsibility fully is the crux of the problem.

Reasons for Optimism

The morale of the troops displays a certain resiliency despite congressional neglect. Indeed, the morale equation for U.S. forces in West Germany in the 1980s is cause for considerable optimism. The available evidence would seem to show that morale in general began to improve in the early 1980s, probably around the time that the poverty crisis started to ease in 1982. Many commanders assert that by 1986 morale had reached its highest level since the mid-1970s, after many of the post-Vietnam problems had been surmounted; others would go even further and assert that the morale picture is better than at any time since the mid-1960s.

Some insight may be gained by looking at further data from the USAREUR personnel opinion survey of the winter of 1982. Table 11.1 displays aggregate data for all ranks, including enlisted personnel, non-commissioned officers, warrant officers, and commissioned officers. In response to the statement "Overall, the morale in my unit is . . . ," only 6.7% rated unit morale very high, though approximately 30% rated morale either very high or fairly high. Approximately 25% believed morale to be neither high nor low, and 41.7% said that morale was fairly low or very low. The different pictures of morale according to the rank of the respondents is displayed in Tables 11.2 through 11.4. Warrant officers and commissioned officers (Table 11.4) had a much more favorable impression of unit morale than did noncommissioned officers (Table 11.3) or enlisted personnel (Table 11.2).

The vastly different opinions of officers and enlisted personnel are striking. Whereas 62.4% of officers believed that morale was either very high or fairly high, only 22% of enlisted personnel agreed. The responses of noncommissioned officers were in between these—34% saw morale as very high or fairly high. Conversely, 50% of enlisted personnel believed that morale was fairly low or very low, whereas only 15% of the officers saw morale in these negative terms. The opinions of noncommissioned officers were again in the middle, with 35.8% rating morale as fairly low or very low. Some differences between officers and enlisted personnel are to be expected. Officers, who are required to fill out reports on readiness, morale, and other matters frequently, are characteristically inclined to see morale in their units in a positive light. The enlisted men at the bottom of the totem pole, who survive the rigors of being a peon soldier as best they can, inevitably take a dimmer view. The survey data reveal, however, that the differences between the two groups amounted to a vast gulf. A substantial majority of the officers believed that morale was high, whereas fully half the enlisted personnel believed that morale was low. Clearly, the status of morale depends upon whom one talks to. The very positive judgment of officers must be tempered by the less favorable views of the enlisted troops.

The West German press began to discuss U.S. morale in more positive terms in the early 1980s. A commentary in *Die Welt* in 1981 was typical of the more sanguine evaluations that began to appear with regularity:

> In view of this assortment of economic and psychological burdens, one must ask what the status is in reference to the morale and combat effectiveness of the American troops. The answer turns out to be surprisingly positive. The troops react as a whole in a manner similar to the allegedly sober stock exchange. With the recovery of the dollar—though not in the first instance because of this—the morale, state of mind, and combat readiness of the troops have improved to such an extent that even senior troop commanders are simply amazed.[1]

Elite groups in Germany also expressed a much more positive view of U.S. troop morale in 1982–1983 than they had a few years earlier, as confirmed in interviews with a series of West German political and military leaders. In a 1982 interview, the chief of the division of the German foreign ministry that deals with foreign military forces, Herr Dr. Rötger, said that he had perceived a major improvement in morale:

> I am convinced that many positive changes have taken place in the last few years. The Wartime Host Nation Support Treaty represents a major increase in our ability rapidly to bring troop reinforcements to Europe in time of emergency. The combat capability of American forces is, I believe, the strongest it has been in many years. It appears to me also that the frame of mind of the soldiers, the level of morale in general, is much better now than it has been at times in the past. Among the experts concerned with such matters in the German government there is no doubt

that reliance upon American forces as a major element of deterrence and
security is a sound policy. The strength and capability of American forces
stands beyond question.[2]

Even officers in the West German army displayed much more enthusiasm
for developments in the U.S. forces:

> The relationships between German officers and American officers have
> always been extremely good. But in recent years I think they have been
> marked by even greater understanding and cooperation, because the Amer-
> ican army has carried out a great deal of reform and modernization. I
> think that at the present time the American army has better soldiers than
> it had in the past. Morale is definitely very high. We have great respect
> for what the Americans have been able to do, and I believe that relationships
> between German and American officers will continue to be extremely
> cooperative and fruitful in the future.[3]

As of 1982–1983, an entirely different tone marked reports and analyses
appearing in the U.S. press. Careful American observers seemed to have
realized that a number of factors related to morale had taken a turn for
the better. An analysis in the *Wall Street Journal* is typical of this more
positive tone:

> But as voices rise in Congress for pulling troops home, American soldiers
> of all ranks as well as German soldiers, businessmen, students, diplomats
> and politicians describe an American army that they say is good and
> getting better. They also acknowledge that many problems, some growing,
> some fading, still persist. . . .
> The army recently commissioned a survey of its press coverage. Of
> 138 articles in German newspapers from June 1981 through last March
> [1982], 74 were deemed favorable. But U.S. press coverage of the army in
> Germany was less positive, and American attitudes worry some U.S.
> politicians. . . .
> As for the fighting ability of the army in Germany, a lot of its members
> say it hasn't been given its due. Capt. Stephen Hawkins, commanding a
> cavalry camp in a forest clearing near the Czech border, says he has "seen
> a vast improvement in the quality of soldiers in the last five years. We
> had soldiers in the past who couldn't learn what to do—couldn't read the
> maintenance manuals for the tanks. Well, there might be half a dozen like
> that now (in his 100-man troop): five years ago there were probably 15."[4]

This evaluation was echoed in a review of the 1982 NATO maneuvers
that appeared in the *Chicago Sun-Times*.

The general impressions of a reporter returning to view the games after four years is that substantial improvements have been made. . . .
Gen. Frederick Kroesen, chief of the U.S. Army in Europe, paints a picture of an army finally emerging from "20 years of neglect" to become a potent fighting force. "Of any peacetime army I have seen in my 40 years in service, this is the one I would rather go to war with," he said. . . .
The soldiers themselves looked to be taking the exercise more seriously this year, a reflection, some said, of improved living conditions and morale in Europe. . . .
The Army also says it has a higher quality soldier in Europe. . . . There were noticeably fewer complaints from sergeants about dull minded troops.[5]

Fred Reed described the positive changes in colorful language for the *Washington Times*:

Somewhat to my surprise, the Army looks pretty good today—to the extent, anyway, that one may judge by units involved in NATO's current exercises. . . . My consistent impression, for what my impression is worth, is that the Army has changed for the better.
Five years ago things were so bad that I got sick of it and quit covering average Army units. Recruits going through basic at Fort Jackson were a bedraggled mob, sullen, uninterested, slovenly. They did a creditable imitation of being on the stupid side. Drill sergeants looked upon them with contempt. . . .
At Fort Hood, I rode with tank crewmen who occasionally parked their tanks and ran into the bushes to smoke a joint. In Panama I went through jungle training with troops who barely understood their equipment. Morale was sorry. . . .
Soldiers in Reforger, the current exercise, have been in uniformly good spirits. Good troops are usually cheerful troops. Guys spending hours on unaccompanied guard duty in the bushes wanted to kid around and get their pictures taken. When our helicopter came swooping over a column of armor, the crews regularly grinned, waved and tried to get their pictures taken.
. . . Race relations look—again, for what an impression is worth—to be much better. This is a hard thing to judge without more time; still, blacks seemed to regard themselves as soldiers instead of as an oppressed group. The old surliness toward white officers was not in evidence. Race was not an early subject to come up in conversation as it used to be. Maybe it's still there out of sight, but five years ago it was on the surface. Large units sometimes seemed on the verge of racial war. If these guys were puzzled by their equipment, it didn't show.
Public Affairs officers had been telling me for months that the Army was making headway. It had never occurred to me to believe them.[6]

Preventing Further Crises:
Continuing Precautions

The general improvement in morale in the mid-1980s is, without doubt, genuine and solid. The dollar's strong recovery played an important role, as did an improved recruiting environment for the military services. Still, however, full credit should be given the army and the air force. The services were able not only to withstand the trauma of severe crisis, but to emerge from crisis with improved credibility, an achievement of major significance. But the generally positive morale equation of the mid-1980s should not lead to the conclusion that morale problems in West Germany have been liquidated. If the value of the dollar should plunge precipitously for a longer period of time, if the services' success in recruiting more highly qualified personnel should dissolve in a more unfavorable recruiting environment, or if a new wave of youthful rebellion should appear on the scene, a new morale crisis might well break out. As we have seen, the morale crises of the 1970s and 1980s were costly. Each new crisis had the effect of increasing the physical and psychological distance between U.S. forces and the West German population, thus undermining the foundation of German tolerance and respect upon which the presence of the U.S. military rests.

If another morale crisis is to be avoided, civilian and military leaders in the Pentagon will need to devise imaginative policies in reference to all of the factors of morale we have discussed. The tools needed to combat problems of drug abuse and criminality must be refined and sophisticated constantly. Discrimination against military personnel must be combatted systematically and quietly without unnecessarily arousing the sensibilities of minority groups. Security measures against terrorism must be tightened up and refined without causing unnecessary separation between U.S. troops and the German civilian population. The housing crisis must be eased by the provision of thousands of new units of government-subsidized housing near military bases. Provision must be made for generous cost-of-living and housing subsidies in order to avoid the poverty conditions that could be generated by a plunge in the purchasing power of the dollar. Most important, perhaps, is the attention that must be paid to the acculturation of soldiers and air force personnel sent to West Germany. If the problem of the isolated "barracks rats" is to be ameliorated and a higher level of respect and understanding between Germans and U.S. military personnel is to be reached, the services will have to make much greater efforts in the areas of language training and cultural sensitivity.

In West Germany it will be difficult, perhaps impossible, to sustain a high level of morale in view of the degraded condition of the physical facilities. As we have seen, the miserable condition of the physical plant gives rise to a latent and permanent morale crisis of serious dimensions. Decisions will have to be made soon regarding the feasibility of the master restationing plan. Intelligent compromises will have to be reached between the Pentagon, the Congress, and the German government. Vigorous negotiations with the West German government must be continued in order to receive as much help as feasible and possible for the building of new facilities. Most important, however, Congress must finally decide on the nature and quality of the commitment the United States will make to maintain its military presence in the Federal Republic and must be willing to support that commitment with sufficient funds for adequate facilities and maintenance.

Notes

1. *Die Welt*, September 18, 1981.
2. Interview with Herr Dr. Rötger, chief, Division of NATO Forces Affairs, Ministry of Foreign Affairs, Bonn, September 17, 1982.
3. Interview with Michael von Schubert, major, German army, Bonn, July 1, 1982.
4. *Wall Street Journal*, May 18, 1982, pp. 1, 20.
5. *Chicago Sun-Times*, October 11, 1982, pp. 1, 8-F.
6. *Washington Times*, September 23, 1982, p. 3.

Table 11.1. Evaluation of Unit Morale-All Ranks

Category Label	Absolute Freq	Relative Freq (Pct)	Adjusted Freq (Pct)
Very High	347	6.7	6.7
Fairly High	1184	22.9	23.0
Neither High Nor Low	1286	24.9	25.0
Fairly Low	886	17.2	17.2
Very Low	1264	24.5	24.6
Don't Know	178	3.4	3.5
	19	0.4	Missing
Total	5163	100.0	100.0

Valid Cases   5144   Missing Cases   19

Source: USAREUR Personnel Opinion Survey, Winter 1982,
        Office of Research and Evaluation, ODCSPER, Headquarters,
        U.S. Army Europe, Heidelberg, Germany.

Table 11.2. Evaluation of Morale-Enlisted Personnel (E1-E4)

Category Label	Absolute Freq	Relative Freq (Pct)	Adjusted Freq (Pct)
Very High	138	5.0	5.1
Fairly High	463	16.9	17.0
Neither High Nor Low	642	23.4	23.6
Fairly Low	531	19.4	19.5
Very Low	832	30.3	30.5
Don't Know	120	4.4	4.4
	15	0.6	Missing
Total	2741	100.0	100.0

Valid Cases   2726   Missing Cases   15

Source: USAREUR Personnel Opinion Survey, Winter 1982,
        Office of Research and Evaluation, ODCSPER, Headquarters,
        U.S. Army Europe, Heidelberg, Germany.

Table 11.3. Evaluation of Morale-Noncommissioned Officers (E5-E9)

Category Label	Absolute Freq	Relative Freq (Pct)	Adjusted Freq (Pct)
Very High	144	7.1	7.1
Fairly High	548	26.9	26.9
Neither High Nor Low	565	27.7	27.8
Fairly Low	312	15.3	15.3
Very Low	418	20.5	20.6
Don't Know	49	2.4	2.4
	3	0.2	Missing
Total	2039	100.0	100.0

Valid Cases   2039   Missing Cases   3

Source: USAREUR Personnel Opinion Survey, Winter 1982,
Office of Research and Evaluation, ODCSPER, Headquarters,
U.S. Army Europe, Heidelberg, Germany.

Table 11.4. Evaluation of Morale-Commissioned Officers (01-06)
and Warrant Officers (W1-W4)

Category Label	Absolute Freq	Relative Freq (Pct)	Adjusted Freq (Pct)
Very High	65	17.1	17.1
Fairly High	173	45.3	45.3
Neither High Nor Low	78	20.4	20.4
Fairly Low	43	11.4	11.4
Very Low	14	3.6	3.6
Don't Know	9	2.3	2.3
Total	383	100.0	100.0

Valid Cases   383   Missing Cases   0

Source: USAREUR Personnel Opinion Survey, Winter 1982,
Office of Research and Evaluation, ODCSPER, Headquarters,
U.S. Army Europe, Heidelberg, Germany.

12

The West Germans and
the All-Volunteer Force

West Germany has been the site of the largest foreign-based component of the all-volunteer force since the advent of the AVF in 1973. As a major purpose of this study is to analyze the sociopolitical dynamics of the relationship between the U.S. military and the German civilian population, the study of morale factors leads to the next important question, which concerns the viability of the AVF structure in the German context. What do the Germans think of the AVF? Are perceptions of the structure and quality of the AVF responsible for the more negative German attitudes toward U.S. forces that seem to have developed during the 1970s and early 1980s?

As we have seen in previous chapters, morale crises—such as periods of heavy drug abuse and periods of severe crime problems—have, without doubt, eroded West German respect for U.S. forces. What is not clear is the extent to which the various morale crises may have arisen from the structure and nature of the AVF regime. Whether or not, however, the AVF regime has indeed exacerbated morale problems, it is important to know whether the Germans think or believe that the AVF has contributed to morale problems and, more important, whether they believe the AVF has eroded the capability of U.S. forces to defend their country against aggression from the Warsaw Pact.

A lively debate has erupted in the United States over the long-term viability of the AVF. Some members of Congress, military commanders, analysts of national security affairs, and some sectors of the public have roundly criticized the AVF as a failed program, whereas others have defended the AVF as the only plausible military regime for the 1980s and beyond. The Reagan administration stood stoutly behind the AVF, as demonstrated by the president's *Military Manpower Task Force Report* of 1982.[1] The arguments for and against the AVF have produced a burgeoning number of carefully researched books and journal articles.[2]

One dimension, however, seems to be missing in this debate. Amidst all the arguments over manpower policy, the morality and political acceptability of the draft, and the combat effectiveness of the forces, no one seems to have investigated the whole range of problems associated with stationing AVF forces abroad. This issue demands attention. It ought to be an important component of the AVF debate because of the crucial importance of the sociopolitical relationships between the United States and countries where U.S. troops are stationed. If, for instance, it should turn out to be true that foreign perceptions of the AVF erode the political acceptability of the presence of U.S. forces abroad, that fact ought to be taken into account when long-range military manpower plans are devised by the Pentagon and Congress.

In this chapter we shall attempt to understand how West German attitudes toward the AVF have affected the social acceptability of U.S. forces in West Germany and hence the texture of the politico-military relationship between the United States and the Federal Republic of Germany. Three sources of evidence have been used extensively in this investigation: 1) public opinion data, 2) coverage of the issue in the West German press, and 3) interviews with German citizens ranging from high-ranking political figures to businesspeople, students, and homemakers.

Public Opinion Data

The public opinion data in this chapter were generated by the Wickert Institute in Tübingen specifically for this study. Though extensive public opinion data exist on many aspects of U.S.–West German relations, little of it has to do directly with issues that concern the all-volunteer force. The Wickert poll attempted to fill this gap by including questions that touched upon major characteristics of the AVF. Twenty-one hundred West Germans, excluding residents of West Berlin, were polled in the spring of 1983. The results are displayed in the tables appended to this chapter.

One question sought to elicit information on the level of awareness Germans have of the demographic characteristics of the army (Table 12.1). When asked whether the U.S. Army in Germany represents an appropriate or a representative cross-section of U.S. society, 41% of the respondents replied affirmatively, 35% replied negatively, and 24% were unable to answer. Of the age groups, the youngest cohort (eighteen to twenty-nine)—the group most likely to have contact with U.S. troops— was also the group with the highest percentage of respondents (65%) who saw the army as unrepresentative of U.S. society. The more highly educated group (high school, abitur, or university degree) were also more aware of the army's unrepresentativeness. Northern West Germans were least aware of the army's unrepresentativeness, while Germans in Bavaria and Baden-Wuerttemberg, where troops are concentrated, were more likely to see the army as unrepresentative. The question does not equate unrepresentative demography with an undesirable military structure, though we might assume that most West Germans, like most Americans, believe that military forces ought to be a more or less representative cross-section of the society from which they are drawn. A plurality of respondents (41%) saw the U.S. Army as representative of U.S. society. Though this is probably good news to planners in the Pentagon, it should be pointed out that such results also indicate a certain amount of confusion or misinformation on the part of the West Germans. It is also true that over a third of the respondents (35%) were aware that the U.S. Army is not very representative of American society, and it may be argued plausibly that this figure is far too high for the maintenance of robust German confidence in the credibility of the AVF.

Table 12.2 probes further into German perceptions of AVF demography by asking a more specific question about black soldiers: "Do you believe that a large number of black soldiers in the American army diminishes the army's ability to defend our country?" For the population as a whole, only 1% replied affirmatively, 87% said no, and 12% were unable to answer. There is little significant variation in the results according to various demographic groups. Slightly higher percentages remained noncommittal among self-employed and retired persons, within the oldest age group, and in the southern states. Otherwise, the variations were minor. In no case did the percentage expressing less confidence in black soldiers rise above 4%. The 4% figure was recorded in the northern states, where the population has had less familiarity with U.S. forces. The results provide much reason for optimism. There is, in the first place, hardly the slightest hint of racism on the part of the Germans. Second, very few Germans saw any connection whatever between the racial characteristics of the AVF and its ability to defend their country.

The data in Tables 12.3 and 12.4 inquire into an important aspect of the social relationships between West Germans and U.S. military personnel—housing. The obvious intent of the questions was to find out how West Germans feel about living in close proximity to U.S. military personnel. The first question asked was, "Would you have any objection if a black American military family moved into the apartment or house next door to you?" Again we see almost no manifestation of racism on the part of the Germans. Only 4% expressed an objection to living next door to a black U.S. military family. An overwhelming 94% recorded no objection at all, and only 3% declined to answer. Among the various demographic groups there were a few minor variations. Slightly higher percentages among self-employed and retired persons by profession, the oldest group by age category, and in North Rhine Westphalia said that they would object, though the results by region show no discernible pattern. What is auspicious here is that black U.S. military families appeared to be quite welcome in almost all West German neighborhoods.

It is tempting to question these results in the light of our discussion in Chapter 8 of West German discrimination against U.S. soldiers. It is quite possible, of course, that the German respondents were less than candid in their responses to poll takers about the emotional racism they actually feel. Nevertheless, as pointed out in Chapter 8, only a small percentage of West German public establishments actively discriminates against U.S. service personnel, and such discrimination is usually the result of violent behavior on the part of service personnel rather than racist attitudes. Even if it is true that the results in the table do not capture accurately the extent of racist sentiment in Germany, the conclusion is still entirely warranted that discrimination because of race is confined to a very small portion of the population.

Table 12.4 poses the same question, for purposes of comparison, in reference to white U.S. military families. For the West German population as a whole, the results were the same; 93% of the respondents said that they would have no objection if a white U.S. military family moved into the apartment or house next door, only 4% said they would object, and 3% declined to answer. Again, there were few significant variations among the demographic groups. Interestingly, however, a much higher percentage of self-employed and retired persons by profession said they would object to a white family (10%); only 7% of this same group had said that they would object to a black military family moving in next door. It could be, of course, that this group simply was not being very honest. They may well have declined to reveal their racism in answer to the first question but felt no constraint in voicing an objection to a military family in answer to the second question. On the other hand, it might well be the case that they would expect a black family to make a greater effort to live quietly as good neighbors, in contrast to the raucous white soldiers they probably had seen more frequently. Retired persons, after all, desire peace and quiet above all else. Whatever the truth, the discrepancy in the responses of retired and self-employed persons leaves some suspicion as to their veracity.

Another discrepancy is apparent for the residents of Hesse, Rhineland-Palatinate, and the Saar by region. Although 11% of these burghers recorded an objection to living next door to a white U.S. military family, only 1% stated an objection to a black military family. These results are puzzling. Either black military families have a better reputation as good neighbors among these Germans, an explanation that is plausible, or the residents of these southern German states were hiding some racism. Even with the discrepancies, the data give a clear indication that almost the entire West German population welcomes U.S. military families in their midst as neighbors. It should be emphasized, however, that the questions clearly specified families, not single soldiers. The results confirm the observations of most military commanders that the difficulties encountered in finding suitable housing for military families relate much more to the limitations of the housing market than to narrow-minded attitudes on the part of West Germans. The results also confirm that West Germans have a general fondness for Americans, as we saw in the data presented in Chapter 3.

The question in Table 12.5 was included in order to compare German attitudes on the two major types of foreign presence in West Germany, military personnel and foreign workers. In 1983 foreign workers constituted a much larger component of the population in West Germany than did foreign military forces. If we count service personnel, members of their families residing in West Germany, and national civilian employees of the six countries that maintain military forces there, the foreign military presence totaled 780,000 persons in a country of 61.5 million people, or 1.2%. The Americans, with approximately 500,000 service personnel, family members, and civilian employees, constituted only 0.8% of the population. By contrast, there were 4.63 million foreign workers and their family members in West Germany (7.7% of the population). As unemployment began to rise in the Federal Republic in the late 1970s, the foreign worker population became the subject of a quarrelsome social and political debate. As in the United States, the competition for jobs and the creation of huge foreign ghettos in major West German cities gave rise to arch-conservative groups that called for the repatriation or expulsion of foreign workers. How do West Germans compare the disruptive effects of the two major foreign populations in their midst? Do they think that the foreign worker population causes greater social disruption than the foreign military population, or is it the other way around?

The question asked was, "Which of the following groups in Germany cause more negative effects upon German society and general conditions of life?" The choices offered were "foreign workers," "U.S. forces," or "neither of these." The results, displayed in Table 12.5, show that 40% of the respondents said that foreign workers caused more negative effects, whereas only 11% selected U.S. forces. Significantly, however, a plurality of the respondents, 45%, said that neither group was the cause of major social disruption. Only 4% declined to answer the question. Only two major variations may be found in the demographic group categories. In the youngest age group, 23% selected U.S. forces as the cause of major disruption, though the data by age group do not seem to show any coherent pattern. The variation by region is perhaps slightly more significant: Only 1% of the respondents in the northern states selected

U.S. forces as the greater cause of disruption, but this is to be expected, as northern Germans rarely come into contact with U.S. military personnel and are consequently less aware of the social disruption they might cause. In Hesse, Rhineland-Palatinate, and the Saar only 5% believed that the Americans caused social disruption, but in Bavaria and Baden-Wuerttemberg fully 20% said that the Americans had negative effects. Probably the fact that U.S. Air Force units are located mainly in Rhineland-Palatinate and to a lesser extent in Hesse, whereas Bavaria and Baden-Wuerttemberg host mainly army units had some bearing on these results. As we have seen in previous chapters, problems of crime, indiscipline, and drug abuse are much more prevalent in the army than in the air force. As these problems often spill out beyond military bases into surrounding West German cities and towns, the location of army and air force units in these states may help to explain the results in the regional categories.

U.S. military analysts may find relief in the fact that the Germans are much more concerned about the social disruption caused by the foreign worker population than by U.S. military forces. These results are to be expected, however, simply by virtue of the fact that the foreign worker population constitutes a much larger segment of the population in West Germany. In addition, U.S. military personnel do not compete in the German labor market for jobs. Hence, at times of high unemployment the question of who takes jobs away from whom does not concern U.S. military personnel. Also, though there are large U.S. military "ghettos" in certain areas—such as Frankfurt, Heidelberg, Nuremberg, and Stuttgart—the cultural life of these ghettos is much closer to West German culture than are the more exotic cultural characteristics of the Turkish, Yugoslav, Greek, and Pakistani communities. And, of course, a plurality of the respondents believed that neither population—foreign workers nor U.S. military forces—caused any particular social disruption. The West Germans ought to be given credit for displaying such a progressive, enlightened attitude. Still, there is room for concern about the 11% of the respondents who registered more dismay over the social disruption caused by the U.S. military. If the social and political acceptability of U.S. forces is to be assured over the long term, that percentage needs to be very small indeed.

The questions shown in Tables 12.6 and 12.7 also probed perceptions of the social impact of U.S. military personnel upon West German society, though without a comparison to other groups. In Table 12.6 the Germans were asked, "What effect does the presence of American troops in Germany have on German society and living conditions?" For the population as a whole, a majority of 51% said they believed that there was no particular effect at all, either positive or negative; 22% said that the effects were either very positive or somewhat positive; and 16% said that the effects were somewhat negative. The pattern of results for the various demographic categories was similar to that shown in Table 12.5. The youngest group once again registered a higher percentage (26%) who perceived negative impacts, though again the results by age group show no very coherent pattern. More males (21%) perceived negative effects than did females (14%). Again, a smaller percentage in the northern states perceived negative effects from the U.S. forces, probably due to lack of contact with U.S. troops. We also find the same unusual pattern for the southern states. Whereas only 11% of the respondents in Hesse, Rhineland-Palatinate, and the Saar perceived negative social effects emanating from U.S. forces, 26% perceived negative effects in Bavaria and Baden-Wuerttemberg. Again, the locations of air force and army units may have some explanatory value. It is, at any rate, good news that for the population as a whole a greater percentage of West Germans perceived positive social effects from the presence of U.S. troops than perceived negative effects.

The question in Table 12.7 focuses on a more specific aspect of social relations—the effect of U.S. troops on West German crime rates. Only 3% of the respondents said they believed that there was much more crime in West Germany due to the presence of U.S. forces; 18% believed that there was somewhat more crime, and 65% said that the presence of U.S. troops has had no particular effect at all on West German crime rates. In the demographic categories, the most significant variations appear in the categories for sex and region. A higher percentage of males than females believed that there was either much more or somewhat more crime because of U.S. forces (30% as opposed to 17%). The pattern of results for the regional categories generally follows that in Tables 12.5 and 12.6. The percentage in the northern states who perceived more crime (14%) was lower than in the southern states. However, the percentage who perceived more crime was rather high for both groups of southern states—37% in Hesse, Rhineland-Palatinate, and the Saar, and 32% in Bavaria and Baden-Wuerttemberg.

It is, of course, good news that only 3% of the respondents believed that there was much more crime in West Germany because of the presence of U.S. troops. But when the categories of much more crime and somewhat more crime are added together, it becomes evident that over a fifth of the Germans (21%) said they believed that crime was worse because of American forces. Such a percentage, it may be plausibly argued, is too high in any case. Crime rates are a sensitive issue in all democratic states. The fact that a significant proportion of the West German population believed that the presence of U.S. forces caused greater crime does not augur well for the future. At times when rising crime rates become a potent social issue with widespread demands for a political response, there may be a greater tendency to view U.S. forces as an unnecessary evil that ought to be removed. It is perhaps highly unlikely that a majority of Germans would reach the conclusion that the disadvantages of American troops outweigh the advantages. It could happen, however, and perceptions of the relationship between U.S. forces and German crime rates represent a sensitive issue that needs constant attention by military planners.

The last table in this chapter touches perceptions of the AVF in a more immediate way. The respondents were asked to compare the defense capability of the U.S. Army today with the situation ten years previously. Though it is probably true that many of the respondents were unsure of the date the AVF was established (1973), the comparison prompted by the question is actually between today's AVF and earlier versions of the army. The results were surprisingly positive for the total population. Thirty-one percent of the respondents said they believed that the army's defense capability today (1983) was either much better or somewhat better than it was ten years previously, 36% believed that it was about the same, and only 9% thought the situation was either somewhat worse or much worse. Interestingly, a much higher percentage (45%) of the youngest age category—the group least likely to be aware of the change from the draft to the AVF in 1973—believed that the army's defense capability was either much better or somewhat better. A higher percentage of males than females (18% vs. 6%) believed that the situation was either somewhat worse or much worse. A higher percentage (14%) of respondents in Bavaria and Baden-Wuerttemberg—the areas where army forces tend to be concentrated—believed that the situation was somewhat worse or much worse.

A review of the data in these tables does not lead to the conclusion that West Germans have adopted more negative views of U.S. forces since the introduction of the AVF in 1973. Indeed, public opinion seems to have moved in the direction of greater mass approval of the American military presence during the last twenty years. Most of the questions in this chapter, however, concern the AVF only indirectly. There is solid evidence, shown in the tables in Chapter 3, that the Germans have become ever more conscious that their country's security is dependent upon the presence of U.S. troops. But this does not tell us much about what the West Germans really think of the AVF. The data in Tables 12.1 and 12.8 mildly indicate at least a couple of ominous trends. First, less than a majority (41%) of respondents believed that the U.S. Army in West Germany represented an appropriate cross-section of American society. A majority of 59% either answered negatively or had no answer. Though we cannot know from these results whether the Germans approved or disapproved of the army's demography, we at least know that there was some awareness that the demography is not representative of the society as a whole. Second, only a minority of 31% believed that the army's defense capability had improved in the last ten years. A larger minority of 33% said that the army's defense capability was worse or did not answer, and 36% believed that things were about the same. Though these results still do not tell us very much about real feelings about the AVF, this is not an opinion profile that inspires great confidence.

West German Press Coverage

A quite different picture emerges from a review of press coverage. In the earlier years of the all-volunteer force the West German press seemed to devote very little attention to the changes that were taking place. During the period from 1974 to 1978, U.S. forces in Germany were in the process of rehabilitation from the ravages of the Vietnam War and were undergoing changes in force structure mandated by the Nunn Amendment. The West German press noted that rehabilitation and improvement were taking place, but only rarely was mention made of the all-volunteer character of the forces. It took the Germans a few years to realize fully that the AVF had actually been implemented and that it was a very different military regime from the previous forces based on the draft. Most likely it was the changing demography of the forces that more than anything else captured the attention of West German commentators on military affairs. By the mid-1970s, a substantial contingent of women could be seen in and around U.S. military bases, and the percentage of black service personnel was also obviously much higher than it had been previously. These changes, and the fact that they were related to the new AVF force structure, were picked up by the West German press, though the news tended to be reported in a simple matter-of-fact fashion without many attempts to analyze the more fundamental differences between the AVF and the earlier draft forces. Only when a serious morale crisis began to grip U.S. forces in 1978 did German commentators pay serious attention to the AVF. In the late 1970s a whole new series of articles began to appear that attempted to analyze possible links between the nature of AVF forces and the problems of poverty, crime, and drugs besetting U.S. forces.

Even in the press coverage since 1978 we find few articles that specifically analyze the AVF as a military structure or discuss the problems associated with alternative military manpower policies. References to the AVF were usually embedded in articles on other subjects, often in articles that discussed the variety of problems associated with morale. When comparisons were drawn between the German Bundeswehr and U.S.

forces, an explanatory note was usually appended to explain that U.S. forces consist wholly of voluntary recruits, whereas West German forces are based on the principle of the draft.

What is striking about the press coverage from the late 1970s until about 1982 is that references to the AVF force structure are overwhelmingly negative. Although no effort to analyze press coverage statistically has been undertaken, an educated guess would be that over 80% of the comments in reference to the AVF force structure were unfavorable. The same applies to quoted statements by West German observers, political leaders, or ordinary citizens. Most of the favorable quotes in reference to the AVF were attributed to U.S. military authorities, though West German journalists seemed to find a greater number of unfavorable comments emanating even from U.S. military commanders. Following are examples of unfavorable comments, beginning with conclusions from a 1981 press commentary on alcohol and drug abuse.

> Tens of thousands of G.I.'s apparently have severe difficulty understanding the real purpose of military service, so they submerge their frustration in the consumption of alcohol and hashish.
> More important than to lament these circumstances is to search for the reasons. Undoubtedly the stationing of forces for years on end in anything but liveable accommodations plays an important role. . . .
> The more profound cause, to be sure, lies in the structure of the American volunteer army. A substantial proportion of the young soldiers are recruited from the lower social classes, for whom service in the army, marines, or air force represents very often the only possibility of escaping unemployment. The Pentagon has chronic difficulties in meeting the need for qualified personnel.[3]

In a lengthy article on the poverty and isolation of U.S. forces in West Germany, Hans-Anton Papendieck wrote in 1980,

> Changes have taken place in the American army which have nothing to do with the inverse decline in standards of living. Since the U.S. army became an army of volunteers, most of the soldiers come from the lower classes of society. Their level of education most often cannot be compared with that of the Europeans.
> Four out of ten army personnel are either black or trace their roots to Mexico or Puerto Rico. For the latter English remains a foreign language, which they learn only with difficulty or not at all because of their deficient educational foundation. They remain strangers.
> They enlisted in the army because it was the only alternative to unemployment. It would be too much to expect them to be able to appreciate

the host country [Germany], to whose defense they would contribute in time of crisis.[4]

Writing for *Die Zeit* in 1979, Margrit Gerste described the AVF forces in the following terms:

A young wife is bored to tears. She would like to register for a language course sponsored by the army. Her husband won't allow it: "There are too many G.I.'s in there." He and his buddy—both are tank crewmen—sit in the kitchen, drink beer, and are bored stiff: two ponderous southern boys, who don't like to talk much. They are in the army because they simply had nothing better to do after graduating from high school. . . .

The army is no better than the society from which it is drawn. Racial integration has not occurred. Approximately 20 percent of the G.I.'s are black, and only a very few of them have reached the higher positions. During working hours they have to cooperate, but at the end of the work day the paths diverge. At the casino whites and blacks sit separated from each other in different corners. And the G.I. bars in Mannheim have exclusively all white or all black patrons.

America has had a professional army since the end of the Vietnam War. Those who sign up do so voluntarily for at least two years. For many the army is a chance to escape from a society which more or less abandons a man to his fate, which does not have enough employment possibilities and no social welfare system, a society in which employment protection and four weeks of vacation annually are rarely the rule, and which does not have a system of universal health care.

The army, however, offers all these things: "The army takes care of you, here you don't have to worry about going hungry, and you always have a place to live," a 23-year-old sergeant said, who has been in the army four years—the last half year in the Federal Republic. He plans to stay in for 20 years, in order to cash in on a pension—50 percent of his final pay scale. The army gives him a job, a defined niche in life, and clear chances for promotion. "It's like a big family. What would happen to me on the outside? It could be a lot worse." Sergeant G. likes the army, "because the rewards are more direct and come sooner." He was recently nominated as a candidate in the competition for "soldier of the year." . . .

An American captain who works most of the time with the younger soldiers said in an interview with the *Mannheimer Morgen*: "Many of them come over here very young, have no education, and have never been away from home before. Out of fear of the 'other' way of life they entrench themselves in the barracks, which then become a wholly American world."

In this depressing little corner of existence conflicts and aggressions build. For example, none of the young men whom I met had a girlfriend. And many simply count the days until their return to the States. "Tomorrow it's only 102 days!" a boy from Vermont exclaimed. He didn't need to think it over, he knew it automatically.[5]

Comments of U.S. military authorities are also printed frequently in the West German press, some positive and some negative in regards to the AVF. The negative comments, such as the following, are never attributed to persons by name:

> American military authorities posit the change in the U.S. army to an army of volunteers and professional soldiers as a major reason for the increase in drug dependence. "Since that time the wave of drug abuse has dramatically increased," a staff officer in Washington said. In his opinion the sociological structure of the army had thereby changed. Young men, who in civilian life were unable to find employment, search for better luck in uniform. "Often the people are so frustrated that it (the military) is the only thing left," a government official emphasized.[6]

The opinions of West German officials and other citizens in reference to the AVF may also be found in numerous U.S. newspaper articles. Few are positive, especially when the subject is the relationship between crime rates and the AVF. For example,

> Fritz Kindervater, a police spokesman in Erlangen, said G.I. crime has fluctuated over the years but that it has risen again in recent months, with increasing cases of taxi drivers and people on the street being threatened with knives.
> Asked what he thought was the cause, Mr. Kindervater said, "I get the impression that over the last two years, because of the all-volunteer army, the quality of the soldier has gone down. Some of them come across totally illiterate and without any internal leadership."[7]

The most damaging comment from a West German government official in reference to the quality of soldiers in the AVF is probably the statement attributed by the *New York Times* in 1980 to Hans Matthöfer, the minister of finance. The indirect quotation was in the context of a hasty and angry reaction to charges that the West German government failed to meet the 3% annual increase in defense spending mandated by NATO. "The 3 percent standard was also deplored by the Finance Minister, Hans Mathofer [sic], who described it as mechanistic. In a thinly veiled criticism of the American forces stationed here, he said that West German soldiers did not use drugs and could read and write."[8]

Demography of U.S. Forces:
Women and Blacks

The changing demography of U.S. forces seems to have been the major factor that directed the attention of West German commentators to the regime of the AVF, not only the higher proportions of ethnic minorities, but also the higher percentage of women. As the West German armed forces contain almost no women at all (a total of twenty-two female medical officers), the larger numbers of women in the U.S. military accentuated the contrast between the West German and U.S. forces. A generous number of articles have appeared in the West German press that discuss the role of women in the U.S. armed forces, the challenges and opportunities of military women, and the relationships between women and their male peers. Although most commentators have attempted to analyze the situation objectively and fairly, a slight discernible bias has been evident against the presence of women, especially when comparisons are drawn between U.S. and West German armed forces. The issue that has attracted the lion's share of attention, however, is that of pregnancy.

The West German press reported in 1979 that there were 13,000 female troops stationed with the U.S. forces in West Germany, and that at any given time between 10 and 20% of the women were pregnant.[9] Since that time the problems with pregnancy have grown steadily worse. In 1983, there were 25,683 female personnel among the 251,161 U.S. military personnel stationed in the Federal Republic (10.2%), with the rate of pregnancy at any one time hovering around 18%. In general, the West German press has taken a very dim view of this situation. Typical of the press coverage is an article in *Die Rheinpfalz* that appeared in 1979, with a subheadline that read, "The Combat Capability of the Troops Stationed in Germany is in Danger." The West German journalists are careful to let U.S. military spokespeople do most of the talking:

"If we are unable to reduce the number of pregnancies in a reasonable manner," a colonel said, "then the problems are likely to reel out of control. Since women in uniform work not only in offices but also function as specialists for highly technical military equipment, the troops are only partially combat ready because of pregnancy. Before and after the birth the young mothers in uniform are usually absent."

"If that continues," a young officer emphasized, "we shall soon have more small children in the army than tanks and planes." As a consequence of the pregnancy boom the Pentagon has now instituted a major campaign which is intended to educate the G.I.'s more intensively as to methods of birth control. "After all, the army isn't supposed to be a kindergarten," a military spokesman said, "but rather an instrument which can decide questions of war and peace."[10]

The presence of women in the U.S. forces is one factor that has sparked a lively debate in West Germany on the issue of an all-male military establishment. As issues of women's liberation have assumed a higher priority on the political agenda, an increasing number of politically active groups in the FRG have demanded that the draft be applied equally to men and women or be abolished altogether. Though this set of issues is not the subject of our concern here, it is worth noting that the presence of women in the U.S. armed forces has served as a powerful example, positive for some groups and negative for others, of a sex-integrated military establishment. The issue of pregnant female soldiers, however, has by and large probably produced more negative than positive images of the AVF. As made clear by the West German government's White Paper on security policy in 1979, official government policy does not in any way contemplate inducting women into the armed forces: "The Federal Government rejects proposals for the introduction of a 'general national service' scheme under which young women would also be required to perform service in the public interest. Such a scheme could be implemented only at enormous expense and would actually amount to nothing more than occupational therapy."[11]

The West German government has been careful over the years to treat the changing demography of the AVF with the greatest circumspection. No government officials or members of the Bundestag have ever made public statements critical of the rising proportions of women or minority groups in the forces stationed in the Federal Republic. To do so would, of course, display the kind of racist or antifemale attitudes government officials or politicians can ill afford. Privately, however, various West German government officials have expressed concern to U.S. officials that the changing demography of the AVF might have the effect of diminishing public support for the stationing of U.S. forces in the FRG. The issue gained credence in the late 1970s and early 1980s when there was a demonstrable increase in cases of discrimination against U.S. GIs by the West German proprietors of rental property and public establishments.

In 1982, the issue boiled over into the public domain, causing considerable acrimony between the West German government and the Pentagon. In June, a conference on the role of blacks in the armed forces was held at Racine, Wisconsin. In the confidential conference report, which was never made public but somehow leaked to the press, it was revealed that a high Pentagon official had stated that the European allies, specifically West Germany, had quietly sought to pressure the United

States into limiting the number of blacks assigned to bases in Europe. The pressures, according to the official, were rejected by the Pentagon. Though the conference report did not identify the Pentagon official by name, a source in Bonn (according to a report in the *New York Times*) identified him as Lawrence Korb, assistant secretary of defense for manpower, reserve affairs and logistics.[12]

For the first time the demography of the AVF had openly become a political issue between the West German and U.S. governments. The incident sent tremors through military headquarters in both countries throughout the summer and fall of 1982. As might be expected, both governments vigorously denied that the West Germans had ever made any such request concerning blacks in the U.S. forces. On June 10, the Pentagon issued a statement saying that no pressure had been put on the United States and that no formal requests had been made. At the same time, however, a Defense Department spokesperson added, "Now what may have been said in an unofficial way, at any given time, I obviously can't speak to."[13] The West German government likewise issued prompt denials that any official request had been made or that the issue had even been formally discussed. Despite the denials, there was little doubt at army headquarters in Heidelberg that, at least in some form, such a request had been made by the West German government.

Speculation was rife as to its source. Though no one would talk about it openly, all kinds of theories abounded as to who the culprits were. Some observers believed that the idea emanated from the Bundestag, primarily from conservative CDU deputies; others believed that the pressure came more likely from the West German foreign ministry or the defense ministry. In actuality, the exact source of the request is immaterial for the simple reason that the general idea behind the request is fairly widespread in the German government. Even high-ranking government officials are quite willing to address the issue off the record and to express views that they believe are neither racist nor offensive. All West German officials are quite willing to concede that U.S. military manpower policy is beyond the purview of the West German government and that the demography of the AVF is also no business of theirs. At the same time, however, they believe that it should cause no offense to the U.S. government to indicate the simple fact that a high proportion of minority group soldiers in the American forces is bound to cause trouble in relationships between German civilians and U.S. military personnel. After all, people are not perfect anywhere, and small-minded people as well as those not used to dealing with peoples of a different culture exist everywhere, in the Federal Republic as well as the United States.[14]

The clash of perspectives here is highly instructive. Ever since the establishment of the AVF in 1973, senior Pentagon officials as well as the higher echelons of U.S. military leadership have been highly sensitive to any adverse comments about the changing demography of U.S. forces. The Department of Defense takes great pride, as well it should, in the fact that it is the largest equal opportunity employer in the world. Especially since the establishment of the AVF, military service has appeared to be a particularly attractive avenue of social mobility to blacks and other minorities. Blacks and minorities are naturally sensitive to any suggestion that they are less qualified for the rigors and benefits of military service than are whites. All major studies of minority participation in the armed services support the conclusion that combat effectiveness and other measures of quality in the forces are not in any way diminished by higher levels of minority participation.[15] Why then should allies of the United States be concerned about minority participation? In the view of senior Pentagon officials, if the United States is willing to undertake the substantial burden of defending its allies by sending a massive number of American troops to their countries, the allies ought to be thankful for such largesse and refrain from adverse comments on the demography of the forces, which is none of their business anyway.

In the mid-1970s, when the black content of the forces began to rise noticeably (19.9% in the army, 14.3% in the services as a whole), the Pentagon was forced to confront the issue of the international repercussions of the demographic changes. Army headquarters in Europe began sponsoring an annual Equal Opportunity and Race Relations Conference. At the 1975 conference, held at Garmisch-Partenkirchen, the relationship between minority participation and force credibility in West Germany occupied center stage. Minton Francis, deputy assistant secretary of defense for equal opportunity, roundly denounced as "a canard" any suggestion that the army had lost international credibility because of too many black soldiers and stated that the debate on the proportion by which any minority should be represented in the army was dangerous.

> The debate seems to center on whether there are too many blacks in our volunteer army for it to be viewed by other nations as a credible military force. We need to combat this notion as being harmful and a wrong concept of our minorities, blacks in particular. Young blacks who are victims of this canard would be expected to respond, like any victim of defamation, with anger and resentment. We can inspect the conditions in our society which would lead anyone to be concerned about the numbers of blacks in the military.[16]

Although anyone committed to the principle of an equal opportunity society can endorse Mr. Francis' statement wholeheartedly, the issue of the international credibility of the AVF has refused to go away. The surfacing of the issue in the form of an unpleasant political skirmish between West Germany and the United States in 1982 bears witness to the inherent intractability of the issue. Whether the West Germans have any right to question the demographic characteristics of the U.S. forces stationed in the FRG is not the point. The point is that the demography of the forces *does* cause problems in the U.S.–West German politico-military relationship. A willingness to confront the issue and to attempt to devise imaginative responses is the better part of wisdom for policy-makers in Congress and the Pentagon. The high ratio of minorities in the forces probably exacerbates the problem of discrimination against GIs in West Germany. It exacerbates the problems of isolation and social distance between West Germans and U.S. forces. And it probably has contributed to the loss of respect experienced by U.S. forces simply because so many West Germans are aware that the forces are demo-graphically unrepresentative of U.S. society. Again it must be emphasized that whether this ought to be the case is not the relevant point for policymakers. The point is that the facts as they are must be faced squarely and dealt with intelligently. If, indeed, it should turn out to be the case that the demography and other characteristics of the AVF have the effect over the long term of undermining the viability of the U.S. military presence in West Germany, hence eroding a basic foundation of the Atlantic Alliance, then the whole issue of stationing the AVF abroad, indeed of maintaining the AVF in its present form must be reconsidered.

Conscription vs. Volunteer Forces

Most important perhaps is that the root principle of the AVF rankles the West Germans deeply and disturbs the U.S.–West German political relationship profoundly. West Germany maintains its armed forces on the basis of general male conscription, whereas the United States relies on the principle of volunteer service. When the Gates Commission issued its report in 1970 urging the switch from the draft to the AVF in line with President Nixon's 1968 campaign promise, the West Germans, while refraining from public comment, issued numerous private warnings to the effect that the alliance relationship would become much more difficult to manage with such widely divergent military manpower policies. The West German press in general was highly critical of the idea. When the changeover from the draft to the AVF was completed in 1973, most West German press commentaries expressed regret that the United States had abandoned the principle of general duty to military service as a result of disillusionment and loss in Vietnam.

There seems to have been little change in West German public opinion and press commentary on this issue in the intervening years. This should come as no surprise to Americans when full weight is given to West Germany's national interests in the unequal security partnership between the two countries. From the West German point of view, the distribution of burdens for the common defense is inherently unequal as long as the Federal Republic maintains the social burden of conscription, whereas the United States relies on the much softer option of an all-volunteer force. In effect, the United States, by paying market-defined wages for military recruits, buys it way out of the societal dilemmas arising from conscription. Conscription is a tough policy choice for any society; it is no less unpopular in West Germany than it was in the United States and no less difficult to maintain as long-term social policy for youth. True, the United States spends a greater percentage of its gross national product on defense than does the Federal Republic (approximatley 5.9% vs. 3.7%). At the same time, however, the cost of manpower consumes over half of the U.S. defense budget, whereas the West Germans spend less than a quarter of their defense budget on manpower. For the Germans, it is not difficult to conclude that the United States avoids the burden of conscription by buying its way out with higher defense budgets, hardly a policy worthy of commendation.

The inequity of conscription vs. volunteer forces causes the West Germans to react sharply when they are criticized by Americans for not assuming a proper share of the burden of Atlantic defense. In 1980, Chancellor Helmut Schmidt expressed German picque in no uncertain terms, according to the *New York Times*: "He also said that NATO's goal of 3 percent growth must be reviewed, and he took aim at the United States, where, he has noted, there is no military draft. 'The freedom of the West will not be defended with paper money but by people,' he said, alluding to the compulsory military training among the alliance members on the Continent."[17] The West German government's official White Paper on security policy also makes clear statements about conscription that might be interpreted as an implied condemnation of U.S. personnel policy based on the AVF principle. They are statements that also ought to give pause to Americans who criticize the FRG's contribution to Western defense:

> The Federal Government will continue to rely on general conscription. Nothing gives clearer evidence of a free nation's firm resolve to safeguard and preserve its independence than the citizens' personal commitment to national defence. Our security interests and our commitments to the North Atlantic Alliance demand that our armed forces be maintained at their present level. In a state of defence trained reservists must be available to augment the armed forces to wartime strength. This is not possible without general conscription.

. . . compulsory military service is not an end in itself, but rather a
civic duty essential for the preservation of the Community. State and
society do not place any unreasonable demands upon young men by calling
them up for 15 months of basic military service. Young people must realize
that they have to accept responsibilities in return for the many rights
guaranteed to them by the Community. Conscripts serve in the armed
forces in order to safeguard our future—they do it in their own interests
and in the interests of our country.[18]

All members of NATO—with the exception of the United States, Great
Britain, and Canada—raise military forces by means of conscription.
Whatever the strengths and weaknesses of an all-volunteer force may
be, the weaknesses appear in a magnified form when the AVF is stationed
in countries that maintain military forces by conscription. The more the
citizens of West Germany realize that U.S. forces are paid volunteers
rather than conscripts, the easier it is for them to jump to the conclusion
that the problems of the U.S. forces in West Germany derive from the
structure and nature of the AVF. Especially when comparisons are drawn
between U.S. forces and the West German Bundeswehr, as they often
are in the press, the conclusion emerges easily that the Americans might
be better able to approach the high-quality standards of the Bundeswehr
if they would abandon the AVF and return to general conscription. The
Bundeswehr has only miniscule problems with drug abuse and alcoholism
as compared to U.S. forces. Rates of serious crime in the Bundeswehr
are but a small fraction of crime rates in the U.S. forces. And the
Bundeswehr does not appear to undergo the periodic crises of morale
that afflict U.S. forces every few years. The more that these comparisons
are brought home to the West German people by the media, coupled
with the message that the Federal Republic has maintained conscription
while the United States has abandoned it, the less favor the AVF is likely
to enjoy among the German citizenry.

Impressions from Interviews

The best evidence that German views of the AVF are more negative
than positive comes from interviews. Interviews provide perspectives
different from those provided by current public opinion data and fill gaps
left in public opinion data by questions that treat the AVF only indirectly.
The major problem, of course, with recording ideas taken from interviews
is that persons in governmental or official capacities who express negative
views usually do not wish to be quoted directly; their comments must
remain strictly off the record. What follows is a summary of impressions
from a lengthy series of recorded interviews with government officials

in Bonn in the fall of 1982. Evaluations of the AVF by these officials ranged from very negative to fairly enthusiastic. In general, however, the more proximity a West German government official had to the domain of security policy, the more likely it is that he had either deep reservations about the AVF or downright disdain. Few officials denounced the AVF in direct terms, as to do so would violate canons of protocol or government regulations. Many, however, expressed in one way or another the idea that there would be fewer problems in the relationship between U.S. military personnel and the German civilian population if U.S. forces were not based on the AVF principle. Another common theme that emerged from these interviews was the idea that, whatever quality American forces may now possess, they could achieve a far higher level of quality and combat readiness if the United States would abandon the AVF and return to conscription. As one official put it, "You would do our alliance a great favor if you were willing, as a society, to put your armed forces on the same basis as those of most of the alliance partners. It is no secret to anyone that the forces with the greatest problems and the least respect in Europe are the forces of those few members who do not bear the burden of conscription."

Perhaps as important as interviews is the capacity of a researcher to listen to all the implicit messages that emanate from diverse segments of a population on a given subject of interest. Although I claim no special gifts in that area, it still may be useful to record general impressions from the cacophony of views expressed about the American AVF by West German businesspeople, labor leaders, professional persons, students, homemakers, and others. In general, it may be said that older Germans are somewhat less aware of the unrepresentative demography of the AVF than are younger Germans, and that older Germans still have a tendency to view U.S. forces the way they were in the 1950s and 1960s. Older Germans are much more likely than younger Germans to express a high level of confidence in basing the country's security on the presence of U.S. forces and to believe that U.S. forces today are as good as they were twenty years ago. Middle-aged West Germans seem to be most aware of the disarray in the forces brought about by the Vietnam War in the late 1960s and early 1970s and to believe that the forces never quite recovered from the turmoil.

Two groups in particular seem to express distinctly more negative opinions of U.S. forces and to relate their dissatisfaction to the character of the all-volunteer force: students and persons who live in close proximity to large U.S. bases. It is hazardous to attempt to categorize the views of students, as their views, like those of other groups, range from very conservative to very liberal or radical. As a group, however, West German students tend to be more dissatisfied than other groups with the country's security arrangements and with the presence of a massive number of U.S. forces. Their dissatisfaction tends to be somewhat more ideologically based than that of other groups, with a higher proportion of students adopting leftist attitudes typical of the left wing of the SPD or the Green party. As a group, students are more likely than others to express negative opinions of the demography of the AVF and of its capability to defend the country. They are also more likely to be in favor of a withdrawal of U.S. troops, though much of this dissatisfaction stems from disapproval of the presence of nuclear weapons in the FRG.

The inhabitants of northern West Germany tend to be less informed and less interested than southern West Germans in issues that relate to the U.S. military presence. This is only natural, as there is only one large U.S. military base in the north, at Garlstedt between Bremen and Bremerhaven. The opinions of northerners tend to be less sharply defined on issues related to the relationships between West Germans and U.S. military personnel or the quality of the AVF. In the south, by contrast, opinions about the Americans are more sharply drawn. In conversations and informal interviews most southerners have a great deal to say about the U.S. presence and, more specifically, the AVF. What they have to say is often unsettling. The impression comes through rather strongly that there has been a definite loss of respect for U.S. forces in the last ten years. How much respect has been lost is difficult to estimate. It is clear, however, that the AVF in the 1980s does not enjoy the prestige accorded to U.S. forces in the 1950s and 1960s.

Especially in regards to the behavior of U.S. troops, many south Germans are sharply critical. In urban areas such as Frankfurt, Heidelberg, and Nuremberg many seem to be under the impression that social problems such as crime and drug abuse are much worse than they otherwise would be because of the presence of U.S. troops. It is not difficult to see why negative impressions are quickly formed. On any Sunday afternoon in Nuremberg, for instance, a large group of GIs may usually be found sprawled out on the steps of the cathedral. They are disheveled, boistrous, and inebriated. Other groups of GIs may be seen sitting at outdoor cafes at the Marktplatz singing lewd songs and making catcalls at passing females. A comment on the scene by a young German civil engineer is not untypical: "We're used to it by now. And we understand that these GIs are the forgotten members of your society who had no other option but the military." The engineer's wife continued, "They have to be here, we understand that. But you can understand, I'm sure, the trepidation we sometimes have knowing that these GI's are our defenders. Things are not like they used to be, before you installed the all-volunteer force."[19] There is an edginess, a certain acerbic tone in many of the comments an American is likely to hear from Germans when the subject is the quality of U.S. forces stationed in Germany. It is disturbing. It does not mean that West German respect for U.S. forces has disappeared or even drastically declined. But it does lead to the question of whether German respect for the U.S. military presence is slowly but surely ebbing away.

The AVF: Can Confidence Be Restored?

Despite foreboding signals, excessive pessimism should not be indulged. The polls still show that the West Germans overwhelmingly approve of the U.S. military presence. A large majority favors a strong alliance with the United States within NATO, and only a small percentage is in favor of the withdrawal of U.S. troops from the country. There is reason to believe that the quality of the U.S. troops in West Germany is improving. Pentagon studies clearly demonstrate that since 1980 a favorable recruiting environment has produced a higher proportion of young military personnel with higher quality attributes, such as high school diplomas and higher scores on military entrance tests.[20] Company commanders report that in the mid-1980s morale is higher and motivation among the troops is stronger. The West German press coverage of U.S. forces has a generally more positive tone now than it did a few years earlier. A comment that appeared in *Die Welt* in 1981 gives room for optimism:

> The American troops in the Federal Republic are a professional army composed of volunteers who serve for longer periods [than the earlier conscript forces]. Surprisingly, however, their political attitudes and their moral quality are not essentially different from those of the conscript army.
>
> The readiness and the morale of the Americans as derived from their democratic tradition depend very much upon the condition that their presence in the host country is welcomed and appreciated, and that one does not proscribe their presence with public, one-sided calls for disarmament. If it should happen that they are not welcomed by the great majority of the German people, then they would not be worth any more than they were in the last years in Vietnam. If that happened the Germans would have lost the protection which has saved them from war for the last 36 years.[21]

Such comments are not frequent, but they have begun to appear, and the more often West Germans read positive evaluations of the AVF in their newspapers, the more likely it is that higher respect for the AVF can be generated.

Still, there are nagging questions about the AVF in West Germany that will not go away. The most pressing question is whether the respect and prestige that U.S. forces in the Federal Republic once enjoyed can be restored. There are two distinct possibilities. It is possible that the positive trends may be converted into a process of growing respect for American forces. If so, however, the process most likely will be slow and halting. It is also possible that public respect for the forces will continue to diminish, as has clearly happened during the past decade. If the latter possibility should materialize, then the viability of the U.S. military presence in West Germany will eventually be undermined. It is this possibility that demands the attention of Congress, the administration, and policy planners in the Department of Defense.

It is inevitable that the coming decade will see a great national debate on military manpower policy. The quality of the AVF and its long-term viability as national policy have come under severe attack. Alternatives to the AVF will continue to be discussed in the press, scholarly journals, and government circles. The missing element that must be added to the debate is the subject of the relationship between the United States and the countries where U.S. forces are stationed. At any one time over one-quarter of total U.S. military forces are stationed abroad. The army has between one-third and one-half of its personnel stationed in foreign countries. West Germany is, of course, the most crucial location, not only because it has by far the largest contingent of U.S. forces outside U.S. territory, but because the U.S.–West German relationship constitutes the heartbeat of the Atlantic Alliance. The indispensable ingredients for the continued stationing of U.S. forces in West Germany are public respect and confidence. Given the crisis of confidence in U.S. forces that has afflicted the U.S.–West German military relationship in the last decade, it is absolutely vital that confidence and respect be restored and strengthened.

At best, the politico-military relationship between the United States and the Federal Republic will continue to be strained by the basic disparity in the social burden of defense: the very fact that Germany maintains military forces by means of conscription while the United States relies on the softer option of the all-volunteer force. Though it is by no means self-evident, there is reason to suspect that the basic nature of the AVF itself constitutes part of the crisis of confidence. The critical question is whether respect for AVF forces can be nurtured. If it cannot, then the whole question of the viability of stationing AVF forces in Germany must be reviewed. If indeed the AVF itself has the effect of undermining German confidence in the alliance relationship, serious consideration must be given to alternative military personnel policies.

Notes

1. U.S. Department of Defense, Military Manpower Task Force, *A Report to the President on the Status and Prospects of the All-Volunteer Force* (Washington, D.C.: Department of Defense, October 1982).

2. See, for instance, Kenneth J. Coffey, *Strategic Implications of the All-Volunteer Force: The Conventional Defense of Central Europe* (Chapel Hill: University of North Carolina Press, 1979); Andrew J. Goodpaster, Lloyd H. Elliot, and J. Allan Hovey, Jr., eds. *Toward a Consensus on Military Service: Report of the Atlantic Council's Working Group on Military Service* (Elmsford, New York: Pergamon Press, 1982); William J. Taylor, Jr., Eric T. Olson, and Richard A. Schrader, eds., *Defense Manpower Planning: Issues for the 1980s* (Elmsford, New York: Pergamon Press, 1981); William Bowman, Roger Little, and G. Thomas Sicilia, eds., *The All-Volunteer Force After a Decade: Retrospect and Prospect* (Elmsford, N.Y.: Pergamon-Brassey's International Defense Publishers, 1986).

3. *Nürnberger Nachrichten*, September 18, 1981.

4. *Hannoversche Allgemeine*, September 13, 1980.

5. Margrit Gerste, "The Poor Devils from Across the Atlantic: American Soldiers in the Federal Republic," *Die Zeit*, June 29, 1979.

6. *Die Rheinpfalz* (Ludwigshafen) July 12, 1979.

7. *International Herald Tribune*, May 31, 1979.

8. John Vinocur, "Lag in Bonn's Arms Outlays Forseen," *New York Times*, November 8, 1980, p. 3.

9. *Die Rheinpfalz* (Ludwigshafen), July 12, 1979.

10. Ibid.

11. *White Paper 1979: The Security of the Federal Republic of Germany and the Development of the Federal Armed Forces* (Bonn: Published by the Federal Minister of Defense on behalf of the Federal Government, 1979), p. 239.

12. John Vinocur, "G.I.'s in West Germany Meet Rising Wall of Bias," *New York Times*, June 25, 1982, p. 6.

13. Ibid.

14. The views in this paragraph are derived from the author's interviews with civilian and military officials at army headquarters in Heidelberg and with officials of the West German government in late August and September 1982. Most officials were willing to discuss the issue only "off the record" on condition that their names not be used.

15. See especially Martin Binkin and Mark J. Eitelberg (with Alvin Schexnider and Marvin M. Smith), *Blacks and the Military* (Washington, D.C.: The Brookings Institution, 1982); *Military Manpower Task Force Report*.

16. Quoted in the *International Herald Tribune*, September 10, 1975.

17. Vinocur, "Lag in Bonn's Arms Outlays Forseen."

18. *White Paper 1979*, p. 239.

19. Comments by Wolfgang Schuler and Inge Schuler, Nuremberg, September 12, 1982.

20. *Military Manpower Task Force Report*, pp. II-1-30. See also Bowman et al., *The All-Volunteer Force After a Decade: Retrospect and Prospect*, Chapters 1, 2, and 5.

21. *Die Welt* (Bonn), September 18, 1981.

Table 12.1. American Army's Representation of American Society

Question: "In your opinion does the American army in Germany represent an appropriate or a representative cross-section of American society?"			
	Yes %	No %	No Answer %
Total Population	41	35	24
Profession:			
Wage-earners, Salaried employees, Civil servants	37	38	25
Self-employed, Retired, Other	47	29	24
Age Groups:			
18-29	27	65	8
30-49	40	28	32
50-69	51	22	27
Education:			
Primary school only	41	27	32
High school, Abitur, University degree	40	45	15
Sex:			
Male	34	39	27
Female	44	33	23
Size of Community:			
100,000 inhabitants or less	41	24	35
Over 100,000 inhabitants	41	45	14
Region:			
Schleswig-Holstein, Lower Saxony, Bremen, Hamburg	33	21	46
North Rhine Westphalia	38	37	25
Hesse, Rhineland-Palatinate, Saar	53	37	25
Bavaria, Baden-Wuerttemberg	43	40	17

Source: Wickert Institute Public Opinion Study, April 1983.

Table 12.2. Black Soldiers and Army Defense Capacity

Question: "Do you believe that a large number of black soldiers in the American army diminishes the army's ability to defend our country?"			
	Yes %	No %	No Answer %
Total Population	1	87	12
Profession:			
Wage-earners, Salaried employees, Civil servants	1	93	6
Self-employed, Retired, Other	3	69	28
Age Groups:			
18-29	1	95	4
30-49	2	89	9
50-69	1	80	19
Education:			
Primary school only	2	84	14
High school, Abitur, University degree	1	90	9
Sex:			
Male	1	93	6
Female	1	85	14
Size of Community:			
100,000 inhabitants or less	2	83	15
Over 100,000 inhabitants	1	91	8
Region:			
Schleswig-Holstein, Lower Saxony, Bremen, Hamburg	4	88	8
North Rhine Westphalia	1	90	9
Hesse, Rhineland-Palatinate, Saar	1	84	15
Bavaria	1	93	6
Baden-Wuerttemberg	1	79	20

Source: Wickert Institute Public Opinion Study, April 1983.

Table 12.3. Living Next Door to Black American Military Family

Question: "Would you have any objection if a black American military family moved into the apartment or house next door to you?"			
	Yes %	No %	No Answer %
Total Population	4	93	3
Profession:			
Wage-earners	1	93	6
Salaried employees, Civil servants	4	94	2
Self-employed, Retired, Other	7	91	2
Age Groups:			
18-29	4	92	4
30-49	2	96	2
50-69	7	91	2
Education:			
Primary school only	3	95	2
High school, Abitur, University degree	6	90	4
Sex:			
Male	3	94	3
Female	5	92	3
Size of Community:			
100,000 inhabitants or less	5	91	4
Over 100,000 inhabitants	3	95	2
Region:			
Schleswig-Holstein, Lower Saxony, Bremen, Hamburg	1	98	1
North Rhine Westphalia	9	90	1
Hesse, Rhineland-Palatinate, Saar	1	94	5
Bavaria, Baden-Wuerttemberg	6	88	6

Source: Wickert Institute Public Opinion Study, April 1983.

Table 12.4. Living Next Door to White American Military Family

Question: "And what about a white American military family?" (moving into the apartment or house next door)	Yes %	No %	No Answer %
Total Population	4	93	3
Profession:			
Wage-earners	1	93	6
Salaried employees, Civil servants	1	96	3
Self-employed, Retired, Other	10	88	2
Age Groups:			
18-29	1	96	3
30-49	5	90	5
50-69	5	93	2
Education:			
Primary school only	6	92	2
High school, Abitur, University degree	1	93	6
Sex:			
Male	1	96	3
Female	5	91	4
Size of Community:			
100,000 inhabitants or less	6	89	5
Over 100,000 inhabitants	2	96	2
Region:			
Schleswig-Holstein, Lower Saxony, Bremen, Hamburg	1	98	1
North Rhine Westphalia	3	94	3
Hesse, Rhineland-Palatinate, Saar	11	84	5
Bavaria, Baden-Wuerttemberg	3	91	6

Source: Wickert Institute Public Opinion Study, April 1983.

Table 12.5. U.S. Forces vs. Foreign Workers in German Society

Question: "Which of the following groups in Germany cause more negative effects upon German society and general conditions of life?"				
	Foreign Workers %	U.S. Forces %	Neither Of these %	No Answer %
Total Population	40	11	45	4
Profession:				
Wage-earners, Salaried employees,				
Civil servants	35	9	50	6
Self-employed, Retired, Other	48	14	36	2
Age Groups:				
18-29	35	23	38	4
30-49	40	5	51	4
50-69	44	10	41	5
Education:				
Primary school only	33	10	52	5
High school, Abitur,				
University degree	49	13	34	4
Sex:				
Male	54	12	33	1
Female	34	10	50	6
Size of Community:				
100,000 inhabitants or less	33	6	55	6
Over 100,000 inhabitants	46	16	34	4
Region:				
Schleswig-Holstein, Lower Saxony,				
Bremen, Hamburg	37	1	54	8
North Rhine Westphalia	50	13	31	6
Hesse, Rhineland-Palatinate,				
Saar	47	5	47	1
Bavaria, Baden-Wuerttemberg	29	20	48	3

Source: Wickert Institute Public Opinion Study, April 1983.

Table 12.6. American Troops and German Living Conditions

Question: "What effect does the presence of American troops in Germany have on German society and living conditions?"

Possible Answers:
A. Very Positive
B. Somewhat Positive
C. No Particular Effect
D. Somewhat Negative
E. Very Negative
F. No Answer

	A %	B %	C %	D %	E %	F %
Total Population	7	15	51	16	0	11
Profession:						
Wage-earners, Salaried employees, Civil servants	6	15	54	16	0	9
Self-employed, Retired, Other	10	14	45	17	0	14
Age Groups:						
18-29	1	15	46	26	0	12
30-49	7	12	56	14	0	11
50-69	12	17	49	12	0	10
Education:						
Primary school only	5	17	49	19	0	10
High school, Abitur, University degree	10	11	53	13	0	13
Sex:						
Male	3	21	49	21	0	6
Female	9	12	52	14	0	13
Size of Community:						
100,000 inhabitants or less	7	20	51	13	0	9
Over 100,000 inhabitants	7	9	52	20	0	12
Region:						
Schleswig-Holstein, Lower Saxony, Bremen, Hamburg	1	17	70	8	0	4
North Rhine Westphalia	9	16	40	16	0	19
Hesse, Rhineland-Palatinate, Saar	10	16	58	11	0	5
Bavaria, Baden-Wuerttemberg	8	11	44	26	0	11

Source: Wickert Institute Public Opinion Study, April 1983.

Table 12.7. American Troops and German Crime Rates

Question: "What effect does the presence of American troops in Germany have on crime rates?"

Possible Answers:
A. Much more crime because of American forces
B. Somewhat more crime because of American forces
C. No particular effect*
D. No answer

	A %	B %	C %	D %
Total Population	3	18	65	14
Profession:				
Wage-earners	1	13	66	20
Salaried employees,				
Civil servants	1	16	70	13
Self-employed, Retired, Other	7	21	58	14
Age Groups:				
18-49	1	20	66	13
50-69	5	15	63	17
Education:				
Primary school only	5	17	62	16
High school, Abitur,				
University degree	1	19	68	12
Sex:				
Male	6	24	55	15
Female	1	16	69	14
Size of Community:				
100,000 inhabitants or less	4	15	64	17
Over 100,000 inhabitants	2	21	64	13
Region:				
Schleswig-Holstein, Lower Saxony,				
Bremen, Hamburg	1	13	82	4
North Rhine Westphalia	3	3	66	28
Hesse, Rhineland-Palatinate, Saar	1	36	47	16
Bavaria, Baden-Wuerttemberg	6	26	60	8

*The actual phrasing of the response was: "Crime in Germany has nothing to do with the presence of American forces."

Source: Wickert Institute Public Opinion Study, April 1983.

Table 12.8. Improvement or Decline of American Defense Capability
Over Time

Question: "In your opinion how does the defense capability of the American army compare today with the situation ten years ago?"

Possible Answers:
A. Much better today
B. Somewhat better today
C. About the same
D. Somewhat worse today
E. Much worse today
F. No answer

	A %	B %	C %	D %	E %	F %
Total Population	9	22	36	6	3	24
Profession:						
Wage-earners, Salaried employees,						
Civil servants	10	21	38	7	3	21
Self-employed, Retired, Other	7	24	33	5	2	29
Age Groups:						
18-29	19	26	35	11	1	8
30-49	7	19	37	5	5	27
50-69	5	22	37	5	2	29
Education:						
Primary school only	6	22	30	3	5	34
High school, Abitur,						
University degree	13	21	44	11	1	10
Sex:						
Male	9	21	30	15	3	22
Female	9	22	39	3	3	24
Size of Community:						
100,000 inhabitants or less	7	19	39	7	4	24
Over 100,000 inhabitants	11	25	34	5	2	23
Region:						
Schleswig-Holstein, Lower Saxony,						
Bremen, Hamburg	20	21	29	8	4	18
North Rhine Westphalia	3	19	50	3	3	22
Hesse, Rhineland-Palatinate, Saar	1	31	37	1	1	29
Bavaria, Baden-Wuerttemberg	11	20	29	11	3	26

Source: Wickert Institute Public Opinion Study, April 1983.

13

U.S. Forces and
West German Security

There is a continuing debate as to whether the United States needs to station a large contingent of forces in West Germany. The answer to the question lies as much in the realm of values as in facts. It depends, in the final analysis, upon one's view of the Soviet threat, which in turn depends upon one's basic understanding of the Soviet system, its nature and intentions. If the Soviet system truly seeks peace and accommodation and does not seek to impose its model of social order on other nations, then there is no reason to suppose that Western Europe is threatened. It follows that U.S. conventional forces and nuclear weapons could be withdrawn from Europe without adverse consequences. If, on the other hand, the logic of the Soviet system or the Soviet national interest requires it to expand the communist order to other parts of the world, then the threat to Western Europe is real and requires a NATO response. Even if the Soviet threat is genuine, must the NATO response include the stationing of a large contingent of U.S. forces in the Federal Republic of Germany? The answer, in my opinion, is an unequivocal yes. That is because the security of the United States and that of Western Europe are indissolubly linked and because Western Europe's security cannot be assured without a U.S. guarantee. The positive proof of the American guarantee, in turn, is the presence of U.S. troops on European soil, primarily at the dividing line between East and West in Germany.

Soviet Intentions and Finlandization

One of the Soviet Union's primary goals for the last two decades has been to achieve a decoupling of the European members of NATO from the United States. Such a decoupling would represent a triumph of Soviet policy, because it would leave Europe vulnerable to Soviet political pressure and perhaps to military threats. The only way to avoid a decoupling is to maintain the strength and vitality of the NATO alliance and to convince the Soviet Union that the U.S. guarantee of Western Europe's security is as ironclad today as it has been for the last thirty-five years. Without a substantial contingent of U.S. forces in West Germany, the credibility of the U.S. guarantee is not convincing, a situation that might tempt the Soviets to exert pressure on Western Europe.

Few people, either experts or laypeople, expect the Soviet Union to undertake outright military aggression against Western Europe. The Soviets need the technology and hard currency that only the capitalist countries of Western Europe can provide. They are hard pressed to maintain control over their East European allies, and they could hardly hope to take political and economic control of Western Europe without a struggle of herculean dimensions. Why then, if Soviet aggression is so unlikely, should the United States continue to maintain large forces in West Germany? It is at this point that an understanding of Soviet intentions becomes so important. In the first place, status and power in the contemporary world depend less upon outright military control or oc-cupation than upon influence over decision-making elites. The point really is not whether the Soviet Union intends to mount an outright invasion of Western Europe. It is whether the Soviet Union might be able over time to achieve paramountcy over the decisions made by governmental leaders in Western Europe. The phenomenon of "Finlandization," as a description of restricted decision-making competence, is as disturbing as the possibility of military invasion.

Some observers have suggested that Finlandization is nothing to be feared and might, in fact, represent a workable solution to the problem of Europe's division into competing alliance systems. If it works fine for Finland, why not for Germany? The question itself belies a profound misunderstanding of the geopolitical realities in Central Europe. West Germany cannot be compared to Finland in any sense at all—geographical, political, or otherwise. And can we suppose that imposing Finland's dilemma upon West Germany would in fact improve security in Western Europe? Finland borders the Soviet Union directly, whereas neither portion of Germany does. The Soviet Union possesses a veto over all important foreign policy and security decisions of the Finnish government. Should any other government in Western Europe be subjected to such restriction on its sovereignty? Should it not have the right to define its values and to select its security options? Would the imposition of the Soviet shadow over West Germany help to contribute to real security in Europe? Would it be in the interest of either U.S. or European security? The answer to all these questions is clearly no, which is why any version of Finlandization ought to be resolutely rejected.

The security of Western Europe lies in the avoidance of Finlandization as well as in deterrence of Soviet military adventures. Both of these objectives can be achieved as long as the link between U.S. and Western European security is clearly maintained and is clearly visible to Soviet leaders. What is too often forgotten is that NATO has succeeded in accomplishing its mission brilliantly for over thirty-five years. The Soviets have not gained any territory militarily, nor have they achieved any visible influence over any part of Western Europe since NATO's founding in 1949. There is no reason why NATO cannot continue to deliver these results in the forseeable future, if its members continue to maintain its vitality.

The vital link between U.S. and European security can only be maintained by a substantial U.S. military presence in Europe. The very presence of large American forces in West Germany gives notice to the Soviet Union that any form of military aggression in Western Europe would immediatley engage the entire armed forces of the United States, as well as the armed forces of the other NATO allies. This is the essence of the American guarantee. Without that guarantee, the Soviets just might be tempted to military adventures at some future date. More important, without the guarantee, European governments would not be in a position to resist Soviet political and diplomatic pressure, with the result that a process of de facto Finlandization would probably occur over a longer period of time.

It is significant that debates over the removal of U.S. troops occur only in the American Congress, never in the German Bundestag or other European parliamentary bodies. The absolute necessity of maintaining substantial U.S. forces in Europe seems to be crystal clear to European leaders of all major political parties. In the case of West Germany, no major political leader in a responsible position has advocated the removal of any U.S. forces in the recent past. Even representatives of the left wing of the SPD have advocated the maintenance of American forces. In a recent article, Karsten Voigt, a former chairman of the Young Socialists and SPD member of the Bundestag for Frankfurt since 1976, wrote:

> We Germans have a vital interest in the prevention of all war— conventional or nuclear. To assure that the nuclear powers take our interest in survival into account in their calculations of their own interests, we want to connect, as far as possible, our risk with theirs. The stationing of U.S. and other allied armed forces on West German territory serves, in addition to strengthening the conventional defense capability, to link the risks of the allies visibly together with our own. The presence of these troops will continue to be in the interest of the Federal Republic of Germany.[1]

Ever since the Mansfield efforts in the late 1960s there have been recurrent initiatives in Congress to withdraw some or all U.S. troops from Germany. Such initiatives are, however, wrongheaded and ought to be abandoned. Either U.S. troops in Germany serve the vital security interests of the United States or they do not. Congress cannot have it both ways. The major reason, of course, that troop withdrawal initiatives are repeatedly introduced is that some members of Congress believe that the Europeans in general, and the West Germans in particular, do not bear their fair share of the burden of Western defense. This is an issue on which vast misunderstanding prevails. It is true that the United States spends much more on defense than do the European allies, either in terms of absolute dollars or as a percentage of GNP. Though various estimates produce widely divergent figures, the figures cited by Congressman Dennis Eckert seem to be the most accurate. According to Eckert's figures, the United States spends approximately 5.6% of its gross national product on defense, while the NATO allies average 3.5%. This means that each American invests $607 per year in defense compared with a NATO average of $434.[2] On the other hand, the United States has a very different global role to play than the European allies. The United States is a vast, continent-sized country with interests to protect all over the world, whereas the European allies are concerned only with the defense of European territory from Soviet attack. It is appropriate that a global superpower spend proportionately more on defense than small countries with limited interests.

European Contributions to NATO Defense

The substantial contributions of the European allies to Western defense are not well understood in Congress. According to a statement issued by NATO headquarters in mid-1984, the European allies provide 90% of the ground forces for NATO, 80% of the combat planes, 80% of the tanks and 90% of the armored divisions in the alliance. Their navies deploy 70% of NATO's fighting ships. The European allies have 3 million men and women on active duty and another 3 million in reserves. The corresponding U.S. figures are 2 million and 1 million.[3] Due consideration of these figures ought to lead to a reassessment of what burdens are being borne by whom. West Germany's contributions to NATO defense are particularly impressive. In the period between 1970 and 1981 the defense expenditures of the Federal Republic more than doubled, from 22.6 billion to 52.2 billion German marks, maintaining an average annual increase of some 3% in real terms. By various NATO criteria—absolute level of defense spending, real increases in defense expenditures, percentage of total national budget, per capita expenditures—West Germany is among the alliance leaders in defense spending. West Germany is also the largest European contributor to the common NATO infrastructure program (26.5% of total costs) and pays the second largest share (almost 31%, behind the United States) of the costs of the NATO Airborne Warning and Control System (AWACS) program. Beside the United States, the Federal Republic is the only NATO member that provides military aid to other NATO countries. Since 1964, 3.3 billion marks have been given to Turkey, Greece, and Portugal in the form of military aid.[4]

The role of the Bundeswehr in NATO is crucial. In Central Europe, the Bundeswehr provides 50% of all NATO ground forces and 50% of all ground-based air defense. It also supplies 30% of the combat aircraft. In the Baltic, 70% of the naval forces and 100% of the naval air forces are West German. No other NATO member has so extensively integrated its armed forces under NATO command. No other country maintains so many NATO troops within its own territory. As former Chancellor Helmut Schmidt put it,

> Germany is about the size of Oregon, with a couple of exceptions. In Oregon you have 2.5 million people and in Germany there are 60 million. In Oregon you have no nuclear weapons, in Germany there are 5,000. In Oregon you have the National Guard and perhaps the Reserve Officers' Training Corps Program and maybe an airbase or two used by the Air Force. In Germany, there are not only the German forces but American forces, French forces, British forces, Dutch forces, Belgian forces, a Canadian detachment and a Danish general. Think of your own country living under such conditions in such a densely populated area.[5]

The presence of so many NATO troops means frequent military exercises with the accompanying damage to property and crops. No other NATO country regularly inconveniences its citizens with so many extensive military maneuvers on its territory.

In addition to its financial contribution to NATO, West Germany also expends considerable sums for the viability and security of West Berlin, over 14 billion marks per year. Not included in the NATO criteria for determining financial contributions are the many nonmonetary contributions West Germany makes to Western defense. The provision of valuable real estate is certainly important. West Germany provides 444 square miles (115,000 hectares) of land, with a market value exceeding 50 billion marks, for the stationing of NATO forces. Finally, West Germany maintains the social burden of general male conscription, whereas the United States does not. If Bundeswehr draftees were to receive the same pay as military personnel in the United States, the Federal Republic would have to spend some 2 billion marks more a year for defense without achieving any increase in military capability. Because of the system of military conscription, West Germany has a substantial military force in reserve. In an emergency, 700,000 reservists could be ready for combat within three days.[6]

If the facts on burden-sharing were given proper credence by members of Congress, especially the hidden contributions not subject to quantification, a more realistic assessment of the burdens of Western defense might emerge. Empathy, the capacity to understand and emotionally sense the situation from another point of view, is needed. Robert Komer, undersecretary of defense in the Carter administration, pinpointed the problem: "When Congress complains about inadequate allied sharing of the burdens of defense, it often turns out that Congress is part of the problem. . . . Unfortunately, those in Congress who beef about inadequate burden-sharing usually don't know the facts."[7] West Germany's contribution to NATO defense is more substantial than that of any other European ally, yet it is Germany that is threatened with troop withdrawals, not the smaller European allies. If the Federal Republic is the big prize, then threats to withdraw troops from that country, precisely the place where Soviet aggression would be most likely to occur, are not in the national interest of the United States.

The Futility of Withdrawal Threats

The big danger of recurrent threats to withdraw U.S. troops from West Germany is that they will eventually backfire. Though they are meant to goad the Europeans into greater defense expenditures, over time they serve to accomplish precisely the opposite result. From the European point of view, which ought to be accorded proper respect in the United States, the European contribution to NATO defense is approximately what it ought to be. If it is not acceptable to the United States, then other security arrangements might have to be worked out. Recurrent withdrawal threats serve mainly to undermine European confidence in the long-standing U.S. guarantee of Europe's security. Europeans fear that a U.S. withdrawal will in fact take place someday, decoupling the United States from the European members of NATO and leaving the Europeans dangerously vulnerable to Soviet machinations. If that is the case, no time is to be lost in seeking alternative security arrangements. The end result of repeated withdrawal threats is not a strengthening of the alliance, but the growth of neutralist sentiment that will bring about the alliance's demise.

Withdrawal initiatives in Congress also undermine the possibility of negotiating reciprocal withdrawals of Soviet and U.S. forces from Central Europe in the mutual and balanced force reduction (MBFR) talks in

Vienna. There is little reason for the Soviet Union to negotiate seriously when the prospect looms large that Congress will withdraw U.S. troops from Europe unilaterally. As Jonathan Dean, a former MBFR negotiator, has pointed out,

> Such [reciprocal] withdrawals are probably the only way American forces in Europe can be reduced without dangerously undermining European defense morale. . . . Unilateral withdrawals would cut into the number of American troops in Europe that NATO has determined might safely be reduced in return for Soviet withdrawals, and would bring down the level of American forces to the point where further reductions by negotiation would no longer be feasible.[8]

There is another false assumption that often surfaces in congressional debates on the withdrawal of U.S. forces from Germany. Members of Congress often ask why the United States must provide so much for the defense of Europe, why the Europeans cannot make a greater effort to defend themselves. Such questions are based on a false premise. The point is that U.S. troops are not stationed in Europe primarily to defend the Europeans. They are there to provide for the defense of the United States as well. The United States is far more secure with a line of forward defense in Central Europe than at the coastline of Manhattan Island. European leaders understand this simple fact quite well. It is no wonder they become impatient with the repeated threats of withdrawal mounted in Congress. European leaders have every right to demand that the United States finally make up its mind about the nature of its vital strategic interests and the level of its commitment to Europe. The exacerbation caused by repeated congressional threats of withdrawal may clearly be seen in a statement to reporters by former NATO secretary-general Joseph M. A. H. Luns, an unwavering friend of the United States. "I told your Congress that if you feel the defense of Europe is not in your interest, my advice is to clear out. Defense is not a question of philanthropy. It is a question of interests, and you are in Europe because it is in your interest."[9]

To say that withdrawal threats are counterproductive is not to suggest that reforms could not or should not be undertaken in NATO. There is much that can be done to revitalize the alliance. The Europeans ought to be encouraged, indeed pressured at times, to commit more resources to defense. Withdrawal threats are simply the wrong way to accomplish this goal. Excellent suggestions for strengthening and revitalizing NATO have been made by expert observers on both sides of the Atlantic. Many of these deserve serious study by NATO governments.[10] There is also legitimate debate over the appropriate number of U.S. troops that must be stationed in Europe. It is possible that a small number could be withdrawn without substantial damage either to European morale or to NATO's conventional defense capability, though the more plausible arguments call for increasing, not decreasing, U.S. troop levels in Europe. In any case, large troop withdrawals cannot be undertaken, which means that the number of U.S. troops stationed in Europe must remain large.

There are two reasons why the present level of approximately a quarter million military personnel must remain permanently stationed in West Germany. In the first place, any troop withdrawals of substantial magnitude would have the effect of undermining the credibility of the U.S. security guarantee and hence lend impetus to the growth of neutralist sentiment. Such withdrawals would also send the wrong signal to the Soviet Union. To the Soviets, American troop withdrawals would imply that the United States at long last was beginning the process of liquidating the security guarantee of Western Europe. The Soviets could only see in troop withdrawals a realization of a long-sought goal of Soviet foreign policy, the decoupling of Europe's security from the United States. Second, the presence of large U.S. forces in Germany raises the nuclear threshhold in the case of hostilities. Anything that contributes to the West's ability to wage conventional warfare convincingly for a substantial period of time lowers the need for reliance on the use of nuclear weapons. The fear of Europe becoming a nuclear battleground is enormous throughout Western Europe, and the stationing of new U.S. intermediate-range nuclear missiles in Europe in the mid-1980s has aroused much controversy. The nuclear deterrent must remain in place as a necessary backdrop to conventional fighting capability and as the ultimate guarantor of European security. At the same time, however, anything that strengthens conventional capability and reduces reliance upon nuclear weapons contributes to peace. Reductions in the number of U.S. troops in Europe would have the opposite result by weakening NATO's conventional capability.

Policy Implications

The evidence presented in this book has three major policy implications. First, the stationing of a large contingent of U.S. forces in Germany should be continued for the indefinite future. The administration and Congress have an obligation to state the nature of the U.S. commitment to European political leaders in clear, unmistakable terms. The Europeans must know that the U.S. security guarantee is genuine and permanent and that it will not be abrogated by future administrations or Congress. Congress especially must make up its mind about the commitment of forces to Europe and must then stand by that commitment unequivocally. Repeated initiatives to withdraw troops from Europe as a means of pressuring the Europeans to ante up more resources for defense are wrongheaded and ought to be abandoned once and for all.

Second, Congress must back up the commitment of forces to Europe by providing adequate funds for equipment, training, and facilities. The present state of physical facilities in Germany, especially barracks and living quarters, is deplorable. It contributes negatively to force morale in a powerful way. A study by the House Appropriations Committee, released in the summer of 1984, points out numerous other deficiencies of the conventional forces in Europe:

> The United States Army cannot be sustained in combat for any extended period of time. . . . While combat forces are capable of initiating a response, the forces do not have the war reserve material and the combat service support to sustain wartime operations. Shortages in aircraft and equipment, spare parts, personnel, fuel storage capacity, casualty care, communications and munitions continue as severe limitations in the capability to sustain war against Soviet forces.[11]

The irony of such a report is that Congress itself is largely responsible for the deficiencies highlighted in the report. Congress has no trouble appropriating billions for big-ticket weapons systems at the same time that it reduces funds for personnel pay increases, training, ammunition, and renovation of living quarters. Congressional budget-cutters, in their unending zeal to "cut out the fat" from the military budget, consistently select the easiest targets, such as funds for spare parts and decent living quarters. The result is that the essential infrastructure necessary for maintaining U.S. troops in West Germany is eroded. There then seems to be no alternative but to call for withdrawals of troops from Europe, using the perverse reason that the Europeans have not contributed their fair share to Western defense. Unless and until Congress is able to straighten out its priorities in reference to the commitment of U.S. troops to Europe, the United States will endure crisis after crisis of European confidence in NATO. The alliance may in fact unravel if Congress is unable or unwilling to state the commitment of conventional forces to Europe in clear and unequivocal terms.

Finally, the debate on the military personnel policy of the United States must be reopened. It is doubtful that the AVF can be a practicable personnel mechanism in the future. In this book we have dealt with only two aspects of the AVF—the effect of the AVF upon force morale in West Germany and the effect the AVF has had upon the military relationship between West Germany and the United States. The limited evidence we have considered does not lead to the conclusion that the AVF, in general, has been a failure. It was, when launched in 1973, a dramatic departure from decades of previous experience and an exciting experiment in social engineering. In many ways it has succeeded extremely well, and in some ways its performance has surpassed the expectations of its creators.[12] There is, however, one aspect of the AVF experience that has received only scant attention and has not been taken into account adequately when overall assessments of the AVF have been drawn up. That is the effect of the AVF upon the sociopolitical relationship between the United States and its major allies.

The most important case study is, of course, West Germany, as that country is the most strategic ally of the United States in the NATO alliance and is the site of the largest U.S. military presence outside of the United States. Even here, we do not have sufficient evidence to conclude that the AVF has been a complete failure. The evidence we have to base our conclusions upon is incomplete, partly subjective in character and subject to divergent interpretations. Nevertheless, it has been a central theme of this study that the AVF has been less than successful in the context of the FRG. There are multiple strands of evidence that lead us to conclude that the AVF has played an important part in the process of undermining the long-term viability of the U.S. military presence in Germany. U.S. forces have lost much of the respect and prestige they enjoyed in former times, and the West Germans are much less inclined in the 1980s to entrust the defense of their country to U.S. forces than they were in the 1960s. There are many reasons why this has happened. Certainly the fault does not lie exclusively with the all-volunteer force structure. At the same time, however, there is much evidence to support the conclusion that the character and quality of the AVF are major reasons why respect for U.S. forces in West Germany has eroded.

There are other important reasons for reopening the debate on the AVF that go beyond the boundaries of this study. An increasing volume of studies is beginning to appear that question the viability of the AVF from many different vantage points. Most disturbing is the probability that a decline in the numbers of military-age youth in the years ahead will lead to massive shortfalls in meeting the recruitment needs of the armed forces, especially if the forces are expanded. In addition, there is much concern that the technologies of sophisticated weapons systems will be beyond the abilities of lesser-educated AVF recruits.[13] In the NATO context, the existence of the AVF will continue to cause serious political strains between the United States and the European allies. The debates on the defense contributions of NATO members can be expected to continue indefinitely. The United States, Great Britain, and Canada are the only members of NATO that rely on volunteer forces rather than conscription. The United States cannot hope to persuade the Europeans

to make greater sacrifices for the common defense as long as it refuses
to contemplate the social burden of conscript forces. The West Germans
in particular will become increasingly angered by U.S. pleas for larger
contributions to support American forces. In their view, they make a
profound contribution to defense through the burden of conscript forces,
at the same time that the United States relies on the softer option of
an all-volunteer force.

The debate on personnel policy will be neither easy nor popular.
Greater sacrifice for the purpose of national defense will not be greeted
with popular approval without a convincing case of absolute need.
Conscription, however, is not the only alternative available to an all-
volunteer force. It would perhaps be much more desirable to discuss the
issue in the context of various plans for universal national service.[14] In
any case, the debate on the viability of the AVF needs to be reopened.
Considering the body of evidence that is accumulating on the difficulties
the AVF will face in the decades to come, it would be wise for concerned
political leaders to begin the debate as soon as possible.

In this volume, we have looked at a plethora of problems besetting
U.S. military forces in West Germany. The problems are real, and they
need to addressed by the administration, by Congress, and by the American
people with courage and candor as soon as possible. At the same time
it should be remembered that the problems are merely the reverse side
of an impressive success story. American forces in Germany have for
forty years been the vanguard of the conventional defense of Europe,
and more important, of the United States itself. They remain so today.
U.S. forces in Germany have a vital mission to accomplish, and they
are fulfilling that mission extremely well. They deserve the full support
of the American people and Congress.

Notes

1. Karsten Voigt, "German Security Policy and European Security Needs," in
Germany, Keystone to European Security: A Symposium, AEI Foreign Policy and
Defense Review 4, nos. 3 and 4 (1983), pp. 26–27.

2. Brian J. Kelly, "NATO Alliance Faces Greatest Strain," Chicago Sun-Times,
October 13, 1982, p. 4.

3. Drew Middleton, "Western Defense: Are Europeans Doing Enough?" New
York Times, September 17, 1984, p. 6.

4. "Focus On The Contribution of the Federal Republic of Germany to Western
Defense," Focus On series, no. 3, May 1982 (German Information Center, New
York), pp. 2–3.

5. Quoted in Time, May 9, 1983, p. 53.

6. "Focus On The Contribution of the Federal Republic of Germany To Western
Defense," pp. 2–3.

7. Robert Komer, "How to Get Less from the Allies," *Washington Post*, October 22, 1981, p. 21.

8. Jonathan Dean, "The Risks in Reducing U.S. Forces in Europe," *New York Times*, October 23, 1982.

9. Quoted in Brian J. Kelly, "NATO Alliance Faces Greatest Strain," *Chicago Sun-Times*, October 13, 1982, p. 4.

10. See, for example, Morton H. Halperin, "Keeping Our Troops In Europe," *New York Times Magazine*, October 17, 1982, p. 82; Jeffrey Record, "Keeping Troops In Europe," *New York Times*, December 3, 1982, p. 31; Jeffrey Record, "The Europeanization of NATO: A Restructured Commitment for the 1980s," *Air University Review* (September-October 1982), pp. 23–28; Henry Kissinger, "A Plan to Reshape NATO," *Time*, March 5, 1984, pp. 20–24; John L. Clarke, "NATO, Neutrals and National Defence," *Survival* 24, no. 6 (November-December 1982), pp. 260–265; many fine suggestions by European scholars and political leaders may be found in *Germany, Keystone to European Security: A Symposium*.

11. "U.S. Forces Inadequate, Report Says," *Montgomery Advertiser*, July 7, 1984, p. 6A.

12. The achievements of the AVF are well documented in Military Manpower Task Force, *A Report to the President on the Status and Prospects of the All-Volunteer Force* (Washington, D.C.: Department of Defense, October 1982). Various measurements of the quality of recruits in the AVF have improved in the early 1980s, and since 1981 the armed services have met or exceeded annual quotas for new recruits.

13. See Martin Binkin, *America's Volunteer Military: Progress and Prospects* (Washington, D.C.: The Brookings Institution, 1984).

14. See, for example, the many excellent suggestions for national service plans in Michael W. Sherraden and Donald J. Eberly, eds., *National Service: Social, Economic, and Military Impacts* (Elmsford, N.Y.: Pergamon Press, 1982).

References—English Language

I. Books

Anderson, Martin. *The Military Draft*. Stanford: Hoover Institution Press, 1982.

———, ed. *Registration and the Draft: Proceedings of the Hoover-Rochester Conference on the All-Volunteer Force*. Stanford: Hoover Institution Press, 1982.

Arkin, William M. *Research Guide to Current Military and Strategic Affairs*. Washington, D.C.: Institute for Policy Studies, 1981.

Bachman, Jerald G., et al. *The All-Volunteer Force: A Study of Ideology in the Military*. Ann Arbor: University of Michigan Press, 1972.

Baker, Kendall L.; Russell J. Dalton; and Kai Hildebrandt. *Germany Transformed: Political Culture and the New Politics*. Cambridge, Mass.: Harvard University Press, 1981.

Beres, Louis Rene. *Myths and Realities: U.S. Nuclear Strategy*. Muscatine, Iowa: The Stanley Foundation, 1982.

Bergsten, C. Fred. *The Dilemmas of the Dollar: The Economics and Politics of United States International Monetary Policy*. New York: New York University Press, 1975.

Binkin, Martin. *The Military Pay Muddle*. Washington, D.C.: The Brookings Institution, 1975.

———. *America's Volunteer Military: Progress and Prospects*. Washington, D.C.: The Brookings Institution, 1984.

Binkin, Martin, and Shirley J. Bach. *Women and the Military*. Washington, D.C.: The Brookings Institution, 1977.

Binkin, Martin, and Mark J. Eitelberg (with A. J. Schexnider and M. M. Smith). *Blacks and the Military*. Washington, D.C.: The Brookings Institution, 1982.

Binkin, Martin, and Irene Kyriakopoulos. *Youth or Experience?: Manning the Modern Military*. Washington, D.C.: The Brookings Institution, 1979.

Blechman, Barry M., et al. *The Soviet Military Buildup and U.S. Defense Spending*. Washington, D.C.: The Brookings Institution, 1977.

Boston Study Group. *The Price of Defense: A New Strategy for Military Spending*. New York: Times Books, 1979.

Bowman, William; Roger Little; and G. Thomas Sicilia, eds. *The All-Volunteer Force After a Decade: Retrospect and Prospect*. Elmsford, N.Y.: Pergamon-Brassey's International Defense Publishers, 1986.

Buck, James H., and Lawrence J. Korb, eds. *Military Leadership*. Beverly Hills: Sage Publications, 1981.

258

Calleo, David P. *The Atlantic Fantasy: The U.S., NATO, and Europe.* Baltimore: Johns Hopkins University Press, 1970.

Carlton, David, and Carlo Schaerf. *Arms Control and Technological Innovation.* New York: Halsted Press, 1977.

Chambers, John Whiteclay, ed. *Draftees or Volunteers: A Documentary History of the Debate Over Military Conscription in the United States, 1787–1973.* New York: Garland Publishing, 1975.

Chapkis, Wendy. *Loaded Questions: Women in the Military.* Amsterdam: Transnational Institution, 1981.

Cleveland, Harlan. *NATO: The Transatlantic Bargain.* New York: Harper & Row, 1970.

Coffey, Kenneth J. *Manpower for Military Mobilization.* Washington, D.C.: American Enterprise Institute for Public Policy Research, 1978.

————. *Strategic Implications of the All-Volunteer Force: The Conventional Defense of Central Europe.* Chapel Hill: University of North Carolina Press, 1979.

Collins, John M. *American and Soviet Military Trends Since the Cuban Missile Crisis.* Washington, D.C.: Center for Strategic and International Studies, Georgetown University, 1978.

Committee for the Study of National Service. *Youth and the Needs of the Nation.* Washington, D.C.: The Potomac Institute, 1979.

Cooney, James A., et al. *The Federal Republic of Germany and the United States: Changing Political, Social, and Economic Relations.* Boulder, Colo.: Westview Press, 1984.

Cortright, David, and Strom Thurmond. *Unions in the Military?* Washington, D.C.: American Enterprise Institute for Public Policy Research, 1977.

Council on Foreign Relations. *Nuclear Weapons and World Politics.* New York: McGraw-Hill, 1977.

Craig, Gordon A. *The Germans.* New York: G. P. Putnam's Sons, 1982.

Cromwell, William C., et al. *Political Problems of Atlantic Partnership.* Bruges: College of Europe, 1966.

Czempiel, Ernst Otto, and A. Dankwart Rustow, eds. *The Euro-American-System: Economic and Political Relations Between North America and Western Europe.* Boulder, Colo.: Westview Press, 1976.

Davis, Franklin M., Jr. *Come as a Conqueror: The United States Army's Occupation of Germany, 1945–1949.* New York: Macmillan Co., 1967.

Dietchmann, Seymour J. *New Technology and Military Forces for the 1980s and Beyond.* Boulder, Colo.: Westview Press, 1979.

Doenhoff, Marion. *Foe into Friend.* Translated by Gabriele Annan. London: George Weidenfeld and Nicolson, 1982.

Endicott, John E., and Roy W. Stafford, eds. *American Defense Policy.* Baltimore: Johns Hopkins University Press, 1977.

Gabriel, Richard A., and Paul L. Savage. *Crisis in Command: Mismanagement in the Army.* New York: Hill & Wang, 1978.

Gallois, Pierre. *The Balance of Terror: Strategy for the Nuclear Age.* Boston: Houghton Mifflin, 1961.

Gatzke, Hans W. *Germany and the United States.* Cambridge, Mass.: Harvard University Press, 1977.

Gerhardt, James M. *The Draft and Public Policy: Issues in Military Manpower Procurement, 1945–1970.* Columbus: Ohio State University Press, 1971.

Germany, Keystone to European Security: A Symposium. AEI Foreign Policy and Defense Review 4, nos. 3 and 4. Washington, D.C.: American Enterprise Institute for Public Policy Research, 1983.

Gimbel, John. *A German Community Under Occupation: Marburg, 1945–1952.* Stanford: Stanford University Press, 1961.

––––––. *The American Occupation of Germany: Politics and the Military, 1945–1949.* Stanford: Stanford University Press, 1968.

Goldman, Nancy L., and David R. Segal, eds. *The Social Psychology of Military Service.* Beverly Hills: Sage Publications, 1976.

Goodpaster, Andrew J.; Lloyd H. Elliot; and J. Allan Hovey, Jr., eds. *Toward a Consensus on Military Service: Report of the Atlantic Council's Working Group on Military Service.* Elmsford, N.Y.: Pergamon Press, 1982.

Gottlieb, David. *Babes in Arms.* Beverly Hills: Sage Publications, 1980.

Goulden, Joseph C. *The Best Years: 1945–1950.* New York: Atheneum, 1976.

Gray, Colin S. *The Soviet-American Arms Race.* Lexington, Mass.: Lexington Books, 1976.

Hartmann, Frederick H. *Germany Between East and West: The Reunification Problem.* Englewood Cliffs, N.J.: Prentice-Hall, 1965.

Hauser, William L. *America's Army in Crisis.* Baltimore: Johns Hopkins University Press, 1978.

Hillenbrand, Martin J. *The Future of Berlin.* Montclair, N.J.: Allanheld, Osmun Publishers, 1980.

Hitch, Charles J., and Roland N. McKean, eds. *The Economics of Defense in the Nuclear Age.* Cambridge, Mass.: Harvard University Press, 1960.

Hoeber, Francis P. *Slow to Take Offense: Bombers, Cruise Missiles, and Prudent Deterrence.* Washington, D.C.: Georgetown University Center for Strategic and International Studies, 1977.

Hoeber, Francis P., et al. *Arms, Men and Military Budgets: Issues for Fiscal 1981.* New Brunswick, N.J.: Transaction Books, 1980.

Hope, Richard. *Racial Strife in the U.S. Military: Toward the Elimination of Discrimination.* New York: Praeger Publishers, 1979.

Huntington, Samuel P. *The Soldier and the State: The Theory and Politics of Civil-Military Relations.* Cambridge, Mass.: The Belknap Press of Harvard University Press, 1957.

Jensen, Lloyd. *Return From the Nuclear Brink.* Lexington, Mass.: Lexington Books, 1974.

Kaiser, Karl. *Europe and the United States: The Future Relationship.* Washington, D.C.: Columbia Books, 1973.

Keely, John B., ed. *The All-Volunteer Force and American Society.* Charlottesville: University Press of Virginia, 1978.

Kelleher, Catherine. *Germany and the Politics of Nuclear Weapons.* New York: Columbia University Press, 1975.

Kennan, George F. *Memoirs 1925–1950.* Boston: Little, Brown and Co., 1967.

————. *Memoirs 1950–1963.* Boston: Little, Brown and Co., 1972.

Kim, Choongsoo, et al. *The All-Volunteer Force: An Analysis of Youth Participation, Attrition, and Reenlistment.* Columbus: Ohio State University Center for Human Resource Research, 1980.

Krendel, Ezra S., and Bernard Samoff. *Unionizing the Armed Forces.* Philadelphia: University of Pennsylvania Press, 1977.

Laird, Melvin R. *People, Not Hardware: The Highest Defense Budget Priority.* Washington, D.C.: American Enterprise Institute for Public Policy Research, Public Policy Project on National Defense, 1980.

Lawrence, Richard D., and Jeffrey Record. *U.S. Force Structure in NATO: An Alternative.* Washington, D.C.: The Brookings Institution, 1974.

Long, Franklin A., and George W. Rathjens, eds. *Arms, Defense Policy and Arms Control.* New York: W. W. Norton, 1976.

Luttwak, Edward N. *Strategic Power: Military Capabilities and Political Utility.* Beverly Hills: Sage Publications, 1976.

Mako, William P. *U.S. Ground Forces and the Defense of Central Europe.* Washington, D.C.: The Brookings Institution, 1983.

Mandelbaum, Michael. *The Nuclear Question: The United States and Nuclear Weapons, 1946–1976.* New York: Cambridge University Press, 1979.

Margiotta, Franklin D., ed. *The Changing World of the American Military.* Boulder, Colo.: Westview Press, 1978.

Margiotta, Franklin D.; James Brown; and Michael J. Collins, eds. *Changing U.S. Military Manpower Realities.* Boulder, Colo.: Westview Press, 1983.

Marmion, Harry A. *The Case Against a Volunteer Army.* Chicago: Quadrangle Books, 1971.

McGeehan, Robert. *The German Rearmament Question.* Chicago: University of Illinois Press, 1971.

Mendershausen, Horst. *Troop Stationing in Germany: Value and Cost* (Memorandum RM-5881-PR). Santa Monica: Rand Corporation, 1968.

Merritt, Anna J., and Richard L. Merritt. *Public Opinion in Semisovereign Germany.* Chicago: University of Illinois Press, 1980.

————, eds. *Public Opinion in Occupied Germany: The OMGUS Surveys.* Chicago: University of Illinois Press, 1970.

Millett, Allan R., and Anne F. Trupp, eds. *Manning American Armed Forces.* Columbus: Mershon Center of Ohio State University, 1981.

Moodie, Michael. *Sovereignty, Security and Arms.* Beverly Hills: Sage Publications, 1979.

Morgan, Roger. *The United States and West Germany, 1945–1973.* London: Oxford University Press, 1974.

Nelson, Daniel J. *Wartime Origins of the Berlin Dilemma.* University, Ala.: University of Alabama Press, 1978.

————. *A History of U.S. Military Forces in Germany.* Boulder, Colo.: Westview Press, 1987.

Newhouse, John. *U.S. Troops in Europe: Issues, Costs, and Choices.* Washington, D.C.: The Brookings Institution, 1971.

Noelle-Neumann, Elisabeth, ed. *The Germans: Public Opinion Polls, 1967–1980.* Westport, Conn.: Greenwood Press, 1981.

O'Sullivan, John, and Alan M. Meckler, eds. *The Draft and Its Enemies: A Documentary History.* Chicago: University of Illinois Press, 1974.

Paul, Roland A. *American Military Commitments Abroad.* New Brunswick: Rutgers University Press, 1973.

Peterson, Edward N. *The American Occupation of Germany: Retreat to Victory.* Detroit: Wayne State University Press, 1977.

Petrov, Vladimir. *U.S.-Soviet Détente: Past and Future.* Washington, D.C.: American Enterprise Institute for Public Policy Research, 1975.

Pierre, Andrew H., ed. *Nuclear Weapons in Europe.* New York: Council on Foreign Relations, 1984.

Potomac Institute. *National Youth Service: What's at Stake?* Washington, D.C.: Potomac Institute, 1980.

Pranger, Robert J., and Roger P. Labrie, eds. *Nuclear Strategy and National Security: Points of View.* Washington, D.C.: American Enterprise Institute for Public Policy Research, 1977.

Record, Jeffrey. *U.S. Nuclear Weapons in Europe: Issues and Alternatives.* Washington, D.C.: The Brookings Institution, 1974.

———. *Revising U.S. Military Strategy: Tailoring Means to Ends.* Elmsford, N.Y.: Pergamon-Brassey's International Defense Publishers, 1984.

Ruhm von Oppen, Beate. *Documents on Germany Under Occupation, 1945–1954.* London: Oxford University Press, 1955.

Sabrosky, Alan Ned. *Defense Manpower Policy: A Critical Reappraisal.* Philadelphia: Foreign Policy Research Institute, 1978.

Sarkesian, Sam C., ed. *Defense Policy and the Presidency: Carter's First Year.* Boulder, Colo.: Westview Press, 1979.

———. *Combat Effectiveness, Cohesian, Stress, and the Volunteer Military.* Beverly Hills: Sage Publications, 1980.

Schlissel, Lillian, ed. *Conscience in America: A Documentary History of Conscientious Objection in America, 1757–1967.* New York: E. P. Dutton and Co., 1963.

Scowcroft, Brent C., ed. *Military Service in the United States.* Englewood Cliffs, N.J.: Prentice-Hall, for the American Assembly, 1982.

Sherraden, Michael W., and Donald J. Eberly, eds. *National Service: Social, Economic, and Military Impacts.* Elmsford, N.Y.: Pergamon Press, 1982.

Shmitt, Hans A., ed. *United States Occupation in Europe After World War II.* Lawrence: Regents Press of Kansas, 1978.

Stockholm International Peace Research Institute. *World Armaments and Disarmament, SIPRI Yearbook.* London: Taylor and Francis, 1980.

Sweet, William. *The Nuclear Age: Power, Proliferation, and the Arms Race.* Washington, D.C.: Congressional Quarterly, 1984.

Taylor, William J.; Eric T. Olson; and Richard A. Schrader, eds. *Defense Manpower Planning: Issues for the 1980s.* Elmsford, N.Y.: Pergamon Press, 1981.

Tax, Sol, ed. *The Draft.* Chicago: University of Chicago Press, 1967.

Thies, Wallace J. *The Atlantic Alliance, Nuclear Weapons and European Attitudes: Reexamining the Conventional Wisdom.* Policy Papers in International Affairs,

No. 19. Berkeley: Institute of International Studies, University of California, 1983.

Thompson, W. Scott, ed. *National Security in the 1980s: From Weakness to Strength*. San Francisco: Institute for Contemporary Studies, 1980.

Treverton, Gregory F. *The Dollar Drain and American Forces in Germany*. Athens, Ohio: Ohio University Press, 1978.

Trezise, Philip H. *The Atlantic Connection: Prospects, Problems, and Policies*. Washington, D.C.: The Brookings Institution, 1975.

U.S. Army War College. *Army Command and Management: Theory and Practice*. Carlisle Barracks, Pennsylvania: Army War College, 1977.

U.S. Defense Policy: Weapons, Strategy, and Commitments. Second Edition. Washington, D.C.: Congressional Quarterly, 1980.

U.S. Defense Policy. Third Edition. Washington, D.C.: Congressional Quarterly, 1983.

Weigley, Russel F. *History of the United States Army*. New York: Macmillan Co., 1967.

Zink, Harold. *The United States in Germany 1944–1955*. Princeton: D. Van Nostrand Co., 1957.

II. Book Chapters

Faris, John. "Leadership and Enlisted Attitudes." In *Military Leadership*, edited by James H. Buck and Lawrence J. Korb. Beverly Hills: Sage Publications, 1981.

————. "The Military Occupational Environment and the All-Volunteer Force." In *Manning the American Armed Forces*, edited by Allan R. Millett and Anne F. Trupp. Columbus: Mershon Center of Ohio State University, 1981.

Joffe, Josef. "Germany and the Atlantic Alliance: The Politics of Dependence, 1961–68." In *Political Problems of Alliance Partnership*, edited by W. C. Cromwell, et al. Bruges: College of Europe, 1982.

Kaufmann, William W. "U.S. Defense Needs in the 1980s." In *Military Service in the United States*, edited by Brent C. Scowcroft. Englewood Cliffs, N.J.: Prentice-Hall, for the American Assembly, 1982.

Martin, Laurence W. "The American Decision to Rearm Germany." In *American Civil-Military Decisions*, edited by Harold Stein. University, Ala.: University of Alabama Press, 1963.

May, Ernest. "American Forces in the Federal Republic: Past, Current and Future." In *The Federal Republic of Germany and the United States: Changing Political, Social, and Economic Relations*, edited by James A. Cooney, et al. Boulder, Colo.: Westview Press, 1984.

Peters, B. Guy, and James Clotfelter. "The Military Profession and its Task Environment." In *The Changing World of the American Military*, edited by Franklin D. Margiotta. Boulder, Colo.: Westview Press, 1978.

"The Post-War Atlantic System and its Future." In *The Euro-American System: Economic and Political Relations Between North America and Western Europe*, edited by Otto Czempiel, and A. Dankwart Rustow. Boulder, Colo.: Westview Press, 1976.

Sarkesian, Sam C. "An Empirical Reassessment of Military Professionalism." In *The Changing World of the American Military*, edited by Franklin D. Margiotta. Boulder, Colo.: Westview Press, 1978.

Segal, David R., et al. "Institutional and Occupational Values in the U.S. Military." In *Changing Military Manpower Realities*, edited by James Brown, et al. Boulder, Colo.: Westview Press, 1982.

Sorley, Lewis. "Prevailing Criteria: A Critique." In *Combat Effectiveness, Cohesian, Stress, and the Volunteer Military*, edited by Sam Sarkesian. Beverly Hills: Sage Publications, 1980.

III. Journal Articles

Altman, Stuart. "Earnings, Unemployment, and the Supply of Enlisted Volunteers." *Journal of Human Resources* 4 (Winter 1969), pp. 38–59.

Anderson, Frederic M. "Weapons Procurement Collaboration: A New Era for NATO?" *Orbis* 20, no. 4 (Winter 1977), pp. 965–990.

Andrews, Michael A. "Women in Combat?" *Military Review* 59, no. 7 (July 1979), pp. 28–34.

Bare, Gordon C. "Burden Sharing in NATO: The Economics of Alliance." *Orbis* 21, no. 2 (Summer 1976), pp. 417–436.

Barlow, Jeffrey G. "Western Europe and the NATO Alliance." *Journal of Social and Political Studies*, Spring 1979, pp. 3–15.

Betit, Eugene D. "Soviet Tactical Doctrine and Capabilities and NATO's Strategic Defense." *Strategic Review*, Fall 1976, pp, 95–107.

Bloemer, Klaus. "Freedom for Europe, East and West." *Foreign Policy*, no. 50, (Spring 1983), pp. 22–38.

Boutwell, Jeffrey. "Politics and the Peace Movement in West Germany." *International Security* 7, no. 4 (Spring 1983), pp. 72–139.

Brooks, William W., et al. "A Current Perspective on Military Unionization: Can It Happen Here?" *Journal of Collective Negotiations in the Public Sector* 8, no. 2, (1979), pp. 97–104.

Brzezinski, Zbigniew. "America and Europe." *Foreign Affairs* 49, no. 1 (October 1970), pp. 11–30.

Callaghan, Thomas A. "Can Europe Be Defended?" *Policy Review*, no. 24 (Spring 1983), pp. 75–86.

Cameron, Juan. "It's Time to Bite the Bullet on the Draft: Both in Number and Quality, Volunteer Forces are Inadequate to Meet a Real Emergency." *Fortune* 101, no. 7 (April 1980), pp. 52–54.

Clarke, John L. "NATO, Neutrals and National Defense." *Survival* 24, no. 6 (November/December 1982), pp. 260–265.

"Controversy Over Proposed Draft Registration: Pro and Con." *Congressional Digest*, April 1980, pp. 99–128.

Cortwright, David. "Our Volunteer Army: Can a Democracy Stand it?" *The Nation*, 223, no. 12 (October 1976), pp. 357–362.

Deporte, A. W. "NATO of the Future: Less is More," *The Fletcher Forum* 7, no. 1 (Winter 1983), pp. 1–16.

Doherty, Thomas. "Don't Sell the Army Short." *Newsweek* 99, no. 5 (February 1, 1982), p. 13.

Douglas, Joseph D., Jr. "What Happens if Deterrence Fails?" *Air University Review* 34, no. 1 (November/December 1982), pp. 2–17.

Doyle, James. "Retreat in the Senate." *The Progressive* 35, no. 7 (July 1971), pp. 26–29.

Enthoven, Alain C. "U.S. Forces in Europe? How Many? Doing What?" *Foreign Affairs* 53, no. 3 (April 1973), pp. 513–532.

Feld, M. D. "Arms and the Woman: Some General Considerations." *Armed Forces and Society* 4, no. 4 (Summer 1978), pp. 557–568.

Fisher, Anthony C. "The Cost of the Draft and the Cost of Ending the Draft." *American Economic Review* 59, no. 3 (June 1969), pp. 239–254.

Fouquet, David. "The Atlantic Arms Race." *European Community*, no. 196 (August/September 1976), pp. 26–29.

Frye, Alton. "Strategic Restraint, Mutual and Assured." *Foreign Policy* no. 27 (Summer 1977), pp. 3–24.

Gabriel, Richard A., and Paul L. Savage. "Cohesian and Disintegration in the American Army." *Armed Forces and Society* 2, no. 3 (Spring 1976), pp. 340–376.

Garnett, John. "BAOR and NATO." *International Affairs* 46, no. 4 (1970), pp. 670–681.

Gray, Colin S. "NATO Strategy and the Neutron Bomb." *Policy Review*, no. 7 (Winter 1979), pp. 7–26.

Gray, Colin S., and Keith Payne. "Victory Is Possible." *Foreign Policy*, no. 39 (Summer 1980), pp. 14–27.

Hanrieder, Wolfram F. "West German Foreign Policy: Background to Current Issues." *Orbis* 13, no. 4 (Winter 1970), pp. 1029–1049.

Haseler, Stephan. "The Euromissile Crisis." *Commentary* 75, no. 5 (May 1983), pp. 28–32.

Hassner, Pierre. "The Shifting Foundation." *Foreign Policy*, no. 48 (Fall 1982), pp. 3–36.

Heiberg, Anne, ed. 'Women as New 'Manpower'." *Armed Forces and Society* 4, no. 4 (Summer 1978), pp. 555–556.

Hoag, Malcolm W. "Economic Problems of Alliance." *Journal of Political Economy*, 65, no. 1 (December 1957), pp. 522–534.

Holmes, John W. "The Dumbbell Won't Do." *Foreign Policy*, no. 50 (Spring 1983), pp. 3–22.

Ingraham, Larry H., and Frederick J. Manning. "Personnel Attrition in the U.S. Army in Europe." *Armed Forces and Society* 7, no. 2 (Winter 1981), pp. 256–270.

Jacob, James B. "Legal Change Within the United States Armed Forces Since World War II." *Armed Forces and Society* 4, no. 3 (Spring 1978), pp. 391–422.

Janowitz, Morris. "The Citizen Soldier and National Service." *Air University Review* 31, no. 1 (November/December 1979), pp. 2–16.

Janowitz, Morris, and Charles C. Moskos, Jr. "Five Years of the All-Volunteer Force: 1973–1978." *Armed Forces and Society* 5, no. 2 (Winter 1979), pp. 171–218.

Jenson, John W. "Nuclear Strategy: Differences in Soviet and American Thinking." *Air University Review* 30, no. 3 (March/April 1979), pp. 2–17.

Jervis, Robert. "Why Nuclear Superiority Doesn't Matter." *Political Science Quarterly* 94, no. 4 (Winter 1979/1980), pp. 617–633.

Joffe, Josef. "Europe and America: The Politics of Resentment." *Foreign Affairs* 61, no. 3 (Winter 1983), pp. 569–590.

Jones, Christopher D. "Equality and Equal Security in Europe." *Orbis* 26, no. 3 (Fall 1982), pp. 637–664.

Klotz, Benjamin. "The Cost of Ending the Draft: Comment." *American Economic Review* 60, no. 5 (December 1970), pp. 970–979.

Koenig, Ernest F. "Force Reduction and Balance of Power in Europe: A Neutral's View." *Military Review* 57, no. 2 (February 1977), pp. 37–47.

Kohl, Wilfrid L., and Willilam Taubman. "American Policy Toward Europe: The Next Phase." *Orbis* 17, no. 1 (1973), pp. 51–74.

Komer, Robert W. "Ten Suggestions for Rationalizing NATO." *Survival* 19, no. 2 (March/April 1977), pp. 67–72.

Kravis, Irving B., and Michael W. S. Davenport. "The Political Arithmetic of International Burden-Sharing." *The Journal of Political Economy* 71, no. 4 (August 1963), pp. 309–330.

Kressler, Diane A. "Germany, NATO, and Europe." *Orbis* 10, no. 1 (1966), pp. 223–239.

Luns, Joseph M.A.H. "A Turbulence of Wind off NATO." *The Atlantic Community Quarterly* 20, no. 4 (Winter 1982/1983), pp. 295–300.

Mansfield, Mike. "Policies Respecting Germany." *Vital Speeches of the Day* 25, no. 11 (March 15, 1959), pp. 335–339.

Moskos, Charles C., Jr. "Compensation and the Military Institution." *Air Force Magazine* 61, no. 4 (April 1978), pp. 31–35.

Moskos, Charles C. "Making the All-Volunteer Force Work: A National Service Approach." *Foreign Affairs* 60, no. 1 (1981), pp. 17–34.

Nitze, Paul H. "Assuring Strategic Stability in an Era of Detente." *Foreign Affairs* 54, no. 2 (January 1976), pp. 207–232.

Novak, Michael. "Moral Clarity in the Nuclear Age." *National Review* 35, no. 6 (April 1, 1983), pp. 354–392.

Nunn, Sam. "Those Who Do Not Serve in the All-Volunteer Armed Forces." *Journal of the Institute of Socioeconomic Studies*, Autumn 1979, pp. 10–21.

Pfalzgraff, Robert L., Jr. "NATO and European Security: Prospects for the 1970s." *Orbis* 15, no. 1 (1971), pp. 154–177.

———. "The United States and Europe: Partners in a Multipolar World." *Orbis* 17, no. 1 (1973–1974), p. 31ff.

Polk, General James H. "The New Short War Strategy." *Strategic Review* 3, no. 3 (Summer 1975), pp. 52–56.

Richardson, Elliot L., and Mike Mansfield. "American Forces in Europe: The Pros and Cons." *The Atlantic Community Quarterly* 8, no. 1 (1970), pp. 5–17.

Rogers, Bernard W. "Improving Public Understanding of NATO Objectives." *The Atlantic Community Quarterly* 20, no. 4 (Winter 1982/1983), pp. 301–306.

Schreffler, R. G. "The Neutron Bomb for NATO Defense: An Alternative." *Orbis* 21, no. 4 (Winter 1978), pp. 959–973.

Schwenk, Edmund H. "Liability of the Stationing Forces for 'Scope Claims' and 'Ex Gratia Claims' in the Federal Republic of Germany." *Military Law Review* 65 (Summer 1974), pp. 57–84.

Seignious, George; James Callaghan; and Raoul Girardet. Symposium on The Present and Future of the Atlantic Alliance: How to Improve Public Understanding of its Objectives. *The Atlantic Community Quarterly* 20, no. 4 (Winter 1982/1983), pp. 307–326.

Seybold, Calvin C. "Mutual Destruction: A Deterrent to Nuclear War?" *Military Review* 59, no. 9 (September 1979), pp. 22–28.

Slobodenko, A. "The 'Bases Strategy'—A Strategy of Expansion and Diktat." *International Affairs*, no. 7 (1981), pp. 75–84.

Stray, Svenn. "Challenges to NATO Cooperation." *The Atlantic Community Quarterly* 20, no. 4 (Winter 1982/1983), pp. 291–294.

Strobridge, Truman R. "USEUCOM." *Armed Forces*, April 1982, pp. 98–107.

"Today's American Army." *The Economist* 279 (April 25, 1981), pp. 23–25.

Taylor, Maxwell D. "Changing Military Priorities." *American Enterprise Institute Foreign Policy and Defense Review* 1, No. 3 (1979), pp. 2–13.

Ullman, Richard H. "The Euromissile Mire." *Foreign Policy*, no. 50 (Spring 1983), pp. 39–52.

Vermaat, J. A. Emerson, "Moscow Fronts and the European Peace Movement." *Problems of Communism* 31, no. 6 (November/December 1982), pp. 43–58.

Vershbow, Alexander R. "The Cruise Missile: The End of Arms Control?" *Foreign Affairs* 55, no. 1 (October 1976), pp. 133–146.

Wallace, William. "Atlantic Relations: Policy Co-ordination and Conflict. Issue Linkage Among Atlantic Governments." *International Affairs* 52, no. 2 (April 1976), pp. 163–179.

Webb, James. "The Draft: Why the Army Needs It." *The Atlantic Monthly* 245, no. 4 (April 1980), pp. 34–44.

Wesbrook, Stephen D. "Sociopolitical Alienation and Military Efficiency." *Armed Forces and Society* 6, no. 2 (Winter 1980), pp. 170–189.

Wiegele, Thomas C. "The Origins of the MLF Concept, 1957–1960." *Orbis* 12, no. 2 (Summer 1968), pp. 465–489.

Williams, Phil. "Whatever Happened to the Mansfield Amendment?" *Survival* 18, no. 4 (July/August 1976), pp. 146–153.

Williams, Phil, and Scott D. Sagan. "Congressional Demands for American Troop Withdrawals From Western Europe: The Past as Prologue." *Journal of the Royal United Service Institute for Defense Studies* 121, no. 3 (1976), pp. 52–56.

Wood, Frank R. "Air Force Junior Officers: Changing Prestige and Civilianization." *Armed Forces and Society* 6, no. 3 (Spring 1980), pp. 483–506.

Yochelson, John. "The American Military Presence in Europe: Current Debate in the United States." *Orbis* 15, no. 3 (Fall 1971), pp. 784–807.

———. "MBFR: The Search for an American Approach." *Orbis* 17, no. 1 (1973), pp. 155–175.

Yost, David S., and Thomas C. Glad. "West German Party Politics and Theater Nuclear Modernization Since 1977." *Armed Forces and Society* 8, no. 4 (Summer 1982), pp. 525–560.

Ypersele de Strihou, Jacques van. "Sharing the Defense Burden Among Western Allies." *Review of Economics and Statistics* 49, no. 4 (November 1967), pp. 527–536.

IV. Government Documents

"Final Report on NATO Offset: Message Transmitted from President Ford to the Congress." *Department of State Bulletin*, 72, no. 1878, June 23, 1975, p. 877.

Goldich, Robert L. "Women in the Armed Forces: Proceedings of a CRS Seminar Held on 2 November, 1979." *CRS Report No. 80-27F*. Washington, D.C.: Congressional Research Service, 1980.

———. "Recruiting, Retention, and Quality in the All-Volunteer Force." *CRS Report No. 81-106F*. Washington, D.C.: Congressional Research Service, 1981.

Jones, General David C., USAF, chairman, Joint Chiefs of Staff. *United States Military Posture for Fiscal Year 1981*. Washington, D.C.: Department of Defense, January 1980.

Nunn, Sam, and Dewey F. Bartlett. *NATO and the Soviet Threat: Report to the Committee on Armed Services*. U.S. Congress, Senate, 95th Cong., 1st sess., 24 January 1977. Washington, D.C.: Government Printing Office, 1977.

President's Commission on an All-Volunteer Armed Force. *The Report of the President's Commission on an All-Volunteer Armed Force*. Washington, D.C.: Government Printing Office, 1970.

———. *Studies Prepared for the President's Commission on an All-Volunteer Armed Force*. 2 Vols. Washington, D.C.: Government Printing Office, 1970.

President's Reorganization Project. *Selective Service System Reorganization Study— Final Report*. Washington, D.C.: Office of Management and Budget, 1978.

Smith, General W. Y. "Reinforcing NATO Rapidly." *Defense 80*. Washington, D.C.: Government Printing Office, 1980.

"U.S. and Germany Conclude Talks on U.S.-Troop Costs." *Department of State Bulletin* 59, no. 1514 (1 July 1968), pp. 14–15.

U.S. Central Intelligence Agency. *Soviet and U.S. Defense Activities, 1970–1979: A Dollar Cost Comparison*. Washington, D.C., 1980.

U.S., Congress, Congressional Budget Office. *The Effect of Foreign Military Sales on the U.S. Economy*. Washington, D.C.: Government Printing Office, 1976.

———. *The Selective Service System: Mobilization Capabilities and Options for Improvement*. Washington, D.C.: Government Printing Office, 1978.

———. *Costs of Manning the Active Duty Military*, 31 May 1980. Washington, D.C.: Government Printing Office, 1980.

———. *Improving Military Educational Benefits: Effects on Costs, Recruiting, and Retention*, Washington, D.C.: Congressional Budget Office, 1982.

U.S., Congress, House, Ad hoc Subcommittee of the Committee on Armed Services. *Hearings: U.S. Military Commitments to Europe*, 93rd Cong., 2nd sess., 15 February–March 1974. Washington, D.C.: Government Printing Office, 1974.

U.S., Congress, House, Committee on Armed Services. *Hearings: Full Committee Briefing on German Offset Agreement.* 93rd Cong., 2nd sess., 7 May 1974. Washington, D.C.: Government Printing Office, 1974.

U.S., Congress, House, Military Compensation Subcommittee of the Committee on Armed Services. *Report: Junior Enlisted Personnel Stationed Overseas,* 95th Cong., 2nd sess., 19 December 1978. Washington, D.C.: Government Printing Office, 1979.

U.S., Congress, House, Special Subcommittee on the North Atlantic Treaty Organization Commitments of the Committee on Armed Services. *Report: The American Commitment to NATO,* 92nd Cong., 2nd sess., 17 August 1972. Washington, D.C.: Government Printing Office, 1972.

U.S., Congress, House, Subcommittee on Investigations of the Committee on Armed Services. *Report: National Defense Funding Levels for Fiscal Year 1981,* 96th Cong., 2nd sess., 21 July 1980. Washington, D.C.: Government Printing Office, 1980.

U.S., Congress, Joint Economic Committee, Subcommittee on Economy in Government. *Hearings: The Military Budget and National Economic Priorities,* 91st Cong., 1st sess., 1–9 June 1969. Washington, D.C.: Government Printing Office, 1969.

U.S., Congress, Senate, Combined Subcommittee of Foreign Relations and Armed Services Committees. *Hearings: United States Troops in Europe,* 90th Cong., 1st sess., S. Res. 49 and S. Res. 83, 26 April and 3 May 1967. Washington, D.C.: Government Printing Office, 1967.

————. *Report to the Committee on Foreign Relations and Committee on Armed Services: United States Troops in Europe,* 90th Cong., 2nd sess., 15 October 1968. Washington, D.C.: Government Printing Office, 1968.

U.S., Congress, Senate, Committee on Armed Services. *NATO and the New Soviet Threat,* 95th Cong., 1st sess., 24 January 1977. Washington, D.C.: Government Printing Office, 1977.

U.S., Congress, Senate, Committee on Foreign Relations. *United States Foreign Policy Objectives and Overseas Military Installations.* 96th Cong., 1st sess., April 1979. Washington, D.C.: Government Printing Office, 1979.

U.S., Congress, Senate, Subcommittee on Arms Control, International Law, and Organization, of the Committee on Foreign Relations. *Hearings: U.S. Forces in Europe,* 93rd Cong., 1st sess., 25 and 27 July 1973. Washington, D.C.: Government Printing Office, 1973.

U.S., Congress, Senate, Subcommittee on Manpower and Personnel, of the Committee on Armed Services. *Hearings: Military Recruiting Practices,* 95th Cong., 2nd sess., 10 and 12 October 1978. Washington, D.C.: Government Printing Office, 1979.

U.S., Congress, Senate, Subcommittee on United States Security Agreements and Commitments Abroad, of the Committee on Foreign Relations. *Hearings: United States Forces in Europe,* 91st Cong., 2nd sess., 25 May–15 July 1970. Washington, D.C.: Government Printing Office, 1970.

U.S. Defense Manpower Commission. *Defense Manpower: The Keystone of National Security*. Washington, D.C.: Government Printing Office, 1976.

U.S., Department of Defense. *Annual Reports, Fiscal Years 1981–1984*. Washington, D.C., 1981–1984.

U.S., Department of Defense, Directorate for Management Information Operations and Control. *Selected Manpower Statistics*. Washington, D.C.: 1980.

U.S., Department of Defense, Military Manpower Task Force. *A Report to the President on the Status and Prospects of the All-Volunteer Force*. Washington, D.C.: Department of Defense, October 1982.

U.S., Department of Defense, Office of the Assistant Secretary of Defense for Manpower, Reserve Affairs, and Logistics. *America's Volunteers: A Report on the All-Volunteer Armed Forces*. Washington, D.C., 1978.

———. *Use of Women in the Military*. 2nd edition. Washington, D.C., 1978.

———. *Manpower Requirements Report for Fiscal Year 1980*. Washington, D.C., 1979.

U.S., Department of Defense, Organization of the Joint Chiefs of Staff. *United States Military Posture for Fiscal Year 1984*. Washington, D.C., 1983.

U.S., General Accounting Office. *Report: Improvements Needed in Army's Determination of Manpower Requirements for Support and Administrative Functions, 21 May 1979*. Washington, D.C., 1979.

U.S., General Accounting Office, Comptroller General. *Report to the Congress: Observations on the United States Balance-of-Payments Position*, Washington, D.C., 1967.

———. *Report to the Congress: Status of Efforts to Offset Balance-of-Payments Deficit for Fiscal Year 1974, Attributable to Maintaining U.S. Forces in Europe*, 7 February, 1975. Washington, D.C., 1975.

———. *Report to the Congress: The Congress Should Act to Establish Military Compensation Principles*, 9 May 1979. Washington, D.C., 1979.

"U.S., G.B., and Germany Conclude Trilateral Talks." *Department of State Bulletin*, 56, no. 1456, 22 May 1967, p. 788.

V. Miscellaneous Publications

Cooper, Richard V. L. "Military Manpower and the All-Volunteer Force." *Rand Report R-1450-ARPA*. Washington, D.C.: Rand Corporation, 1977.

Federal Republic of Germany, Federal Minister of Defense. *White Paper 1979: The Security of the Federal Republic of Germany and the Development of the Federal Armed Forces*. Bonn: Federal Ministry of Defense, 1979.

———. *White Paper 1983: The Security of the Federal Republic of Germany*. Bonn: Federal Ministry of Defense, 1983.

"Focus On U.S. Troops in Germany." *Focus On* series, no. 3 (July 1983). New York: German Information Center, 1983.

Harris, Lewis. "Support for Reinstatement of the Draft Growing." *ABC News-Harris Survey* 2, no. 102 (18 August 1980).

NATO: Facts About the North Atlantic Treaty Organization. Paris: NATO Information Service, 1965.

NATO Handbook. Brussels: NATO Information Service, 1980.

Truitt, Wesley Byron. "The Troops to Europe Decision: The Process, Politics, and Diplomacy of a Strategic Commitment." Ph.D. dissertation, Faculty of Political Science, Columbia University, 1968.

References—German Language

I. Books and Monographs

Dettke, Dieter. *Allianz im Wandel.* Schriftenreihe des Forschungsinstituts der Deutschen Gesellschaft für Auswärtige Politik, Bonn. Rüstungsbeschränkung und Sicherheit, Bd. 12. Frankfurt: A. Metzner, 1976.

Haftendorn, Helga. *Abrüstungs- und Entspannungspolitik zwischen Sicherheitsbefriedigung und Friedenssicherung: Aussenpolitik der BRD 1955–1973.* Düsseldorf, Verlagsgruppe Bertelsmann Gambit, 1974.

Joffe, Josef. *Europapräsenz und Europapolitik der Vereinigten Staaten. Eine Untersuchung über Motivation, Funktion und Evolution der Amerikanischen Stationierungspolitik in Europa.* Ebenhausen: Stiftung Wissenschaft und Politik, November 1968.

Löwenthal, Richard, and Hans Peter Schwarz, eds. *Die zweite Republik. 25 Jahre Bundesrepublik Deutschland—eine Bilanz.* Stuttgart: Seewald Verlag, 1974.

Rehbinder, Manfred. *Die Rechtsnatur der Arbeitsverhältnisse deutscher Arbeitnehmer bei den ausländischen Streitkräften unter besonderer Berücksichtigung der Verhältnisse in West-Berlin.* Berlin: Dunker and Humbolt, 1969.

Thiel, Elke. *Dollar Dominanz, Lastenteilung und Amerikanische Truppenpräsenz in Europa.* Internationale Politik und Sicherheit, Band 6. Baden-Baden: Nomos Verlagsgesellschaft, 1979.

Witzsch, Günter. *Deutsche Strafgerichtsbarkeit über die Mitglieder der U.S.-Streitkräfte und deren begleitende Zivilpersonen.* Karlsruhe: C. F. Müller Verlag, 1970.

II. Chapters from Edited Works

Czempiel, Ernst Otto. "Die Bundesrepublic und Amerika. Von der Okkupation zur Kooperation." *Die Zweite Republic. 25 Jahre Bundesrepublik Deutschland— eine Bilanz,* edited by Richard Löwenthal and Hans Peter Schwarz. Stuttgart: Seewald Verlag, 1974, pp. 554–579.

III. Journal Articles—Authored

Arndt, Claus. "Zu einem Problem der deutsch-alliierten Truppenverträge." *Aussenpolitik* 10, no. 1 (1959), pp. 29–31.

272

Arnolds, Josef. "Die Geltendmachung von Entschädigungsansprüchen nach dem Stationierungsschadensrecht. Eine Kritik an der Rechtssprechung des BGH." *Neue Juristische Wochenschrift* 15, no. 28 (1962), pp. 1234–1235.

————. "Die Abgeltung von Truppenschäden nach dem NATO-Truppenstatut." *Deutsche Richterzeitung* 41, no. 8 (1963), pp. 249–255.

Ball, George W. "Atlantische Partnerschaft im Werden." *Europa-Archiv* 17, no. 8 (1962), pp. 251–262.

Baumann, Gerhard. "Devisenausgleichsabkommen als rechtlich-wirtschaftliches und strategishes Problem." *Wehrkunde* 15, no. 12 (December 1966), p. 628.

————. "Devisenausgleich und Sicherheit." *Wehrkunde* 17, no. 5 (May 1968), pp. 245–251.

Baur, Gieselher. "Beitrag zur Problematik des Truppenschmuggels." *Zeitschrift für Zölle und Verbrauchssteuern* 33, no. 13–14 (1957), pp. 199–201.

Birrenbach, Kurt. "Der europäisch-amerikanische Dialog." *Europa-Archiv* 28, no. 10 (1973), pp. 699–710.

Bleckmann, Albert. "Deutsche Zuständigkeit zur Scheidung amerikanischer Soldatenehen." *Neue Juristische Wochenschrift* 15, no. 50 (1962), pp. 2283–2286.

Boeck, Klaus. "Zahlungsbilanzeffekte und Kosten des Devisenausgleichs." *Wehr und Wirtschaft* 15, no. 12, pp. 587–589.

Boeck, Klaus, and Henry Krägenau. "Truppenstationierung. Devisenausgleich und Burden-Sharing." *Wirtschaftsdienst* 51, no. 2 (1971), pp. 91–94.

Borner, Silvio. "Die Dollarkrise in amerikanischer Sicht." *Aussenwirtschaft* 26, no. 4 (December 1971), pp. 368–391.

Brunn, Jochen. "Dollars für Divisionen: Devisen- und Lastenausgleich in der NATO." *Loyal, das kritische Wehrmagazin* no. 11 (1970), pp. 7–8.

Czempiel, Ernst Otto. "Entwicklungslinien der amerikanisch-europäischen Beziehungen." *Europa-Archiv* 28, no. 22 (1973), pp. 781–790.

Diebold, William, Jr. "Europa und die Vereinigten Staaten. Perspektiven der Wirtschaftlichen Beziehungen." *Europa-Archiv* 25, no. 15–16 (1970), pp. 597–608.

Duckwitz, Georg Ferdinand. "Truppenstationierung und Devisenausgleich." *Aussenhandelspolitik* 18, no. 8 (August 1967), p. 473.

Ehlers, Kurt. "Übergang vom Ersatz—zum Entschädigungsanspruch (bzw. umgekehrt) im ardentlichen Verfahren bei NATO-Truppen-Schäden." *Neue Juristische Wochenschrift* 17, no. 32 (1964), pp. 1461–1462.

Erbenbach. H. "Strafverfolgung im Rahmen des NATO-Truppenstatuts und der Zusatzvereinbarung." *Kriminalistik* 18, no. 3 (1964), pp. 130–132.

Friedel, Alois. "Amerikanische Truppenpräsenz in Europa und ihr Preis." *Wehrkunde* 19, no. 12 (December 1970), pp. 620–624.

Geissler, Markus. "Die Geltendmachung und Betreibung von Ansprüchen aus Truppenschäden nach dem NATO-Truppenstatut." *Neue Juristische Wochenschrift* 33, no. 48 (1980), pp. 2615–2620.

Grafe. Horst. "Die Abgeltung der Truppenschäden nach dem NATO-Truppenstatut in der Bundesrepublik Deutschland." *Neue Juristische Wochenschrift* 14, no. 41 (1961), pp. 1841–1846.

Grossmann, Otto. "Zur Problematik des Aufenthaltes ausländischer Streitkräfte in Deutschland." *Wehrkunde* 17, no. 8 (1968), pp. 399–401.

————. "Allierte Truppen in der Bundesrepublik Deutschland und ihre Bewaffnung." *Europäische Wehrkunde* 30, no. 11 (1981), pp. 500–501.

Joffe, Josef. "Amerikanische Truppenpräsenz und europäische Stabilität." *Europa-Archiv* 25, no. 6 (1970), pp. 191–204.

Kalckreuth, Jurg von. "Zu Problemen der U.S.-amerikanischen Landstreitkräfte in der Bundesrepublik Deutschland." *Europäische Wehrkunde* 31, no. 2 (1982), pp. 61–63.

Maier, Bernhard. "Zur Frage der Verjährung in den Fällen des Art. VII Abs. 3 des NATO-Truppenstatuts." *Neue Juristische Wochenschrift* 27, no. 43 (1974), pp. 1935–1936.

Marenbach, Ernst. "Aktuelle Probleme des NATO-Truppenstatuts." *Neue Juristische Wochenschrift* 27, no. 10 (1974), pp. 394–396, and no 24, (1974), pp. 1070–1073.

Neubauer, J. "Die Rechtsstellung ausländischer NATO-Streitkräfte in der Bundesrepublik Deutschland." *Archiv des Völkerrechts* 12, no. 1 (1964), pp. 34–65.

Nordheim, Manfred von. "Der amerikanische Kongress und die Stationierung von U.S.-Truppen in Westeuropa." *Wehrkunde* 24, no. 12, pp. 618–621.

Nothlichs, Matthias. "Zivile NATO-Bedienstete." *Arbeitsschutz* 4 (1975), pp. 121–124.

Otto, Franz. "Neuregelung für Schäden durch ausländische NATO-Truppen ab 1. Juli 1963." *Staats- und Kommunalverwaltung* no. 1 (1964), pp. 17–18.

Pursch, Ernst-Richard. "Die Regelung von Truppenschäden. Stand nach dem Beitritt der Bundesrepublik zum NATO-Truppenstatut." *Der Städtetag* 15, no. 4 (1962), pp. 190–193.

————. "Die Rechtsstellung der Stationierungsstreitkräfte. Auswirkung für Polizei und Verwaltung." *Die Polizei* 54, no. 11 (1963), pp. 335–339.

Reichel, Hans. "Die Arbeitsrechtlichen Bestimmungen des NATO-Truppenstatuts und seiner Zusatzvereinbarung." *Bundesarbeitsblatt* 12, no. 20, pp. 711–721.

Rieger, Walter. "Klagen der Arbeitnehmer bei den ausländischen Streitkräften vor den Sozialgerichten." *Die Sozialgerichtsbarkeit* 5, no. 9 (1958), pp. 275–276.

Rumpf, Helmut. "Zum Problem der Übungsplätze für die NATO-Streitkräfte." *Bulletin*, No. 70 (1973), pp. 690–692.

Schauer, Hartmut. "Die Kampf- und Kampfunterstüzungstruppen der Vereinigten Staaten in der Bundesrepublik Deutschland." *Kampftruppen* 24, no. 1 (1982), pp. 31–33.

Schneider, Fritz. "Scheinbare Unzulänglichkeiten: Wann kann die deutsche Justiz gegen Mitglieder der NATO-Streitkräfte Strafverfahren durchführen?" *Staatszeitung* 15, no. 39 (1964), pp. 7–8.

Schroer, Friedrich. "Zur Anwendung deutscher ordnungs- und sicherheitsrechtlicher Vorschriften auf Truppen der Stationierungsstreitkräfte." *Deutsches Verwaltungsblatt* 87, no. 13 (1972), pp. 484–489.

Schweizer, Jochen. "NATO-Partner zweiter Klasse?" *Der Volkswirt* 22, no. 41 (1968). p. 9.

Schwenk, Edmund H. "Die strafprozessäulen Bestimmungen des NATO-Truppenstatuts, des Zusatzabkommens und des Unterzeichnungsprotokolls zum Zusatzabkommen." *Neue Juristische Wochenschrift* 16, no. 32 (1963), pp. 1425–1430.

————. "Zustellung und Vollstreckung in nichtstrafrechtlichen Verfahren nach dem NATO-Truppenstatut." *Neue Juristische Wochenschrift* 17, no. 22 (1964), pp. 1000–1004.

————. "Die zivilprozessäulen Bestimmungen des NATO-Truppenstatus und der Zusatzvereinbarung." *Neue Juristische Wochenschrift* 29, No. 35 (1976), pp. 1562–1566.

————. "Strafprozessäule Probleme des NATO-Truppenstatuts." *Juristenzeitung* 31, no. 19, (1976), pp. 581–583.

Thiel, Elke. "Truppenstationierung und Wirtschaft: Betrachtung zum Devisenausgleich." *Wehrkunde* 17, no. 9 (1968), pp. 470–474.

Thiel, Elke. "Truppenstationierung und Devisensausgleich. Vorverhandlung für ein neues amerikanisches Offset-Abkommen." *Europa-Archiv* 24, no. 7 (1969), pp. 221–228.

Thiel, Elke. "Der Preis für währungspolitische Selbstständigkeit." *Wirtschaftswoche* 25, no. 33 (1971), pp. 19–22.

Thiel, Elke. "Devisenausgleich und Lastenteilung im Atlantischen Bündnis." *Europa-Archiv* 26, no. 10 (1971), pp. 353–362.

Thiel, Elke. "Dollarkrise und Bündnispolitik." *Europa-Archiv* 28, no. 11 (1973), pp. 373–381.

Tolmein, Horst Günter. "Stationierungstruppen. Unsere schussbereiten Gäste." *Dialog* 4, no. 2 (1973), pp. 32–36.

Tschinsky, Nikolaus. "Devisionen und Devisen." *Loyal* 5 (1974), pp. 3–4.

Volger, Gernot. "Devisenausgleich als militäre und zahlungsbilanzpolitisches Instrument." *Konjunktur-politik* 20, nos. 5–6 (1974), pp. 346–381.

Wenski, Carl, Lt. Colonel, U.S. Army Europe. Kräftestruktur sowie taktische Führungs- und Einsatzgrundsätze, mit denen die 'erste Schlacht' gewonnen werden soll." *Truppenpraxis* 21, no. 9 (1977), pp. 670–678.

Wieck, Hans-Georg. "Politische und militärische Probleme ausgewogener Truppenreduzierungen in Europa." *Europa-Archiv* 25, no. 22 (1970), pp. 807–814.

IV. Journal Articles—No Author

"Amerikaner in Berlin. Was GI's in der geteilten Stadt erleben." *Information für die Truppe* 6, no. 80 (1980), pp. 3–10.

"Amerikaner in Deutschland." *Loyal, das kritische Wehrmagazin* 6, no. 11, pp. 3–6.

"Der höchste Devisenausgleich, den es je gab. . ." *Wehr und Wirtschaft* 16, no. 1, (1972), p. 15.

"Devisenausgleich: Schmidts Kontertaktik." *Wirtschaftswoche* 25, no. 50 (1971), pp. 22–25.

"Devisenausgleich und U.S. Truppenreduzierungen." *Wehr und Wirtschaft* 14, no. 10 (1970), p. 535.

"Rechtsstellung der Stationierungsstreitkräfte im Bundesgebiet und Aufgabenbereich der Polizei." *Ministerialblatt für das Land Nordrhein-Westfalen*, Ausgabe A, 25, no. 66 (1972), pp. 1115–1119.

"Truppenstationierung—ein Anachronismus?" Editorial. *Wehr und Wirtschaft* 14, no. 9 (1970), pp. 457–458.

"Zur nächsten Devisenausgleichsrunde." *Wehr und Wirtschafft* 15, no. 9 (1971), p. 409.

V. Government Documents

Abkommen über das Ausserkrafttreten des Truppenvertrages des Finanzvertrages und des Steuerabkommens. Verträge der Bundesrepublik Deutschland, Serie A, Bd. 20, No. 229, 1965, pp. 468–473.

Abkommen zur Änderung des Zusatzabkommens vom 3 August 1959 zu dem Abkommen zwischen den Parteien des Nordatlantik Vertrages über die Rechtsstellung ihrer Truppen hinsichtlich der in der Bundesrepublik Deutschland stationierten ausländischen Truppen. BGBP, 1973, 2, No. 41, 8 August 1973.

Bundesrepublik Deutschland. Presse- und Informationsamt der Bundesregierung. *Jahresbericht der Bundesregierung. (Jahre 1970 durchgehend bis 1981).* Bonn: 1970–1981.

Bundesrepublik Deutschland. Presse- und Informationsamt der Bundesregierung. Referat III A2. *Die Alliierten Stationierungs-streitkräfte in der Bundesrepublik Deutschland.* Bonn: 1981.

Bundesrepublik Deutschland. Presse- und Informationsamt der Bundesregierung. *Die Alliierten Streitkräfte in der Bundesrepublik Deutschland.* (Aktuelles Basismaterial Chroniken, Nrs. 4 und 5, 1982.) Bonn: 1982.

Gesetz zu der Vereinbarung zwischen der Regierung der Bundesrepublik Deutschland und der Regierung des Vereinigten Königreichs von Grossbritannien und Nordirland über eine Devisenhilfe an Grossbrittanien gemäss Art. 3 des Nordatlantik Vertrages vom 19. Mai 1959. BGBP, 1959, 2, No. 22, 30 Mai 1959.

Gesetz zu den Vereinbarungen zwischen der Regierung der Bundesrepublik Deutschland und den Regierungen der Vereinigten Staaten von Amerika, des Vereinigten Königreichs von Grossbrittanien und Nordirland, der Republik Frankreich, des Königreichs Dänemark, des Königreichs Belgien, und des Königreichs der Niederlande über gegenseitige Hilfe gemäss Art. 3 des Nordatlantik Vertrages vom 11.3.1959. Bundesgesetzblatt (BGBP) 1959, 2, No. 17, 21.4.1959.

Zusatzabkommen zu dem Abkommen zwischen den Parteien des Nordatlantik Vertrages über die Rechtsstellung ihrer Truppen. Verträge der Bundesrepublik Deutschland, Serie A, Bd. 20, No. 228, 1965, pp. 142–467.

VI. Miscellaneous Publications

Die deutschen Devisenausgleichs-Abkommen mit den U.S.A. dpa Hintergrund-Archiv- und Informationsmaterial. Hamburg: Deutsche Presse Agentur, 1971.

Kaufmann, Bernhard. "Amerikanische Soldaten und ihre Angehörigen als Opfer strafbarer Handlungen in Deutschland." Diss. Johannes Gutenburg Universität, Mainz, 1963.

Rumpf, Helmut. *Das Recht der Truppenstationierung in der Bundesrepublik.* Vortrag gehalten vor der Juristischen Studiengesellschaft, Karlsruhe. 23. Januar 1969. Karlsruhe: C.F. Müller Verlag, 1969.

Schneider, Gerhard. "Die Extraterritorialität der Truppen in strafrechtlicher Hinsicht, unter besonderer Berücksichtigung der das deutsche Territorium betreffenden Truppenverträge." Diss. Albert Ludwig Universität, Freiburg im Breisgau, 1964.

Index